BEING A FINANCIAL ADVISER
The book I wished I'd read 10 years ago!

Mike Grant

Copyright © 2020 Mike Grant
All rights reserved.
ISBN-13: 9798638650292

Contents

1. Becoming a financial adviser 1
2. What makes a good financial adviser? 11
3. What type of financial adviser should you be? 42
4. Charging for financial advice 56
5. Giving financial advice - fact finds and risk 87
6. Giving financial and investment advice - dynamics and processes 109
7. Regulation - a 30 year personal review 127
8. An adviser's response to regulation 153
9. Marketing and finding clients 173
10. Dealing with platforms and providers 181
11. Principles of investment advice 195
12. Principles of protection advice 234
13. Principles of pensions' advice 270
14. Closing comments 299
15. Glossary of abbreviations 320
16. Acknowledgements 325

1. Becoming a financial adviser

Introduction

So you want to be a financial adviser or a better one? Whatever your starting point, it will need to be a journey of self-discovery as you furrow your own path in the industry. Every adviser I have ever met is unique, a product of their life skills, personality, values, intelligence, financial nous, technical knowledge and training.

Expect it to take time. In my experience you will not become a good financial adviser overnight for example at the point you achieve the minimum qualifications as specified by the Financial Conduct Authority (FCA), when you reach "competent adviser," status or even after a couple of years successfully advising clients on your own. It is a long process of small steps not success in a few key staging posts and it may take five to ten years for you to mature into a truly good adviser.

Your thinking, processes and practices initially will be influenced by those who train and mentor you but this will change. In time you will develop your own values and convictions and challenge things you have been taught, rejecting those elements that do not sit well with you, whilst continuing to embrace the good. Slowly you will become a unique adviser with your own modus operandi.

Not a how to guide

This book is not a "how to guide," in which the author sets themselves up as an expert and dispenses wisdom from the lofty height of their success. My message is not, if you copy my methods you will become an outstanding financial adviser. First and foremost I do not claim to be an expert; that is for others to decide. Then I don't want you to become a clone of me because you must be who you are, or who you are destined to become. Moreover you can't become an outstanding financial adviser solely by reading books and manuals, adopting the tactics of others or copying an individual role model. There is much more required, principally doing the job and gaining valuable experience whilst giving advice. Finally if you copy me in entirety you'll certainly pick up some bad habits, especially if you don't learn from my mistakes!

It is also important to say there are various ways to deliver good quality advice and I am not suggesting this book is complete or the only guide to being a financial adviser that you will need. My ways may work for me but others do things very differently and successfully. It is not the case that one model of being an adviser is right and another wrong. So whatever you pick up from these pages remember others will have something to teach you as well.

An old hand passing on his experience

What then do I have to offer if not a "how to guide?" I am someone who has been in the industry for more than 29 years and having learnt a thing or two from giving financial and investment advice I want to pass my experiences on to anyone willing to listen. These pages will set out my thinking, convictions, discoveries, experiences and methods which I hope will benefit you on your journey as an adviser.

In the book I have tackled industry hot potato issues head on, like timed charges versus percentage fees, active versus passive investment and restricted versus independent advice. I have strong opinions on all these subjects. You may disagree with my views but that's fine. I want my readers to be thinkers not followers. You may shift to a new understanding or you may find fault in what I argue and become more convinced that your views are correct. Either way that is good, you will be a better adviser.

You'll learn from what I have done badly, from my weaknesses as well as my strengths. The older you get the more you become entrenched in your own ideas and habits. At 65 I may be long in the tooth or old school but I still reckon I have something useful to say even if there are some subjects that I know zilch about such as promoting a business on Facebook or LinkedIn. That said the importance of having a bespoke website and investment blog are key elements to my business and are described in Chapter 9.

This book is for you!

So who is this book for? Primarily, but not exclusively it is for aspiring financial advisers, those in training or newly qualified. You should have no shortage of work as the industry is desperate for new blood. The adviser community is an ageing bunch heading for retirement, at a time when the need for high quality advice is as great as ever. You could have a great career.

If you are a new entrant, taking your first steps to become an adviser, these pages will inform, guide and hopefully inspire you. They will give you plenty of material to consider. Take the ideas that you are curious about, think about them, discuss them with your colleagues and mentors, then apply, adapt or reject them outright. I am pretty sure something good is bound to stick.

I am also writing for the benefit of experienced financial advisers. Maybe you are stale and feel you are in a rut. Perhaps you have lost your first love for the job and need a reboot. Maybe you are weighed down by problems of your own making, excessive demands from your bosses and out of touch regulation. Perhaps there are things in your thinking and advice processes that don't sit well with you but you are not sure how to articulate what the problems are, let alone solve them. I hope you find my ideas bring clarity and benefit.

The book may also be of value to a variety of other people, for example the investment and insurance companies who mainly distribute their products through advisers, and their representatives in administration and sales that have day to day contact with advisers. I have included a chapter on my experiences and perceptions on what makes their service good and what at times is a pain in the *derriere*.

The book may also be of some value to regulators who often seem out of touch with the advice community and the public they seek to protect. That assumes they are willing to let go of the sense of their self-importance and are wanting to learn.

People looking for a financial adviser may also benefit from reading this book. If that is you, by the end you should better understand the key principles of financial and investment management and what good financial advice looks like. Read on and you will be much better prepared when deciding who you want to manage your money.

Finally the book may be of interest to financial journalists. They may be surprised that I agree with a fair bit of their criticisms of the advice industry although I hope they will also gain a better understanding of the difficult job we face.

The book is about?

So what is in the book? First I discuss the qualities that make a good financial adviser, including being client focussed, having integrity and good communication skills. I then go on to describe the different types of adviser, including the meaning of independence and why I think it is better to be an IFA than a restricted adviser. I then tackle the thorny issue of charging for financial advice and how to demonstrate the value of advice. Be prepared for some controversial and unpopular ideas.

Moving on, in Chapters 5 and 6 I explain the principles of giving financial advice. Bite size is best in my view. The complexity of investment risk is discussed and I explain why meeting clients' financial needs is normally more important than meeting their financial objectives.

The next two chapters about regulation are to the book what vindaloo is to a curry - hot and spicy and likely to make some break out in a sweat. New advisers will learn how much the industry has evolved and why you should not ask a fish what water is. I describe my radical but client centric approach to regulation.

Marketing and finding clients follows. If you don't have clients you don't have a business.

A chapter on dealing with investment and insurance companies is next and to end I cover principles of investment, protection and pension advice with plenty of technical analysis, practical advice and tips.

As you read the book it should be clear that I am a contrarian financial adviser, doing things differently to most others. This is not because I am a contrarian for the sake of it but because I have a view of business and giving advice that is pretty unique. I didn't go out with a plan, looking to create the "left field" adviser I have become. The adviser I am found me or at least the path I walked on led me to it. The path is described below.

Being a contrarian generates lots of controversy. The pot gets a good stir on all sorts of issues, salesmanship, percentage fees, adviser charges, over-regulation, centralised investment propositions and risk profiling.

The other theme you will pick up throughout is that pretty well everything I do is bespoke – the advice I give, the compliance regime I operate, the way I manage investment portfolios and my website. Bespoke is best because it focuses on the individual, not a group or crowd. Shoehorning is out or at least left at the doors of Clarks or Skechers.

Throughout the book I have included various examples of advice I have given my clients. In addition there are practical suggestions, templates and documents to assist you with your administration and record keeping. Even that is bespoke.

The practical advice should help you make fewer mistakes, reduce the potential for complaints and omissions and buy you a very valuable commodity, time.

Becoming an IFA

At age 36 I was looking for a career change. Up to then I had gone to university and became a biology and maths teacher in a secondary school in south London. Just over three years later I left teaching and went to do a PhD in plant pathology at Imperial College. I wasn't sure what might follow but I ended up working for a Christian organisation I had been involved with in my spare time. It involved a variety of functions including Bible teaching and mentoring, mainly working with students and graduates. However by the time I was 36 it was time for a career change.

I applied for jobs in the business world on the back of management and personnel skills I had acquired but had no joy. I don't think my credentials were transferrable to the world of business and commerce.

At that time in 1990 the only people who were recruiting misfits like me were financial service companies looking for salesmen. Although I had a term assurance policy and a pension acquired via the Christian organisation I worked with, I knew next to nothing about money. Not having any didn't help! My wife and I were used to living a frugal existence having relied on gifts from friends and other donors to support us.

After one or two unsuccessful applications I landed a self-employed position with Liberty Life, a small life assurance company. I was based at an office in central London. Dressing up in a suit gave me an air of respectability but not much else about the job did. I would be paid commission only if I made sales. It was a tough existence, cold calling, making awkward approaches to friends and family and visiting commercial premises unannounced to try and drum up business.

With hindsight the company's products were terrible, the norm in the industry - savings plans or whole life contracts with very high charges, borne out of a requirement to pay commission. The culture of the business was about flogging financial products.

The rag tag bunch of people who were my colleagues in the main were wholly unsuited to being financial advisers. The branch manager was an amiable and enthusiastic man who taught us some tricks designed to win over clients. He advised us not to make appointments bang on the hour or half hour but at say ten to or five past the hour. The idea was to communicate you were so busy seeing clients you could only fit them in in 20 minute slots. Also he lived in south east London and when he met new prospects in his patch he would say something like this:

> "I am Berat Tekin (not his real name). Have you heard of me?"
>
> "No."
>
> "Oh! That's a surprise because I am very well known as a financial adviser in south east London."

The cheek of the man was outrageous. Bull shitting was an important sales technique in those days.

However there was some decent formal training at Liberty Life which gave me a good grounding in financial planning. Somehow I eked out a living although I was supported by a very small but timely inheritance from my father who died shortly before I entered the industry.

It didn't take me long to realise that being tied to a single company and a suite of poor products was not a great idea and that I should become an independent financial adviser. I was fortunate that at that time the Liberty Life office was in the same building as *Financial Adviser*, a leading industry newspaper and from time to time I picked up free copies reading them avidly. Along with interesting articles about money in the Saturday's Daily Telegraph, I realised there was a whole new world out there for a new adviser like myself - higher quality products and the lure of independence.

My interest in investment was sown. I remember reading a supplement from a broadsheet about investment trusts. I didn't understand much at the time but they were certainly fascinating. In my days at Liberty Life giving investment advice was very simple. You always recommended the Managed fund, the ubiquitous plain vanilla life company investment offering, consisting of equities, bonds, property and cash. You didn't dare take a position on global stock markets and recommend say the North American or Asia Pacific fund. In those days the concept of an adviser making asset allocation calls or using platforms or wraps where you could pick funds from a multitude of fund managers did not exist. Each life company had a very limited range of in house funds and advisers were instructed to opt for the neutral Managed fund. You can have it in any colour providing it is black.

In 1992 I joined a firm of IFAs based in New Malden in south west London called the Investment Practice. Finding clients was a lot easier, some were provided by the firm, others came from so called "drugs' lunches." These were lunchtime presentations to junior doctors in local hospitals put on by pharmaceutical companies. We copied the concept of these. A free lunch was provided in the common room, followed by a talk on financial planning. Appointments were arranged with those who showed enough interest.

Thereafter it was about selling products, some good, some not so good.

For young professionals in their mid to late twenties the best thing we did was to advise income protection. I have always viewed this insurance as foundational to all good financial plans especially for younger clients in employment or self-employed. I write extensively about this in Chapter 12.

I immediately became aware that I was very different to the 15 or so advisers at the IFA practice. It confirmed that I was a terrible salesman and normally came bottom or close to the bottom of the monthly commission league tables. Selling made me feel uncomfortable at times. I much preferred giving advice and even in the 1990s I charged the odd fee for generic financial planning. I was also an avid student of the technical side of the business - tax, pensions and investments. The advisers in the firm were regularly tested and I normally came top of the class.

A big influence on me in the three years I worked at the Investment Practice was one of the partners, David Flowers. He was very well thought through on investments and he sparked my love of the subject, something that has continued to this day. In my early days as an IFA I was a generalist advising on mortgages, protection, savings, investments and pensions but as I got older, as did my clients, my advice shifted towards investment planning as a speciality.

Running the gauntlet of networks

In late 1995 I decided to go it alone and set up my own business under the auspices of an IFA network, called Burns-Anderson Ltd. I was still self-employed but worked as an appointed representative of the company. They took 15% of what I earned. Whilst I had a lot of autonomy network compliance was excessive. Gold plating the rules was common, principally to protect the network from claims of mis-selling.

After nearly 15 years at Burns-Anderson I left in 2010 to join a different network called Financial Ltd. They uniquely allowed appointed representatives to retain all commission and fees but their compliance became too oppressive and I left in 2013. My firm, Montgo Consulting Ltd become directly authorised by the Financial Conduct Authority (the FCA) in November 2013 where I am today.

I certainly got out of the two networks at the right time. About nine months after leaving Burns-Anderson, their parent company, Honister Capital went belly up and not long after leaving Financial Ltd they fell foul of the regulator. The firm no longer exists and the founder Charlie Palmer was banned from the industry. Oddly Financial Ltd was accused of weak regulation, something which was definitely not my experience. The level of knit picking over suitability reports was frustrating and even worse than at Burns-Anderson. Many types of business had to be pre-approved and a full case file had to be sent to compliance for approval. My reports might come back with 20 points for correction, most of them were trivial. It was a slow and cumbersome process getting cases approved. No wonder network compliance departments earned the title of "business prevention units."

The problem with networks is that the good advisers are hindered by the bad apples. Networks end up setting the compliance bar at a higher level than the legislation requires, adding burdens for the good guys. What needed to go into suitability reports was a case in point, everything plus the kitchen sink said the networks, much less said the regulator. I write more on this later. In the case of Financial Ltd some IFAs were arranging risky unregulated investments and unsuitable pension transfers and the lack of controls brought the network down. The only way I can resolve this contradiction in my mind is that to conclude that Financial's compliance department focussed on the trivial, the easy things to nit-pick on but they failed to see the really big dangers of unsuitable advice given by some unscrupulous advisers. There is a life lesson here.

Freedom from becoming directly authorised by the FCA

Becoming directly authorised by the FCA was the best move I had made in my financial services career and the application itself was straightforward with help from SimplyBiz, my firm's compliance and support provider. It gave me real freedom to run my business the way I wanted and ensure my own compliance was fit for purpose. I should have made the move years earlier. This is one of the major regrets in my career. Unfortunately for too long I believed the hype that it was too difficult and too costly for a one man band to go directly authorised. I guess there is another life lesson here. It is very easy to be bound by our own misconceptions that create non-existent barriers, deterring us from taking bold and liberating steps that will greatly benefit our lives and businesses.

That said I shouldn't be too hard on myself. By the time I threw off the shackles of network membership my business had become mature. I had a loyal client bank. Reviews and servicing these people was more important than finding new clients. Being in a stable if not entirely satisfactory environment in networks for nearly 18 years enabled me to achieve this good state of affairs.

To conclude the introduction, I'm going to take you on a journey through my eyes as a financial adviser. At the end I hope you will be informed, enlightened and inspired to be a first rate financial adviser with a difference. Please read on.

2. What makes a good financial adviser?

Before I cover the question of what makes a good financial adviser I want to briefly ask why should anyone consider becoming a financial adviser in the first place?

Why become a financial adviser?

This is an important question to ask because being a financial adviser is not an easy job. Unless you are given clients to service, finding new ones in the early stages of your career is difficult. The financial advice industry has been tainted by mis-selling scandals in the past and the public, the consumer lobby and journalists have long memories. New legislation continues to pile in on top of the mountain of rules that already exists. There are constant pressures from the regulators and industry critics who expect more and more from advisers. Margins are being driven down by bureaucracy, non-productive work, competition from robo-advice, direct to consumer platforms and DIY investing, aided by the vast amount of financial information that is available online.

The work of a financial adviser may involve long hours, it generates mountains of paperwork (or the digital equivalent) and administration and there are worries and stresses galore, from too much regulation, technology not working, poor service from product providers, stock markets collapses, constant interruptions from people inside and outside the industry trying to sell you something and a multitude of opportunities for advisers to make mistakes.

Finally there are big financial risks if you make serious errors. Complaints may lead to costly Financial Ombudsman Service (FOS) claims and without the protection of a legal long stop, claims against advisers who have long retired are not uncommon. The PPI claims brigade now need a new source of business as the deadline for claims ended in August 2019 and they are turning their attention to investment advice.

Despite all the downsides I have thoroughly enjoyed my time in the industry. It is very satisfying engaging with clients, identifying their financial needs and coming up with creative ideas and solutions that work. Building good long term relationships with clients and providing financial advice that they really appreciate is one of the best parts of the job, as is seeing clients make money on the back of my investment advice. I have also experienced people benefitting from a pay-out from an insurance policy but of course I would rather my clients did not suffer a critical illness or die. Finally knowing you've protected your clients, especially the elderly and vulnerable from failed investment schemes, tax traps, DIY financial blunders, exorbitant fees and charges, scammers or you have obtained redress for poor service from investment and insurance companies is very satisfying.

I enjoy a great balance between working on my own in the office, undertaking research, writing reports or composing e-mails on one hand and interaction with and meeting clients on the other hand. Being an IFA is not all a paper job nor is it all a people job, either of which would probably drive me nuts if that's all it entailed. I love the technical side of the business and writing but not too much to be a reclusive nerd and a total bore. I need and enjoy interaction with people, but not all the time.

Focusing on investments has been a real pleasure and it has enabled me to develop my interest through writing a blog. Working from home, being my own boss and running my own business has given me a lot of freedom. I work flexibly, taking time off when I want. I get to work in casual clothes and thankfully I rarely need to put on a suit. In short my job satisfaction has been very high. In fact at times it feels as if I am being paid to pursue a hobby.

I have made an OK living from being an IFA although I could have earned a lot more had I been more ambitious or greedy. However for me it has been imperative that the quality of my advice trumps the quantity of my advice. This attention to detail and a very high standard of service has been satisfying but it has limited my earnings.

What makes a good financial adviser?

Let's return to the main question. In my view to be a good financial adviser there are various key qualities that you must have. I have listed 15. Despite the large number they don't add up to perfection! You should:

1. Be client focussed

To use a variation of a Warren Buffet quote there are two rules to being a very good financial adviser. The first is to be client focussed. The second rule is don't forget rule one!

The best financial advisers are client focussed. It means you put your clients first above everything, your earnings, any business targets you are set and meaningless regulation or bureaucracy that adds no value for your client but racks up costs for them. You are there to give your clients the best of your abilities and service and ensure the best financial outcomes for them. This is not to say you should not be fair on yourself. You should be paid for your efforts. Also it does not mean being at your clients' beck and call, 24/7. For example the vast majority of my clients don't have my mobile number. Those that do, tend to be friends.

As a client focussed adviser you will develop good relationships with your clients. You will become trusted, even a friend. Your clients will have no hesitation in contacting you for advice or recommending you to family and friends. There is a real dividend from a client focussed mindset.

Being client focussed is not just a slogan. It means being outcome focussed. It is ensuring that the end result of your advice leaves your clients financially better off, hopefully much better off, than they were before you came along. If you are successful they will be suitably protected, their investments will deliver good returns, wealth will be created, the tax they pay will be minimalised, legally of course and suitable plans will be put in place for a comfortable retirement. Moreover your clients will not only be financially better off but they should feel it too.

The opposite is to be process focussed where the adviser is overly concerned about best practice, tasks, regulation, disclosures and ticking boxes and where the end goals and benefits gets lost in the detail. Your job is to guide your clients through the jungle of financial complexities, noise, confusion and endless choices, navigating and hacking your away through the bush to your desired destination, a clear and beneficial financial end goal. And one they can see and feel. It is always a pleasure getting unsolicited notes or comments from clients saying how much they appreciate my advice.

Finally being client focussed means being a good listener. You need to understand how your clients think and feel, what they like and dislike, what motivates them and scares them, what they expect from their investments and what they expect from you. You must respect and address their real concerns and needs. One of the best ways to do this is to create an open atmosphere so your clients feel free to express themselves and can raise awkward or apparently trivial questions. You then need to respond with clear and compelling answers.

That said, the scope of your advice should not be restricted by your clients' goals and priorities, meaning if necessary you should be prepared to lead them into unfamiliar territory.

2. Have something to say

You need to know your stuff to be able to give advice. This means having a good knowledge of money, investments and financial planning. You must have something to say - good quality and relevant content to pass on to clients that will improve their financial position, whether it is about investment, retirement planning, family protection or inheritance tax planning. You need to be seen to be competent in your field in the eyes of your clients. If they know more than you or they don't feel you have sufficient depth of financial knowledge why should they get advice from you?

I should clarify being a competent adviser is not a know all, a specialist in all subjects. A financial adviser is like a GP, who has a good, all round understanding of medicine. He or she will handle most patient conditions on their own, diagnosing and recommending suitable treatment plans but occasionally patients have to be referred to specialists. For a financial adviser it means recommending a client to a trusted accountant, solicitor or an actuary. I write more on this subject later.

3. Always be willing to learn

One of my experiences over the years is constantly being made aware of gaps in my knowledge and understanding. The more I learn the more I realise there is lots I don't know. Usually it is a technical deficit of pensions, tax, trusts or investments.

Fortunately I have an inquisitive mind and this has driven me to try to plug the gaps in my knowledge. Continuous voluntary learning has made me and will make you a better adviser, keeping you fresh and interested in the subject of finance. It will also contribute to your ongoing enjoyment of being an adviser.

Becoming aware of my lack of knowledge may arise in the course of research and written advice to clients or it may come at very inopportune times in a client meeting. The discussion may arrive at a point where I realise my technical knowledge on a subject is on very thin ice. It can be highly embarrassing. In these circumstances it is best to put your hands up and tell the client, *"I am not sure on that point. I will check that out and get back to you,"* rather than bluff your way through and risk giving wrong information or advice. You are not perfect, your knowledge is incomplete and you do not have to try and kid your clients you know it all.

Knowing you're stumped on something is good as the subsequent learning is more likely to stick. Over the years I have attended numerous seminars and webinars on pensions, trusts or inheritance tax for personal development and to satisfy continuous professional development (CPD) requirements. I generally go away with notes and a good understanding. The problem is the more technical aspects have a very short half-life in my memory. A classic example is the residential nil rate band with its complex rules. During a presentation I seem to get it but grill me two weeks later and my knowledge on the subject will be fuzzy. I find it is only when I apply technical knowledge to a specific client advice scenario that it truly sticks. It is a case of use it or lose it.

My advice for all financial advisers is to be inquisitive. Recognise gaps in your knowledge and plug them with targeted study. For the experienced adviser burdened by the weight of regulation, rediscovering a love of learning may help revive your enthusiasm for the job.

4. Be able to identify financial needs

A good adviser must be able to identify clients' financial needs, perhaps ones they haven't spotted themselves. This requires fact finding and discussion with clients but also thinking outside the box, viewing client situations from angles that they have not considered.

You are likely to be taught that being a financial adviser's job is to meet your clients' financial objectives. This would appear to be the FCA's take or at least it used to be. Back in 2014 I had some e-mail correspondence with Rory Percival, who at that time was a senior technical and compliance specialist at the FCA. Now he is an independent consultant whose advice is highly sought after. I had asked him to clarify what the FCA required in suitability reports. He wrote:

> "...there are, in fact, only three things the rules require firms to include in their suitability reports:
>
> - *The client's objectives*
>
> - *Why the recommendation is suitable*
>
> - *Potential disadvantages.*"

I plan to come back to this concise and important clarification later but the point here is that whilst I agree meeting client objectives is important, and this question is specifically asked on my fact find, it is not the whole story. This is because clients' financial objectives are not the same as their financial needs. Sometimes the two are not aligned and it is your responsibility to make your clients aware that certain financial needs should take priority over their perceived financial objectives. A financial planner should not merely be an instruction taker but an advice giver. You are primarily an adviser meeting clients' financial needs not an executive taking action to meet their objectives.

As an example if a young single client comes to me for advice about savings or pensions I will raise the issue of income protection and recommend some of their budget should be allocated here, unless they are covered under a group scheme from their employer. It is based on my conviction that income protection is foundational to all good financial planning. The loss of income through long term ill health can be devastating for your clients' financial wellbeing.

On the point about financial needs in 2018 I took on the husband of a client of mine who had died. On the fact find he stated his only financial objective was to *"cash in"* his pension plan, valued at around £155,000. Looking at his situation I couldn't see any reason for him draw on the pension as his current income was sufficient for his needs. In fact it was £1,500 p.m. more than his monthly expenditure. Moreover he was asset rich with properties, cash and investments in excess of £1,750,000 and he had no debt. By crystallising his pension it would have increased his estate, by the tax free cash taken, but more if he went the whole hog and cashed in the whole pension. This would be aside from a huge income tax charge. He would also pay more inheritance tax and reduce the amount available for his children's and grandchildren's inheritance. If he bought an annuity it would also limit his ability to pass on his pension on his death.

In my view his financial need was inheritance tax planning and this trumped his financial objective. As we discussed and explored these issues and the advice required it was clear there was a misconception at the heart of his financial objective. He thought that tax free cash could only be taken before his 75th birthday. He was 72. This restriction ended in 2011.

The outcome of our discussions was he agreed for us to undertake an inheritance tax review and park his objective to cash in his pension.

As an aside it should be noted that although the legislation allows for tax free cash to be paid after 75, not all pension schemes have amended the rules to allow this freedom. In fact the Aviva pension he holds permits it up to the day before his 76th birthday. I explained it would be possible to transfer his uncrystallised pension before this date should he wish to defer drawing benefits and retain the right to tax free cash indefinitely.

The principle is that a good financial adviser will sometimes need to challenge clients' thinking about their financial planning and steer them in a different, dare I say a better direction. It means an adviser sometimes needs to set the agenda not just implement the agendas your clients come to you with.

5. Be able to argue your case well

A good financial adviser must communicate clearly and convincingly especially if recommending something different to your clients' financial objectives. It is about presenting your case in a compelling manner so that your clients get a clear picture of the facts and realities and want to follow your advice, assuming of course it is correct!

In my view the case for a specific course of action will be more persuasive if the disadvantages or potential risks are explained as opposed to just presenting all the benefits. Firstly it shows you are not just pushing an uncritical solution onto your client and have taken a balanced and holistic view. Then it anticipates and addresses the downsides that clients themselves identify and reassures them you understand their concerns.

Presenting your case well is not about being forceful or having arguments with clients. At times you need to back off if a client doesn't see it your way and is determined to go down a different track. It is their money after all. However in my experience very few clients when presented with the facts and compelling arguments insist on a choice I think is flawed. The vast majority of clients seeking advice from you do so because they are open to it and see the need for an expert to guide them through the complex choices they face.

In very rare cases your client may insist on a course of action that you think is not just flawed but is fatal. In these circumstances you should not be party to such a transaction or course of action and you must be prepared to walk away, as it could lead to a complaint later on. Make sure though you have presented your case, logically, clearly and compellingly. Your insistent client may come to see it your way.

6. Be a terrible salesman

Salesmanship in its purest form is the dark art of persuading someone to buy something they may neither want, need or can afford, or all three. The goal of a salesman is to make a sale primarily for their financial benefit, not their customers' well-being. That was the culture of financial services when I first joined the industry and it was driven by commission, targets and promises of riches for the best salesmen. Then they were wolves in wolves' clothing, today they are wolves in sheep's clothing. Commission has gone but it has been replaced by adviser charges, some of which are excessive as I explain in Chapter 4. The industry has certainly become more professional but it has a veneer of respectability in some quarters.

When I first started as an adviser a whole industry existed to train salespeople. They taught you how to win confidence of your customers, how to make your pitch, how to handle objections and how to close the deal. Perhaps an overt sales culture still exists in other industries where you have to threaten to set the dog on a persistent conservatory salesman who refuses to accept no and leave your house, but no longer in much of the financial services industry as far as I can tell.

I take the view that a good adviser does not need to sell in a traditional sense. That is not to say you do not seek to influence your client to take a specific course of action. It is selling the need not a product. An adviser's job is to get alongside your client, fully understand their financial needs and objectives and recommend suitable solutions. This may of course involve the purchase of a product, a pension to start saving for retirement, a life assurance policy for family protection or an Enterprise Investment Scheme (EIS) for inheritance tax planning. The difference here is your client may take your advice or reject it. If you are truly a fee based adviser you will be paid for your time. If however your pay depends on the client taking a specific course of action i.e. buying a product there will be an inevitable conflict of interest and you will be tempted to push the sale. This is a type of contingent charging which I cover in more detail in Chapter 4.

Advice is about bringing your clients on board with your thinking. Your arguments are made with conviction but gently. If it is sound advice and makes sense, in most cases they will accept it willingly without feeling under compulsion. Having tension free dealings with your clients certainly makes for better long term relationships.

7. Have integrity and trust

So what else makes a good financial adviser? Absolute honesty and integrity are crucial. You need to be a trustworthy human being who will be a faithful steward of your clients' wealth. It is about doing the right thing. Without these attributes your clients will not trust you. Win their trust and they will stick with you for the long term and recommend you to their friends and family. This is essential for building a successful business.

Trust takes time to become embedded in a client adviser relationship. Clients will form a view of you when they meet you for the first time. You may have a winsome personality and they may like you and take to you immediately but it is what happens afterwards that counts. Do you put their interests first? Do you treat them fairly and with respect? Do you give them good financial advice that they want to embrace? Are your charges transparent and fair? Do you provide good service and are you diligent to sort out problems that arise? Do you address their concerns and queries? Moreover it is not just doing these things once but repeatedly, so it becomes the norm over the years. This however doesn't mean being perfect. We all fail and make mistakes, some small, others more significant. At these times we need to own up, apologise and correct the problem. This may require making financial compensation or an offer of such. In these circumstances I have found my clients have been very understanding and forgiving.

A culture of service, integrity and honesty should not be a tactic you adopt in order to build trust and a successful business. It should come from within and reflect who you are in life in general. In my view people either have an ethical compass or they don't. People are inherently trustworthy and honest or not. My drive for excellence comes from my values and character. I am a perfectionist and want to help people and do the right thing. I also want a clear conscience and to be able to sleep well at night.

Interestingly Andrew Bailey, the then Chief Executive of the FCA was reported in the 2018 winter edition of the Personal Finance Society (PFS) magazine to have given a speech in which he advanced the notion that trust has a moral and ethical dimension. Well if that is not blindingly obvious I don't know what is! I am left wondering if the FCA and their predecessors the FSA actually thought that you can magic trust and integrity into existence through rules and regulations.

Here is a question for you, a test of your moral compass. What would you do if at a cash machine you asked for £50 and out popped £150? The receipt showed £50 and your bank account was debited £50. Would you keep quiet about it and hope there was no comeback or would you report it to the bank and offer to return the extra £100? Well if I was a client I would want my financial adviser to own up and pay it back. It would give me confidence that he or she would be honest with my financial affairs, they would not be tempted by fraud and would own up and rectify mistakes that benefitted them.

If you answered you would own up and pay back the £100 I have a second question. Would you do this because it was the right thing to do, full stop, or because you were not sure about a possible legal comeback and sanctions? The question touches on the difference between an inner integrity arising from a genuine moral compass and integrity as a tactic, one that is driven by self-interest. Such integrity is a veneer.

I appreciate this is a simplistic test. For example if the machine paid out £55 instead of the £50 requested would the time cost to rectify the error be justified given the small amount? If so where do you draw the line?

One of the great benefits of regulation in the time I have been in the industry is there are more good guys now than bad. Most of the sharks have been driven out. Commission driven salesmen, the norm for many years were more interested in lining their own pockets than improving the financial position of their clients. It is much better now that commission has gone from investment based business and pensions. However that is not to say that a fees system is not open to abuse especially as adviser charges look worryingly like commission. You could still be ripped off even though it is harder to do so with the greater regulation and professionalism in the industry and that adviser charges must be individually agreed with clients.

8. Have relevant qualifications

Are qualifications a sign of a good financial adviser? Yes and no in my view. It is essential that advisers have at the very least the minimum industry qualifications based on formal training and passing exams, otherwise people might as well get advice from the bloke down the pub. Advisers must prove they are highly knowledgeable and competent and are putting in the effort to continuously improve. Rising educational standards and qualifications have certainly helped raise the profile of the advice industry as a profession in recent years.

That said I am less convinced about the gold standard that is Chartered Financial Planner status awarded by the Chartered Insurance Institute. I admire those advisers who have dedicated hours and hours of time to study for the relevant exams. Undoubtedly the experience will have improved their technical knowledge and financial planning skills but there are no exams that lead to a qualification in honesty and integrity, financial acumen nor that buy automatic trust with clients. Chartered planners are likely to give good advice but they are not immune from giving bad advice or overcharging their clients, just like advisers with fewer qualifications.

I haven't attempted to become a Chartered Financial Planner. I undertook seven years' full time University education before I entered the industry and plenty of study after I joined, culminating in the Advanced Financial Planning Certificate in July 2001 six exams later. I guess I became tired of studying for exams and was uncertain what I would gain. Instead I preferred to focus on mandatory and voluntary CPD and to study specific technical issues arising in the course of my work. As explained above my interest and curiosity has remained undimmed, so bite size study is not generally a chore.

Crucially I cannot recall a single time when I have had a potential new client ask me if I was a chartered adviser. In my experience people are looking for trust in your name not letters after it. Many of my new clients come by recommendation. That said for young advisers I recommend you attempt to achieve chartered status for several reasons.

First the technical and practical knowledge you will gain will benefit you even if no-one asks you for details of your qualifications. Second you will be more attractive to a firm you seek employment with in future. Finally the bar for minimum qualifications required to give advice could be raised by the regulator in the future.

9. Provide excellent service

I have touched on the issue of service. A very high standard of service is absolutely essential for being a good financial adviser but what does it look like? In no particular order here are some random things I think are important. Other areas are highlighted elsewhere in the book. A good financial adviser should:

- Under promise and over deliver. You should surprise your clients about how exceptional you are and exceed their expectations. Under promising avoids appearing to blow your own trumpet.

- Respond quickly to telephone messages and e-mail queries from clients. If you can't provide an immediate answer, acknowledge receipt and say when you will get back to them. Make sure you keep your promise.

- In response to queries answer all the client's questions point by point, thoroughly and clearly. Take your time and don't fob clients off with brief or simplistic comments that don't provide the information and assurance clients are looking for. Remember they are contacting you for a reason, they have a genuine concern. So make sure you appreciate the importance of these issues to your clients and give them the due attention they deserve.

- Be proactive not just reactive, highlighting financial issues clients should consider. This could be inheritance tax planning, a need for life assurance if your client has dependents, increasing pension contributions or using the current year's ISA allowance.

- Recommend and agree financial or investment reviews with

clients. You should put the dates in your diary and make sure you initiate the process at the relevant time. Not all clients however will want annual or regular reviews preferring *ad hoc* ones. Being flexible to your clients' needs and preferences is important rather than having a one size fits all offering. How this relates to the FCA's rules on product governance (PROD) and the EU's second Markets in Financial Instruments Directive (MIFID II) requirements is discussed later.

- If you identify an error in your advice or in a transaction carried out by a platform or other third party ensure it gets corrected and ask for compensation to be paid. Recently I discovered I accidentally put a client into a share class of a fund that had a higher ongoing charges figure (OCF) than an alternative share class available on the platform. I notified the client, advised a switch to the cheaper share class and added a credit to their timesheet for the inconvenience and an adverse movement in the share price.

- Ensure complete transparency on your fees (more on this later).

- Keep clients informed of important relevant changes in the financial services landscape, be that regulation, changes to taxation or global stock markets. The use of occasional newsletters and investment blogs are especially useful here. Aside from providing useful information writing to your clients reminds them that you are still around and are on the ball with what is going on in the world of money.

- Acknowledge receipt and offer thanks when a client makes a BACS or cheque payment to you to settle a fee and express special appreciation when a prompt payment is made. This is just common courtesy.

10. Have good literacy and communication skills

A good financial adviser will also have good literacy and numeracy skills. E-mails, letters and reports should be of a high standard of English, written in clear and crisp language with good grammar and spelling. Sloppy communication will give a bad impression and signals your advice processes, record keeping and attention to detail are equally poor. In contrast high standards of English show you are professional and thorough.

You should also avoid using abbreviations and acronyms without first explaining what they mean. It always irritates me when reading an article that the author assumes that everyone understands what an acronym stands for. In many cases I do because they are widely used financial terms but in others cases I haven't a clue. Whilst you might have explained what an OCF (ongoing charges figure) is for a fund in a suitability letter six months ago, don't assume your client will remember next time around. Given I am likely to have missed defining certain acronyms please refer to the glossary of abbreviations at the back of the book.

You also need to work hard to communicate your content clearly so your message is not vague or misunderstood. Reports and letters with your advice need to be comprehensive, balanced and compelling. Your client should be left in no doubt what your recommendation is and why it is good. As stated, for balance you also need to spell out the potential disadvantages and risks to avoid over-selling or presenting a one-sided picture. Finally it is essential to pre-empt and address queries and concerns that your clients may raise.

As an example consider e-mail correspondence with a client regarding uninvested cash within his pension. At the date of writing this chapter in mid-January 2019 global stock markets were settling down after a big sell-off in the autumn and winter of 2018. A confluence of negative issues had hit equities - notably rising interest rates in the US, US/China trade wars, concerns over the Italian economy and Brexit uncertainty.

In the last six months following a transfer from a paid-up money purchase employer's scheme we had invested the bulk of his pension cash but had held back some money for tactical investment purposes. This was due to concerns about equity valuations in the summer of 2018, which proved to be well founded shortly afterwards. I don't always get to call markets right but this time I did. A high allocation to multi-asset and other cautious risk investments in July 2018 was agreed with a further £30,000 invested in October 2018.

Here is our e-mail chain with my greetings and footers taken out:

E-mail on 27/12/18

To Client:

> As you are no doubt aware markets have continued to slide since we undertook investment of £30,000 of SIPP cash at the end of October. Whilst the value of these investments has fallen in the last two months, at least we know we bought in at significantly lower prices than if we had invested all the cash at outset in the summer. Currently you hold £26,385 in cash. I recommend we invest £25,000 of this into equity funds now to benefit from even lower stock prices than two months ago. Such investment naturally carries the risk that markets will fall further as it is impossible to say when the bottom will be reached. However history teaches us that recovery follows stock market sell-offs and crashes and the benefit of acquiring assets cheaply becomes evident. In my experience being a contrarian and buying when everyone is selling will pay off for an investor in time. However to assess the success of an investment strategy it may require a three to five year view.

You will see I was brief, to the point but explained clearly what my advice was, why it was pertinent and the potential pitfalls.

Email on 10/1/19

From Client:

> Re your advice - yes please, go ahead on the basis you propose. I have been uncertain about investing any more for a while, given recent events in USA, China and with Brexit. However I read your recent blog about JP Morgan's take on things, which if not that upbeat is not in despair either about 2019.
>
> Please go ahead as you propose and we'll see where things stand at the end of the first quarter this year.

His response highlighted two important points for me. Firstly that my regular investment blogs covering the global economy and stock markets play an important role in undergirding my investment advice (more on this later). Secondly behind his explicit consent I sensed uncertainty and concern about his pension investments. So despite his consent to go ahead I decided to offer some reassurance before I proposed my recommended equity funds for the £25,000 of SIPP cash.

E-mail on 11/1/19

To Client

> *I think that although you are relatively close to retirement or at least consideration of retirement and therefore a call to draw on your pension may be required in the next few years, you do have considerable time for your investments to ride the volatility and recover from the recent stock market sell-off. I say this because a move from a wholly uncrystallised pension to a partially crystallised one, where tax free cash only is taken will allow you to remain invested for the medium to long term especially if much of the tax free cash is immediately re-invested. In addition the considerable level of cash savings that I understand you still retain does permit you to defer drawing on your pension for several years at least. That is why I don't think you are taking on undue investment risk by investing the residual £25,000 of SIPP cash now.*

Since the summer the client's portfolio fell 3.78%. To put this in context I wrote:

> *Whilst I do not wish in any sense to trivialise this loss it is relatively small compared to market corrections of -10% and bear markets of -20% that some equity sectors and markets experienced. Your portfolio has been insulated to some degree by the cautious risk funds you are invested in. More importantly the loss is a paper loss and is just a snapshot of the portfolio today. Paper losses only become real losses when crystallised and there is certainly no need to consider doing this now.*

Subsequently the client came back to me with a comment about Brexit.

> *Yes, it all sounds good and I am in agreement with your proposals. The fly in the ointment of course is Brexit and the current political impasse, but as*

> you say, a longer term perspective is sensible (and the hope that our politicians don't do something stupid …).

The second sentence was a "but." Sensing the client still had some residual concerns I wrote:

E-mail on 14/1/19

To Client

> *Thanks for your e-mail. One important factor relating to Brexit is that all four funds I have recommended are global investments. In other words the companies the funds invest in either are based in non-UK jurisdictions or are UK domiciled companies with significant earnings outside the UK. In other words they are much more Brexit proof than UK funds with companies which are leveraged to the UK economy for example retailers or housebuilders. I don't want to down play the risks of Brexit but it is unlikely in of itself to derail the global economy and hence the earnings of global companies.*

His reply was positive with no hesitancy or caveats. Had I picked up any doubt the client was reluctant I would have asked whether he would prefer to delay the investment.

What this demonstrates is a principle that communication is not what you say, but it is what people hear. You can set out a compelling case for a course of action but just because you feel you have communicated well does not mean that the client gets it or accepts it. You may be saying this is good advice but what the client hears is something different – "this is risky and I don't feel comfortable with it." So listening to their responses, reading between the lines, gauging hesitancy and picking up signals is essential to ensure you directly address their concerns. Only then can we say we have truly communicated.

Of course even with perfect communication there is no guarantee your clients will always agree with you and wish to proceed with your advice. In my experience this is however very rare.

I write e-mails formally addressing the recipient as Dear or Hi, depending on the relationship, avoiding text speak, unexplained jargon and acronyms unless as I have said I have spelt out their meaning first.

I like to see apostrophes used correctly in material I read, not because I am a grammar zealot but because when I see good English I judge the person writing to be intelligent, educated and articulate. That they have taken good care in their English means I am more likely to trust that the content of what they write is true and fair.

A recent survey by HR Review, a leading UK human resources company found nine out of 10 CVs had spelling or grammatical errors. The most common were misuses of apostrophes, notably *GCSE's* and *KPI's* (key performance indicators) which are plurals, not possessives. Some CVs mentioned the *A Level's* the applicant had achieved. As a prospective employer I would not be impressed if a candidate's CV listed an A Level in English and they misused apostrophes. (Please note I have not spelt out what a CV or GCSE means. There is no need to explain commonly used acronyms. It is the technical ones my comments above apply to).

The message is very clear for any aspiring adviser looking for a position. You only have one chance to make a first impression. Make sure your CV is up to scratch. Check and check it again and get someone with a good knowledge of English to review it. And it should go without saying, that your CV should be truthful in all respects. If you feel a need to embellish your CV with lies you should look for an alternative career.

Similarly for those already advising, you should aim for a high standard of English at all times. Bad English could be a turn off for potential new clients especially if you are competing with other firms who are more professional in their communications. You may have a great business proposition but your message might lose its credibility by poor English.

High standards are also essential once they become clients. Sloppy grammar and spelling I suspect reflects a casual attitude in your communications in general and your message is likely to be unclear. Claims of professionalism and high standards of service are less likely to be believed.

I certainly don't wish to set myself up as a model of perfection here as I frequently come across typographical errors in my e-mails and letters subsequent to sending them to clients despite running them through a spell checker and reading through the document prior to sending. It can be embarrassing but if I spot the mistakes shortly afterwards I'll e-mail the client with a correction or corrected version, unless they are trivial and self-evident.

One problem I particularly need to take care with is a frequent omission of a very important word, "not." Failure to include it flips the meaning of what I am saying 180 degrees. For example a statement, *"you should not invest all your available cash,"* becomes dangerous advice if the word "not" is excluded. I don't know why it happens but it may be due to a very mild form of dyslexia, I sometimes switch numbers in a sequence. Alternatively it may be because my mind rushes ahead in what I write missing out the small vital word, not. Fortunately I normally spot the omission before I send out most e-mails or letters. I suspect this is a unique problem to me but if not it may be one for you to look out for.

Despite being serious about writing I occasionally slip in light hearted or humorous comments to make what can be a dry technical communications a bit more interesting. Typically I do this in client newsletters and investment blogs. Targeted humour in small quantities does not equate to being flippant but it shows you are human. It brings colour and taste to what you write. Humour and analogy is a good way to make your point and make your writing more readable.

As an example I wrote an investment blog post on 16/10/17 with the title, *"Eeyore Gets Onto The Dance Floor."* Now I could have used *"Upbeat Stock Market Assessment,"* which was what the article was about. However if nothing else clients receiving notice of the publication of my article might have smiled at the title and asked, what the heck is that about? Of course I am trying to encourage my clients to read the article and reduce the expectation it will be a hard slog. Well the bulk of it was an analysis of stock markets following my reading of an upbeat assessment by Trevor Greetham from Royal London Asset Management. However I was more cautious being concerned about the potential for a sell-off.[1].

---

[1] *http://montgo.co.uk/873-2/*

My readers had to wait to the end of the article to learn what had cheered Eeyore, A A Milne's pessimistic character from *"Winnie the Pooh."* What I wrote was this:

> *"Finally I said above that the equity sell-off hasn't materialised. I could have added the word "yet." I sincerely hope for the sake of my clients that Greetham is right and I am wrong. We might then see two iconic pessimists Eeyore and Private Fraser from Dad's Army both getting to the dance floor to do a tango."*

11. Be good with figures

Aside from good literacy a financial adviser should be very comfortable with figures and have a good working knowledge of everyday maths especially that which comes up in the course of giving financial advice. Here are some test questions. See if you can calculate the correct answers and show your workings. You can use a calculator. The answers and workings are at the end of the chapter.

1. A client's investment portfolio rises in value from £159,320 to £197,500. What is the percentage increase?

2. A fund grows by 5.6% p.a. compound net of charges. If £5,000 is invested at outset what is the value of the fund after five years?

3. A unit trust has an offer (buying) price of 444.57 pence a bid (selling) price of 443.26 pence. What is the bid-offer spread in percentage terms?

4. An individual has earned income of £18,000 in 2019/20. How much tax will he pay on £17,000 of dividends he receives from non-ISA investments in that tax year? An understanding of the taxation of dividends is required here.

5. A cash deposit of £10,000 earns 1.3% p.a. compound interest for three years. Over that period the Retail Price Index (RPI) rises from 257.1 to 278.3. Work out the inflation rate and then calculate the value the £10,000 would need to have increased by after three years to have kept pace with inflation at the end of

the period. Finally how much has the investment lost in cash terms from inflation?

Over the years I have either developed spreadsheet calculators or had friends who devised them that help me with my financial planning advice, notably life assurance, annuity and savings calculators.

12. Use technology appropriately and well

Like most advisers and people in general I spend my life on my computer, whether it is typing reports, composing e-mails, checking online accounts, transacting business or fund switches online or undertaking research.

I grew up in a world before computers and the internet. The most technical devices I had to deal with when I was at school were slide rules and log tables. Fortunately when PCs came out I was still young enough to take technology on board with a little help from others.

I guess however I am still old school and no doubt some people will consider me to be behind the times. I am not paperless and I don't use a back office system, preferring to create my own digital files such as spreadsheets. I occasionally use Microsoft Office for example Excel and Word but I mainly use an old programme called Microsoft Works which I find very user friendly. The technology I use generally works. It serves me well.

With the growth of the online digital world there are clever clogs who have devised programmes and tools, for a monthly charge of course, to make life easier for advisers. There are lots of systems available including investment research and product comparison tools. Over the years I have looked at a number of these but have rarely adopted any. One of the problems is that the software can normally do much more than I need or want. Consequently I tend to get lost in the complexity and find the programmes difficult to navigate and use. Moreover the added functionality, unless it is ignored, can end up creating new tasks and work that you would have not dreamed beforehand that you needed in order to service your clients. To cap it all in my view financial software is very expensive on the whole and the cost is rarely justifiable.

The point is that technology should work for you. It should be your servant not your master. A garden should be a place to relax and chill, but it easily becomes a chore. The grass never stops growing and constantly needs mowing, the hedge needs cutting and the annoying weeds keep coming. I have a small manageable garden now but in a previous home I might sit down outside with a drink at the end of the day and see 101 things that needed doing. The garden is constantly demanding your attention. It can be the same with technology. You can't adopt it all, no matter how good it is and so you have to be selective.

My long term favourites are Microsoft Works, Google Chrome, the Exchange from Iress for protection quotes and Unipass. The latter is an industry created digital security certificate enabling advisers to log on to multiple insurance company websites without having to remember passwords.

I have looked at or used Intelligent Office when I was with one of the networks, Synaptics and FE Analytics. I trialled the latter for a while and whilst I liked its investment research functions, my clients told me they did not want the additional reporting it could produce. So my message is be careful and selective what technology you buy and make sure it truly serves and helps you, rather than becoming an expensive burden.

13. Know your limits

A good financial adviser should know his or her limits. You are primarily a pension, protection and investment adviser and a financial planner. These are your specialisms, what you have trained to do. However you have to dabble in all sorts of other related areas of finance. You need to have a working knowledge of economics although you have no formal training in the subject. You need to understand taxation although you are not an accountant and you need to know something about legal matters such as trusts and contracts although you have never studied law. In one sense you need to be a jack of all trades in these peripheral areas of finances, although you will be a master of none. Given this, care is needed as a little bit of knowledge can be dangerous.

Even in the core areas it means being realistic about your competencies, accepting you are not an expert in everything and you need help at certain times, for example on the more technical aspects of pensions. If you have colleagues or friends in the industry who know their stuff, ask for their advice. Sometimes you will need to refer clients to a tax specialist or solicitor. I have a friend who is an actuary. I have occasionally asked him to undertake some technical calculations for me when I wanted to check returns from with profits policies.

In addition there are free high quality resources out there to assist you, notably technical services desks provided by a number of life companies and our ever present friends, internet search engines. If you are in doubt google it.

Knowing your limits also means having the ability to say no. This may manifest itself in various ways. You may need to turn down the opportunity to advise certain clients if you know you are going to lose money because the amount they have to invest is so small. Taking on everyone who knocks at your door may feel like an act of charity but it is likely to leave you dissatisfied and use up valuable time that is better employed elsewhere. Do this frequently and it could create a financial pressure for you.

Similarly knowing your limits requires managing your workload and not allowing anybody to impose impossible burdens on you. If you don't take control and you are overloaded, you'll become overwhelmed and stressed and the quality of your work and life will suffer. In these circumstances you may need to decline or delay taking on a new client, say no to non-essential or least important tasks or pass on work and responsibilities to others. You will need to prioritise client advice and good client outcomes over everything else.

Knowing your limits is about being kind to yourself and being your own person. It is rooted in your values and convictions and being prepared to stand up for what you believe is right. It means being willing to challenge rules, practices and people, who try to impose burdens on you that neither serve you nor crucially your clients. Unfortunately the history of regulation is littered with examples of unintended consequences, normally because they have been ill thought through or poorly implemented, even if the intentions were good. An example here is the "advice gap." As a result of increased regulation and the Retail

Distribution Review (RDR), access to affordable financial advice has become more difficult in recent years, as adviser numbers have dropped and the cost of giving advice has risen.

As financial advisers we need to remember our prime responsibilities are to our clients and ourselves. Having that view has enabled me to stand up to and filter out a lot of the nonsense and do what is right. Being clear on what is right will serve your clients' best interests and keep you sane! I write more on this below.

14. Learn to filter the important from the clutter

I have covered this to some extent in the sections about technology and knowing your limits. You need to be selective and learn to say no. Filtering out the mass of e-mails coming into your inbox which demand your attention is an obvious application here. Fortunately I never seem to get spam or nuisance e-mails these days about fake lottery wins or from fraudsters who want to give me a shed load of free money. My e-mail service provider filters them out. Perhaps also the scammers have moved on to newer more sophisticated scams.

No what I am referring to is the daily barrage of genuine industry e-mails about products, funds, market news, investment commentaries or seminars. I click quickly through these from the titles without opening the message and delete the 95% that are of no interest to me. I can get through and delete 30-40 messages in a minute. Don't be tempted to open and read everyone on the spurious expectation it may contain something useful. You'll simply waste a lot of time. If something however piques my interest from the title I may take a look and read the contents. If it doesn't I hit the delete button.

The other filtering out you will need to do are the multitude of company representatives demanding your time. I write about this in Chapter 10.

15. Stay healthy and have a good work life balance

Staying healthy as far as it is in your control will ensure you are always available and fresh to help your clients when they need it. If you are frequently ill and are unable to service your clients they may get frustrated by the delays and look elsewhere for advice. I have been very fortunate with hardly a day off work from illness in the 27 years that I have been an IFA.

Sleeping well helps too. If you are frequently tired you won't be able to give your best.

Having a good life work balance will help prevent you becoming exhausted and stressed. In my experience my best advice is given when I am relaxed and at peace with myself and life in general. My mind will then be full focussed on the client and the advice at hand. In this state I avoid being distracted and am less likely to make mistakes.

Achieving this state of mind has not always been easy as I have struggled with an anxiety condition for the last 19 years. Moreover having a good work life balance has kept me fresh and interested in what I do. On the whole I thoroughly enjoy my work and as I said earlier it feels like I am being paid to pursue a hobby. Love is a strong word, but I can honestly say I have loved being an IFA. I often look forward to Monday mornings on Sunday evenings! Yes I am that weird.

A key to a good work life balance is not to work every waking hour. I typically do about 8 a.m. to 5 p.m. Monday to Friday but I take time out during the day to walk the dog. I never do client meetings in the evenings, although I may very rarely have a telephone appointment with a client if they are unavailable during the day. I also normally do some work on Saturday mornings, typically catching up on administration or writing investment blogs.

I am fortunate that I am able to determine my own hours. Being directly authorised by the FCA as opposed to being an appointed representative of a network or a registered individual of another adviser firm means I am free from targets, the controls of top down management and the burden that comes from the gold plating of regulations. No one is breathing down my neck and putting pressure on me to carry out their agendas.

Having interests outside work is also important. For me physical exercise helps clear the mind. I play football on Sunday mornings and walk the dog in Eastbourne and the South Downs. These are welcome diversions from what is a sedentary existence, sitting in my office in front of a computer screen, engaging in purely mental tasks.

There has been a cost to my fairly laid back approach. I am not overly driven and know I could have earned more money if I was. What I can confidently say however is that I am a very happy financial adviser and that has been crucial in sustaining me in the long term in my chosen career. If you aspire to be a financial adviser for the long haul you need to be content and have a good work life balance. It will be a firm foundation supporting everything you do.

What clients expect from financial advisers

To conclude this chapter on what makes a good financial adviser I want to look at it from a different perspective, what qualities do clients consider is most important in IFAs.

Since the summer of 2018 I have been meeting informally with a young aspiring IFA who left the Army in December 2019. On his own bat and in his spare time he has attained a Level 4 qualification that permits him to give financial advice. He also gained the Certificate in Mortgage Advice and Practice (CeMAP) and has secured a position with a local IFA firm in Eastbourne. In preparation for moving into his new career he devised a survey and sent it to around 200 of his own contacts. He asked what qualities they would look for in a financial adviser. He presented a long list of choices. The three most important attributes his contacts chose were trustworthiness, knowledge and good communication skills.

I found that very interesting. The first quality is about ethics, doing the right thing. It is the essential foundation on which everything else about your relationship and dealings with your clients is built. If your clients trust you, you will gain the right to advise them.

But it is more than being trustworthy. You can be the most selfless moral person in the world but if you don't understand money you are not fit to be a financial adviser. I suspect for example people never sought financial advice from Ghandi or Mother Theresa! Knowledge is essential to being an adviser. You need to know your stuff and be competent in your technical grasp of financial matters. You need to understand investment and pensions and ensure you are *au fait* with how tax works.

Finally you must have good communication skills to get your knowledge across. You may be a financial genius but if you speak double Dutch it will be of no value to your clients. You will be required to highlight the financial needs of your clients and how your recommendations will help them. You have to be able to get your message across clearly and succinctly in a way they can understand. Good verbal and written communication is essential. You can't leave your clients baffled by jargon and complexity and with unanswered questions.

To finish here there is another interesting point. My friend undertook the study for a purpose. It wasn't an academic exercise. He wanted to learn from his contacts and potential future clients what they think are the most important characteristics in a financial adviser. He would then focus on developing these in his own life. That is what being client focussed means, the very thing I highlighted above as the most important attribute.

Appendix - Answers to Financial Calculations

1. A client's portfolio rises in value from £159,320 to £197,500. What is the percentage increase?

The answer is 23.96% to two decimal places. The workings are as follows:

First deduct the end value from the starting value, £197,500 - £159,320 = £38,180. That is the gain in cash terms.

To calculate the percentage gain, you need to express the cash gain as a percentage of the starting value i.e.

$$\frac{£38,180}{£159,320} \times 100 = 23.96\%$$

That should have been pretty easy.

2. A fund grows by 5.6% p.a. compound net of charges. If £5,000 is invested at outset what is the value of the fund after five years?

The answer is £6,565.83. To calculate this you need to multiply £5,000 by 5.6% five times. The calculation is:

£5,000 x 1.056 x 1.056 x 1.056 x 1.056 x 1.056.

Such a calculation is relatively simple if there are five years, but to do it manually over 25 or 30 years would be time consuming and prone to error. This is where a scientific or google calculator can be used. Try the latter. To increase a figure, in this case £5,000 by 5.6% p.a. you multiply it by 1.056 and to get the power (i.e. multiplying by 5.6% five times) you press the x to the power of y button next to the 0 button. Enter five and press = and up pops the answer.

Incidentally it is worth trying the same calculation over 25, 30 and 35 years to see the power of compounding. This is something that younger clients should see to encourage them to start investing on a monthly basis as soon as possible. A five year delay can be very costly. There is more on this in Chapter 12 on pensions.

3. A unit trust has an offer (buying) price of 444.57 pence a bid (selling) price of 443.26 pence. What is the bid offer spread in percentage terms?

This follows the same procedure as question 1. The bid-offer spread is:

$$\frac{Offer\ Price - Bid\ Price}{Offer\ Price} \times 100$$

i.e.

$$\frac{444.57 - 443.26}{444.57} \times 100 = 0.295\%$$

This is to three decimal points. An alternative way is to calculate it is:

$$1 - \frac{444.57}{443.26} \times 100 = 0.295\%$$

= (1- 1.00295) x 100% = 0.295%. It is necessary to deduct the 1 from 1.00295 to get how greater 444.57 is than 443.26.

4. An individual has earned income of £18,000 in 2019/20. How much tax will he pay on £17,000 of dividends he receives from non-ISA investments in that tax year? An understanding of the taxation of dividends is required here.

The answer is £1,125.

In 2019/20 the individual has a £2,000 dividend tax allowance. All of his personal allowance of £12,500 is used up by his salary and he is a basic rate taxpayer. This means £15,000 of dividends are taxable at 7.5% i.e. £15,000 x 0.075 = £1,125.

5. A cash deposit of £10,000 earns 1.3% p.a. compound interest for three years. Over that period the Retail Price Index (RPI) rises from 257.1 to 278.3. Work out the inflation rate and then calculate the value the £10,000 would need to have increased by after three years to have kept pace with inflation at the end of the period. Finally how much has the investment lost in cash terms from inflation?

This is the toughest question.

We have to compare the cash return against inflation. Cash return over 3 years: £10,000 x (1.013) to the power of 3 as in question 2 = £10,395 to the nearest pound. Inflation over 3 years: The RPI factor at the start was 257.1, the RPI factor at end of the period was 278.3. Inflation over the period therefore is:

$$\frac{278.3 - 257.1}{257.1} \times 100 = 8.246\%$$

What this means is if the £10,000 had kept up with inflation it would now be worth 8.246% more after three years i.e. £10,000 x 1.08246 = £10,825 to the nearest pound.

In conclusion by keeping the £10,000 in cash for three years at an interest rate of 1.3% it has resulted in the client losing £10,825 -£10,395 = £430 to inflation. Another way of saying this is the £10,000 has lost £430 of purchasing power. As an aside the inflation over the period can also be calculated as:

$$1 - \frac{278.3}{257.1} \times 100 = 8.246\%$$

RPI inflation factors can be obtained online for example on this website:

http://www.michaellever.co.uk/retailpriceindexrentcalculator/

By clicking the relevant years you can work out the RPI inflation between any two dates. It is very useful.

3. What type of financial adviser should you be?

I am only going to cover UK authorised and regulated financial advisers here. These pages are not for unauthorised advisers, those that work in non-UK jurisdictions or those that provide financial information or guidance but not client specific recommendations based on personal circumstances. The latter is the true definition of advice.

There have been major changes to the status and definition of financial advisers over the years, the history of which I will not cover in detail. Currently there are two types of authorised financial adviser in the UK, independent and restricted.

Independent financial advisers

An independent financial adviser or IFA must offer unbiased advice from the whole market. This has two elements, independence of product and provider.

Retail investment products

In respect of products anyone holding themselves out as being an independent financial adviser must consider the whole range of what the FCA call "Retail Investment Products." The FCA's list is as follows:

(a) a life policy; or

(b) a unit; or

(c) a stakeholder pension scheme (including a group stakeholder pension scheme); or

(d) a personal pension scheme (including a group personal pension scheme); or

(e) an interest in an investment trust savings scheme; or

(f) a security in an investment trust; or

> (g) *any other designated investment which offers exposure to underlying financial assets, in a packaged form which modifies that exposure when compared with a direct holding in the financial asset; or*
>
> (h) *a structured capital-at-risk product.*[2]

Over the years it has been difficult to get definitive information on what is and what is not a Retail Investment Product (RIP), whilst the term "unit" is not one I associate as being a financial product. It conjures up thoughts of some of the big units I play football with!

The concept of RIPs was borne out of the Retail Distribution Review (RDR) which came into force on 31/12/12 (just the sort of thing we should be celebrating on New Year's Eve). As far back as November 2011 in the run up to the RDR the regulator at the time, the Financial Services Authority (FSA) failed to provide clarity and seemingly was unable or unwilling to provide a full and definitive product list despite calls from the industry. An article in Professional Adviser in early November 2011 stated:

> *"From 2013, independent advisers must have a working knowledge of all 'retail investment products'. There's just one problem: the FSA has been slow to define what they are.*
>
> *A lack of clarity from the regulator on the definition of a "retail investment product" (RIP) is hampering advisers' preparations for the Retail Distribution Review (RDR), it has been claimed.*
>
> *In an RDR policy paper last year, the Financial Services Authority introduced the term to reflect the "range of products that a consumer would expect an IFA to have knowledge of". The regulator said RIPs would include not just packaged products, but also structured investment products, all investment trusts and unregulated collective investment schemes.*
>
> *Also included are, "any other investment that offers exposure to underlying*

---

[2] FCA handbook www.handbook.fca.org.uk/handbook/glossary/G2763.html
© Financial Conduct Authority

assets, but in a packaged form which modifies that exposure compared with a direct holding in the financial asset".

Despite repeated calls for it to do so, the FSA did not provide a comprehensive list of what product types would count as RIPs, although it said it would respond to queries from firms on an individual basis.

But firms now claim the regulator is not providing the clarity it promised it would. Services provider Threesixty has been attempting to seek clarification on whether certain products would be classed as RIPs, including film partnerships, enterprise investment schemes and 100% protected structured products.

However, managing director Phil Young said the FSA has not been able to provide clear answers, hitting its preparations for gap fill sessions next year, and preventing advisers from getting a full picture of the whole of market requirements to be independent.

He said:

'We do think it's a bit ridiculous that these things have not been defined yet.'[3]

Eight years on I am not a whole lot clearer and consider this is to be a failure of the regulator, a subject I will come back to. However my core list of RIPs that I consider could be suitable for most retail clients is as follows:

- Investment bonds

- Personal pensions and Stakeholder pensions

- Open Ended Investment Companies (OEICs), unit trusts and NURS (Non-UCITS Retail Schemes, see the note at the end of the chapter)

---

[3] https://www.professionaladviser.com/professional-adviser/news/2122104/-retail-investment-product

- Investment trusts

- Structured products - deposit based and capital at risk

- Venture Capital Trusts (VCTs) and Enterprise Investment Schemes (EISs)

- Exchange Traded Funds (ETFs) and Exchange Traded Commodities (ETCs), notably physically backed ETCs that are not subject to rolling derivatives contracts

- Cash based products including National Savings and Investments (NS&I).

It is important to understand that not all these RIPs are regulated products. The R in RIPs is retail not regulated. Take investment trusts for example. Although they are collective investments with similarities to unit trusts and open ended investment companies (OEICs) and are subject to certain EU wide regulations, notably PRIIPs, (Packaged Retail Insurance-based Investment Products, see the note at end of chapter) investment trusts are companies listed on the London Stock Exchange (LSE) just like BP, HSBC and Vodafone are.

This means an investor who buys shares in an investment trust, whether direct or via an adviser has no recourse to the Financial Services Compensation Scheme (FSCS) if the trust becomes insolvent. In contrast an investor in a unit trust or OEIC that becomes insolvent is covered, up to £85,000 per person per investment company.

That said advice on investment trusts is a regulated activity and clients have a right to complain and have recourse to the Financial Ombudsman Service (FOS) if they think they were mis-sold by an authorised adviser. If the firm itself has gone bust they may have a valid claim from the FSCS for the bad advice and their losses.

In any event investment trusts are mainstream products that all IFAs need to consider when giving advice to clients. They offer significant benefits that unit trusts and OEICs do not, for example the ability to borrow to invest and to retain a proportion of their earnings to pay out future dividends. [4]

Whilst they carry some additional risks compared to open ended collective investments, before the RDR, many IFAs avoided recommending investment trusts to their clients primarily because they did not pay commission. For advisers who charged fees this was not a barrier.

Another reason why IFAs eschewed advising investment trusts was a reluctance to step outside their comfort zone due to their extra complexity, so they avoided them altogether. In some cases they justified it on the basis that they were too complex and risky for their clients. Aside from split capital investment trusts traditional generalist trusts are not that complex or risky and to be honest I think these were lame excuses.

The RDR was a game changer because those excuses will no longer wash. You cannot hold yourself out to be an independent financial adviser if you don't consider investment trusts. An IFA may not think them suitable for many of their clients or recommend them frequently but they can't be dismissed out of hand in advance for the whole of your client bank. Even if you can't demonstrate advice or sales on investment trusts say in the last 12 months the FCA will expect IFAs to have relevant CPD to demonstrate their knowledge is up to date.

Unregulated collective investment schemes

Before I move off the subject of RIPs we must consider the issue of Unregulated Collective Investment Schemes (UCIS). This term should not be confused with UCITS, Undertakings in Collective Investment in Transferable Securities. UCITS are open ended authorised and regulated funds and they can be marketed in the EU. New advisers may feel they are drowning in an alphabet soup of jargon but think what it is like for

---

[4] I have written two investment blogs on investment trusts which you may wish to read:
http://montgo.co.uk/investment-trusts-part-1 - this covers the technical aspects and difference between investment trusts and open ended funds such as unit trusts.
http://montgo.co.uk/investment-trusts-part-2 - this explains the practical benefits and uses of investment trusts for investors.

clients.

According to the Financial Times lexicon UCIS is defined as:

> "A Ucis fund is an investment vehicle set up for asset classes that are unable to follow the UK's Financial Services Authority's (FSA's) specific rules on matters such as liquidity, leverage or cash reserves. Although Ucis themselves are not directly authorised by the FSA, persons carrying on activities related to Ucis funds are themselves subject to FSA regulations."

Originally the FSA, the architects of the RDR considered UCIS to be an RIP as noted above. Now UCIS does not appear on the current list in the FCA handbook. Instead they have been placed in a special sector called "non-mainstream pooled investments," (NMPIs). These are:

> "...any of the following investments:
>
> (a) a unit in an unregulated collective investment scheme;
>
> (b) a unit in a qualified investor scheme;
>
> (c) a security issued by a special purpose vehicle, other than an excluded security;
>
> (d) a traded life policy investment;
>
> (e) rights to or interests in investments that are any of (a) to (d)."[5]

This change of status arose from concerns about the high risk nature of UCIS and other NMPIs. Research had found that only one in four advised UCIS sales was suitable for retail customers and a number of unregulated schemes had failed with clients losing all their money. So the FCA banned the promotion of UCIS and other NMPIs to most retail clients in January 2014. They can however be promoted to experienced, high net worth clients for whom they may be suitable.

In summary NMPIs have been relegated to a fringe category of esoteric

---

[5] https://www.handbook.fca.org.uk/handbook/glossary/G2763.html © Financial Conduct Authority

products outside the main list of RIPs. It seems to me they are not quite in but neither not quite out. I conclude the FCA are likely to take a soft line if an IFA never recommends a UCIS or other NMPI but to maintain consistency with the principle that independence means an adviser must be aware of all the potential products that could meet a client's needs they are unlikely ever to say this.

Restricted advisers

In contrast to an IFA, a restricted adviser chooses not to give advice on the full range of RIPs. This may be for a variety of reasons. They may feel they lack the competency to advise on more complex investments such as investment trusts, VCTs and EISs. Alternatively their client bank may be relatively unsophisticated and low net worth and have financial needs that do not warrant the use of these products.

Restricted advisers may be pension specialists and have taken a business decision to specialise in that market and not give advice on the full range of investments.

Finally there may be barriers to being an independent adviser, access to suitable research, compliance issues or restrictions on their professional indemnity insurance that prevent them giving advice on all RIPs. Being an independent adviser is certainly more complex and onerous.

Quite frankly I think the term restricted adviser introduced by the RDR is not fit for purpose. It is negative, misleading and off putting. Remember an adviser or firm must disclose to clients their status as independent or restricted at the outset of the advice process. It is a bit like calling cardiac surgeons or cancer consultants, restricted doctors. Yes it is true they do not provide medical treatment on the full range of human illnesses, that is what GPs do but as specialists there is no ambiguity what they do and don't do. I think restricted advisers would be better called something else such as specialists. They may be specialists in pensions or in mainstream investments or specialists in core products - life, pensions and investments.

Although the current term restricted gives independent advisers a big competitive advantage I would not complain if the term specialist adviser was used instead of restricted providing it was made abundantly clear what the nature of their product restriction means. For example you could have the following disclosure:

> *"Your adviser specialises in providing advice on the following core financial planning products - investment bonds, personal pensions, stakeholder pensions, OEICs, unit trusts, structured products and cash based products including National Savings and Investments, but not on VCTs, EISs, investment trusts or ETFs."*

Product provider

The other element of being an independent adviser relates to product provider. The RDR did not change that. Once an IFA has decided a particular product is suitable for a client whether that is a personal pension, OEIC, investment trust or VCT, they must then consider the whole market before recommending a specific provider's product.

A restricted adviser limits the product types they give advice on but the range of providers can take several forms. The FCA give examples of what restricted advice looks like:

- *the adviser works with one product provider and only considers products that company offers*

- *the adviser considers products from several – but not all – product providers*

- *the adviser can recommend one or some types of products, but not all retail investment products*

- *the adviser has chosen to focus on a particular market, such as pensions, and considers products from all providers within that market.*

- *Restricted advisers and firms cannot describe the advice they offer as "independent."*[6]

---

[6] https://www.fca.org.uk/consumers/types-investment-adviser © Financial Conduct Authority

Prior to the RDR most IFAs were restricted in the product types they gave advice on but were independent in terms of product providers they could recommend. Now you can't call yourself an IFA if you are not independent for both products and providers.

It can be a burden for an IFA to have to consider all products and all product providers. A perfectionist can become overwhelmed by the choices and the need to discount a multitude of options. Research can become a nightmare as it is easy to get bogged down in the detail and complexity. For your own sanity and to avoid racking up large fees for your client if you charge on a time cost basis, an IFA must have effective and efficient filtering mechanisms. I will explain mine later but it is worth noting that the search for the perfect can be the enemy of the good.

In the comments section on the Professional Adviser article from November 2011, cited above, IFA, Gillian Cardy offered some wise words:

> "Advisers are required to be "aware of" the range of potential options which could meet a client's needs. This does not equate to exploring / detailing / discounting whole rafts of patently unsuitable products."[7]

Conclusion - independent or restricted?

I chose early on in my career to go down the independent route and I have never regretted it. I also welcomed the broadening of the definition of independence from product provider to product and product provider that the RDR introduced and I would hate to ever have to call myself a restricted adviser.

Surely the ability to say to your clients and potential clients you are unrestricted and offer unbiased and independent advice is best. However I appreciate that for many new entrants you won't have the choice to go down the IFA route if the firm you work for only offers a restricted advice service.

Alternatively to learn your craft you may decide initially to focus on

---

[7] Gillian Cardy in Professional Adviser, November 2011

giving advice on the core financial products only and not on the more esoteric ones such as investment trusts, VCTs or EISs. In any event I would recommend that you aspire to become an independent adviser in time. That is the gold standard. Yes there is more to get to grips with, but the earlier you jump in the better. You have come a long way to become Level 4 qualified. You don't need to be afraid of the extra complexities of learning about investment trusts or VCTs. They are not that difficult to get to grips with.

The concept of independence does have cache amongst the general public and many high net worth clients will choose IFAs rather than restricted advisers. Finally solicitors and accountants may only refer their clients to IFAs due to their regulators' requirements, so if you are looking to develop professional connections being restricted will be a turn-off.

Employed or self-employed?

There are various ways you can work as a financial adviser. You may be with a firm that is directly authorised by the FCA. Once you have reached competent adviser status and can be "let loose" on the general public you will be a Registered Individual (RI) of the firm and you will be authorised to give advice.

The firm you work for will dictate how you operate and whether you offer restricted or independent advice. Given the choice, other things being equal, it won't surprise you that I recommend you opt for a firm that is an IFA.

I am not familiar with modern contracts that you may be offered by directly authorised firms but the contract will invariably be weighted in favour of the firm. After all it was written by them primarily for their benefit. Study the contract carefully, ask questions, get the opinions of close friends in the industry and especially consider what happens to your clients when you leave the firm. If you don't like something in the contract try and get the terms changed. It costs nothing to ask and depending on supply and demand for quality advisers and your own talents you may have some bargaining power.

In the past before the RDR employed financial advisers were thought to be a departure from a pushy sales culture associated with self-employed advisers. This is of course was a myth. No-one was going to pay an adviser a salary of £30,000 p.a. and provide a car and benefits for them to swan around seeing clients, have nice chats over coffee and dispense pearls of financial wisdom. In order for the salary and extras to be paid the adviser had to earn it by bringing in commission from product sales. It may have required a target of up to £100,000 p.a. to justify the remuneration and the costs the firm incurred i.e. office space, professional indemnity insurance and administration staff. If advisers didn't bring in the bacon they were destined for the chop. Employed advisers were under pressure to sell.

Post the RDR, commission has gone from pension and investment business but the targets have not. An employed adviser's target will be fees not commission. Those fees mostly will be adviser charges rather than invoiced fees for example for general financial planning. And where do adviser charges come from? You've guessed it product and investment sales. So what has changed? Not much I suggest - adviser charges are arguably just commission in disguise. The old 3% initial commission plus 0.5% p.a. trail for investments looks very similar to many fee structures today, except that the 0.5% p.a. for ongoing services is more likely to be 0.75% p.a. or 1% p.a.

The only real difference is that adviser charges are not automatically built into the product like commission was and all fees have to be agreed individually with clients.

I can only conclude therefore that to be an employed financial adviser you will need to be a salesman. For IFA like myself who charged invoiced fees long before the RDR there was a clear focus on general holistic advice rather than product sales and this continues today. If you hanker after that model and wish to be free of targets you will probably need to strike out on your own.

At this point you could become a self-employed Appointed Representative (AR) of a network, where you will have a degree of control over your business, for example how you spend your time. You will also be free from targets. However you will face an onerous compliance regime from the network.

I highlighted the problems of networks with their excessive control and bureaucracy and if I could wind the clock back and changed my timelines I would have taken bolder steps much earlier. I would have become independent straight away. I would have also ditched membership of networks sooner and gone for direct authorisation quicker. So please consider learning from my mistakes. My advice is bite the bullet as soon as possible and go down the directly authorised route on your own or with a few trusted other advisers.

Finally on the subject of what type of financial adviser you should be, Andrew Goodwin suggests a different way of looking at it. He is managing director and co-founder of Truly Independent Ltd and in 2017 he published a book called *"The Happy Financial Adviser."* He bangs the drum for independence which I support but then describes two types of adviser - someone who hankers after running a multi-adviser business and someone who wants a lifestyle business. The former is an entrepreneur and driven to achieve something big and make an impact. Goodwin has achieved that with his partner and the firm has a target to have 100 self-employed IFAs on board. In contrast Goodwin defines a lifestyle adviser as follows:

> *"A lifestyle adviser business is a business that is set up primarily by a sole trader financial adviser with the aim of sustaining a particular level of income and no more; or to provide a foundation from which to enjoy a particular lifestyle."*

That describes me to the tee. I have a fantastic work life balance. Work itself is a pleasure not a chore so why change it?

Goodwin then goes on to explain that the risks for a lifestyle adviser are lower.

> *"With no staff, no management and only regulation to abide by, being a lifestyle adviser is a safer bet by following the crowd...The purpose is simply to enjoy what you're doing."*

Goodwin then concludes that a lifestyle adviser business is best positioned through a support firm like Truly Independent Ltd. He rightly points out that there are no start-up costs compared to being directly authorised by the FCA:

> "...you simply join the established firm as a registered individual."

I see his point and for many lifestyle advisers this may be the way to go. For me however being my own boss, determining my own compliance regime and business practices is more important. It is an integral part of being completely independent. I consider the time and money applying for direct authorisation, and expenses of running a compliance regime and undertaking other non-productive business administration is a cost worth paying. That said for newly qualified advisers striking out on your own this is not possible whilst more experienced advisers may also wish to avoid the hassle of running their own business.

Notes

NURS

This stands for Non UCITS Retail Schemes. UCITS is an EU directive and stands for Undertakings in Collective Investments for Transferable Securities. They are funds regulated by the EU and include unit trusts and OEICs. NURS are regulated funds but cannot be marketed outside their home country. Many common multi-asset funds opt for NURS status for the additional investment powers they permit.

PRIIPS - Packaged Retail Insurance-based Investment Products

This is another major piece of EU regulation which came into force on 1/1/18. It relates to advice on investment bonds, structured products and investment trusts and requires advisers to provide their clients with a standardised document called a key investor document (KID), not to be confused with a key investor information document (KIID). The latter are for authorised and regulated unit trusts and OEICs.

According to HSBC private banking:

> *"The Regulation is intended to make it easier for retail investors to understand and compare the key features, risk, rewards and costs of different products in scope of PRIIPs through the provision of the KID. This is a free-of-charge pre-contractual, stand-alone document that is to be shared with the investor prior to the conclusion of any transaction."*[8]

Like much regulation PRIIPs is well intended but poorly thought through and it has created real problems for the investment industry as I explain in Chapter 7.

---

[8] https://www.hsbcprivatebank.com/en/about-us/priips

4. Charging for financial advice

Initial free consultation

Whilst there are a multitude of fee charging structures pretty well all advisers offer potential new clients an initial consultation without charge or obligation. I describe this on my website:

"An initial telephone discussion or meeting of up to an hour is offered without charge or obligation. The purpose of this session is to help you decide if you want to appoint me as your IFA but also for us to clarify your financial objectives and needs and the nature of the work that is required. I will not take you on as a client unless I am sure the advice has greater value than its cost. Value normally means the expected benefits from good investment returns or tax savings but it also includes assurance and guidance through complex financial planning decisions."

In summary the introductory meeting or telephone discussion is like a blind date. The potential new client may have come by recommendation or liked my website enough to make contact but I still need to win his or her confidence. Normally I don't give too much advice at these sessions. Not that I am too cagey or stingy to do so, but the initial discussion is primarily about getting to know the person and assessing if we can and should work together. The decision naturally has to be mutual.

If I feel I can help the client, this depends on three criteria, and he or she wants to appoint me as their IFA I ask them to sign my Client Agreement. This is a combined terms of business and fee agreement, a copy of which you can find as an appendix at the back of the book. At that point all work becomes chargeable.

The three criteria I refer to in deciding if I want to take on a new client are:

1. We have a good rapport and we communicate well.
2. I am confident that the work needed is within my field of expertise and scope of authorisation, and that I can give relevant

and beneficial advice. For example I do not give advice on defined benefit pension transfers or mortgages. Incidentally there no requirement to advise in these areas in order to call yourself an independent financial adviser.

3. The value of my work will exceed its estimated cost for the client.

One point to make here which is expanded on in the next chapter is that I don't travel to potential new clients' homes for the initial consultation. It either happens at my home office or by phone. I have taken a position that the consultation is free but my travel time is not.

Timed charges v percentage fees

This is a controversial topic and is highly nuanced. Like most advisers I have strong views on it.

I am in a small minority and I have taken a strategic view to charge for my services solely on an hourly basis, which is £160 per hour. This used to be about the going rate for advisers in the south east of England, however I may be charging less than the average as my fee rate hasn't increased since 2012.

I do not need to charge VAT as my firm's turnover is below the threshold for registration. However it is worth noting that not all fees are liable for VAT even if a firm is VAT registered. Fees that are deemed to be for intermediation are exempt whilst advisory work is liable for VAT.

Intermediation would include advising and arranging an investment portfolio or a pension. Advisory work includes an inheritance tax assessment or an investment review although either could lead to advice on products which would be intermediation. It is complex and you may need to take a view or advice if your firm is VAT registered on what the predominant service is or whether you can legitimately split the fee into two parts, advisory and intermediation with VAT added to the former element only.

Whilst I have always favoured and almost exclusively used a time charge for the vast majority of my clients I previously had a few with larger portfolios on a fixed fee for annual investment reviews. This was calculated as 0.6% p.a. of the value of their portfolio. However I scrapped this in 2018 and moved to an hourly fee for everything, a method of charging which the industry has largely eschewed in favour of percentage fees. So what are the pros and cons of the various fee options?

A time charge is common in other professions such as the legal and accountancy and arguably adopting it raises the profile and professionalism of IFAs. Solicitors and accountants may also feel more comfortable in making referrals to an IFA knowing their charging structure is similar to their own.

A time charge is highly transparent if a timesheet is provided. An example is attached as an appendix to this chapter. It enables some work items to be cross checked by clients. For example if I record a 40 minute telephone conversation on a particular date the client can judge if this is reasonable and accords with their estimate. They may also take a view on the time recorded to produce a report they receive. Of course they can't check everything, for example the time spent on research or administration. It would be easy for advisers to cheat and inflate the time spent on the multiple work items that go onto timesheets but this is where ethics and trust come into play.

The principle benefit however of an hourly fee is that for advice on large investment sums the cost is invariably cheaper and represents significantly better value for clients. According to an article in Money Marketing on 28/10/16 data released by the FCA showed:

> "The average charges for initial advice are 1% minimum and 3% maximum. For ongoing charges, the average rates are 0.5% minimum and 1% maximum. For firms charging an hourly fee, national average minimum and maximum rates vary between £150 and £195 per hour.[9]"

Consider a portfolio of £500,000. An adviser charging 2% upfront will

---

[9] https://www.moneymarketing.co.uk/fca-reveals-advisers-charging-clients/

receive £10,000 and if they charge 3% the fee is £15,000.

I estimate on average I could undertake the work in researching, advising and arranging a suitable investment portfolio in around 15 to 17 hours. At £160 p.h. that equates to a fee of £2,400 to £2,720, much less than the percentage fees quoted above and almost half if the minimum 1% initial fee is paid.

The problem with percentage fees for large investment sums is there is a major disconnect between the fee and the work undertaken. I would suggest in the majority of cases if those who charged percentage (*ad valorem*) fees actually timed their work and multiplied the number of hours spent by their charge out rate, if they have one, or an average charge out rate, if they don't, the cost would be significantly less than the £10,000 to £15,000 cited.

Paul Lewis financial journalist and presenter of BBC Radio 4's Moneybox programme thinks percentage fees are a rip off. He penned an interesting article in Money Marketing in February 2017 entitled,

> "*Percentage charges are destroying client wealth,*" [10]

In the article he rightly lays into the advice industry for high charges. Whilst I share his sentiment and do not favour percentage fees they do have some actual benefits. Other advantages are claimed by their proponents but these are disputed.

One real benefit is that a percentage fee is fixed and provides certainty for clients. They will know exactly how much they will pay in advance. In contrast an hourly charge is open ended. Whilst I provide estimates of the cost of the work before it commences it is easy to underestimate as invariably unforeseen complications arise and the work may prove more extensive than it appears at outset. This is especially the case when I take on a new client for a financial or investment review. At the start I have very limited information on their finances. I won't get a full picture until I have a completed fact find and obtained comprehensive information

---

[10] https://www.moneymarketing.co.uk/issues/9-february-2017-2/paul-lewis-percentage-charges-destroying-client-wealth/

on their investments, pensions and protection policies. The work required initially is not well defined. It is a bit like a builder opening up the floor boards of a house or examining the roof space for the first time, he is never sure what he might find. If a client's affairs are comprehensive and complex you may discover the financial equivalent of damp or dry rot which results in additional work and cost for the client to rectify.

Overshooting a fee estimate requires management by advisers - if possible by warning a client in advance, explaining why it has happened and in some cases discounting the final bill, especially if the original estimate is way out. However in time clients will come to trust you as they experience you normally deliver advice on or around budget and you are not overcharging them.

A benefit claimed by advocates of percentage fees is that investor and adviser interests are aligned. There is an incentive for the adviser to give high quality investment advice at outset and to undertake regular reviews. This is because the adviser's fee is directly correlated with their clients' investment returns and portfolio growth. A percentage fee is a reward for success. Similarly an adviser's fee is reduced if their clients' investment returns falls. That said there is a potential conflict of interest if the adviser takes more investment risk with clients' portfolios than would be warranted in order to boost their fees. In contrast a time charge is unrelated to portfolio performance and is free from this potential bias.

In addition Paul Lewis challenges the idea that percentage fees mean adviser and client interests are aligned. He writes:

> "It is also a myth that a percentage fee somehow aligns the adviser's interests with their clients'. If a client's wealth falls from £1m to £900,000, they lose £100,000 – but the fee is just £1,000 less at £9,000. In fact, it can misalign interests. Buying a property to let out or paying off debt may be the best advice. But the adviser's interest is for the client to maintain the invested assets on which the percentage fee is charged."

A second real benefit of percentage fees is that they are very good value for small investment sums. However at a certain level they become uneconomic for the adviser. For a client who wants advice on investing say £5,000, a 3% fee will generate just £150. This cannot cover the true cost of the advice. Some firms may however take on the work as a loss leader or subsidise the cost from clients with very large portfolios. However in the article above Paul Lewis queries why these latter clients should pay over the odds so the firm can take on smaller investors.

In fairness many adviser firms will have minimum fee amounts. A quick search on the web found the following fee structure for one IFA:

> *"Our fee for this service is based on a percentage of the amount you invest and/or transfer. These fees are applied as follows but are subject to a minimum of £300:*
>
> - *Up to £150,000 – 3%*
>
> - *£150,001 to £250,000 – 2.5%*
>
> - *£250,001 to £500,000 – 2%*
>
> - *£500,001 and above – 1.5%*
>
> - *Over £1m – By negotiation."*

Even though a minimum fee of £300 applies it is still not high enough to meet the true cost of the work for a £5,000 investor.

Unfortunately for me the regulatory cost to advise a client with £5,000 to invest means it is not worth my while taking them on. Even working very efficiently with slim line advice the full time cost might be three hours, costing £480. I simply can't justify a fee that is equivalent to 9.6% of the amount invested. As stated it is axiomatic for me that the value of the work exceeds its cost and if it doesn't there is no point in the client getting advice from me. I'll come back to the issue of how to communicate the value of advice later.

The other point to note from the charging structure quoted above is that percentage fee structures are frequently tiered as the amounts invested increase. Even so in this case the cost of advice on investments up to £1 million ranges from 1.5% to 3% which is still too high in my view.

I explained I previously used a 0.6% p.a. fee for a set annual review service for a small number of clients with large portfolios typically £300,000 to £700,000 but I have since ditched it for an hourly charge. Not operating by the clock has the benefit that you are not constantly monitoring and recording your time but on the other hand a fixed fee structure creates pressures of its own. This is because there is no limit on the work that can be included. A conscientious adviser could undertake more analysis, research, reporting and compliance than is needed in pursuit of perfection. It is easy to get bogged down trying to find the right funds for a client and spend inordinate time discounting other options. Finally a fixed fee has to accommodate unexpected complications that arise or whatever demands your clients makes on your time unless you set limits on it. Most clients are very reasonable. However you may have some who have endless questions about minor or even trivial issues. A fixed or percentage fee compels you to address these plus and all new regulatory requirements for no extra charge.

In contrast a time charge means an adviser can focus on the essentials and work efficiently as it regulates the instinct to undertake more work than is necessary. The regulator is the fee estimate you have provided your client. In my experience if I aim for perfection I am going to way overshoot my quote. A time charge means an adviser has to constantly ask, is it worth the client paying for this extra non-essential work, bearing in mind the law of diminishing returns? Does the cost of this represent good value?

The other benefit of a time charge is that I can tailor my reviews so they are varied, bespoke or shortened as appropriate. In contrast when I used a 0.6% p.a. fee I provided a set and extensive investment review each year which largely followed the same pattern. What I cover in investment reviews is discussed later in the book.

Under my old charging structure as portfolios values increased over the years so did my fees. This meant less time consuming or simplified reviews were not possible because the work done had to be extensive enough to justify the high fee. Of course the fee was known in advance once I had updated clients' investment valuation statements. So if a portfolio was valued at £500,000 the fee would be £3,000. The review undertaken then had to be of sufficient length to ensure that fee represented good value for the client.

With a time charge the fee is not known in advance and the starting point is to ask what work is required for this client's review, based on their current financial needs, portfolio valuation and profitability, their asset allocation, their attitude to risk and market conditions. It avoids the pressure to undertake additional work or the temptation to pad reports to justify the high fee.

On a time charge basis I find reviews can be varied to keep them fresh, make them more interesting or simplified if appropriate, leading to lower fees. The point I am making here is a percentage charge or any other fixed fee starts with the cost and the work undertaken has to fit that. The charge drives the work. With an hourly charge it is the other way around, the starting point is the work that needs to be done and this determines the fee. I think that is a better way to work.

Another benefit of an hourly charge is that if a client decides to abort the work part way through the advice process or does not wish to go ahead with the new investments, which incidentally virtually never happens, I will invoice them for the work I have done to date. This is made clear in my Client Agreement. The client will receive a copy of my timesheet and there is normally no disputing how much they owe. If however you charge a percentage fee what do you do if the client aborts the work part way through or decides against going ahead with your investment advice? *"Sorry Mike I have decided to go for a buy to let property instead of investing with you."* You simply cannot charge your initial fee of 2% or 3% as this is contingent on the investments going ahead.

The firm I quoted above also refer to a set financial review fee of £450. This is waived if the client then asks for advice on arranging investments and the implementation fee exceeds this. For example for a £100,000 investment the implementation fee is 3% or £3,000 and this exceeds the £450. The latter presumably would be charged if the client aborted the investment advice but the adviser might have done 7-10 hours of work already on creating an investment portfolio, and that will mean a financial loss for the firm. My method of charging ensures I am fully remunerated in these circumstances.

To keep costs down I normally ask clients to undertake certain administration tasks themselves. The most obvious example is I request that clients complete the fact find. I don't see the point in charging them for a one to two hour meeting to do this. On receipt I will check the details and clarify various points if necessary, naturally charging for my time. The cost is less expensive for the client doing it this way. It may also be appropriate for clients to complete certain application forms depending on their complexity.

Advocates of percentage fees will argue their case. One proposed that charging an hourly rate is restrictive to growth of a firm's income. Supposedly it is incompatible with becoming more efficient because the quicker the work is completed the less fees clients are charged! That may be true, however being more efficient buys more time and enables an adviser charging by the hour to take on new clients and undertake more chargeable work. In addition being more efficient means the client pays lower fees. That is a good client outcome, is it not?

That said the fairness to clients of an hourly charge has been challenged. The argument goes that the lack of incentive to be efficient means advisers will simply take longer to conclude a piece of advice business. Whilst unscrupulous advisers may string out work in the same way some lawyers might do to bump up their fees, this would be an anathema to honest advisers. Moreover there is an incentive to work efficiently because lower fees are beneficial to clients and they are more likely to consider the cost of the work to be good value. Happy clients are repeat clients and they are more likely to recommend you to their friends and family.

The flip side of the argument is that firms on fixed percentages have a big incentive to be efficient. This is because the quicker the work gets done the higher the equivalent fee rate per hour. So if an adviser charges a 3% fee on an investment of say £50,000, i.e. £1,500 and does the work in eight hours as opposed to the normal 10 hours, due to efficiency savings the effective hourly fee rate increases from £150 per hour to £187.50 per hour. However the benefits of efficiency passes solely to the adviser, the client gets none. How is that a good client outcome? In contrast the hourly charging adviser automatically passes on efficiency savings in reduced fees to their clients. I know which model seems fairer to me.

Finally on a comparison between hourly charges and percentage fees there are risks to a firm's income for those who operate on percentage fees. I explained one earlier, what happens if the client does not proceed with the advice and hours and hours of work have already been done? The 2% or 3% initial fee does not get paid.

The second risk is what happens if stock markets crash and remain at depressed levels. It slashes fee income in cash terms if charges are set at 0.5% to 1% p.a. This was a point made powerfully by Paul Armson in an article in Money Marketing.[11]

Paul is the creator of the "Inspiring Advisers Lifestyle Financial Planning Online Coaching Programme," a bit of a mouthful if you don't mind me saying so Paul! He writes:

> *"Why create a service proposition that depends on the one thing you cannot control - the performance of the money? It is suicidal."*

With regulatory and PII costs rising, poor investment returns can devastate a firm's income. It is a brutal but accurate assessment. Of course this problem does not arise for advisers working on an hourly charge. If markets fall sharply then their income is protected assuming the same work is done for ongoing reviews.

Paul Armson also explained a recurring theme in conversations he was having with advisers when asked, what is the most worrying challenge that they face. The response is that fee discussions with clients are starting to hurt and they are being lost to other advisers who are willing to undercut them. He notes:

> *"...now many advisers are finding their 1 per cent a year fees are sticking out like a sore thumb."*

The more clients' portfolios grow the larger the adviser's fee. If stock markets soar, investment returns will be good but the fees start to look unjustifiably high compared to the work undertaken. For large portfolios the cost disparity between an hourly fee and a percentage

---

[11] www.moneymarketing.co.uk/paul-armson-time-to-step-away-from-the-suicidal-value-proposition/ (12/2/19)

charge is huge as I demonstrated above.

In conclusion the argument that percentage fees are aligned with client interests is on somewhat shaky ground.

The next section also continues on the theme of percentage fees and their relationship with contingent charges.

Contingent charges and percentage fees

I don't like or use contingent fees. These are where an adviser is paid only if the advice is acted on by the client. The examples of percentage fees described above for investment advice are types of contingent charges, as the adviser's earnings vary widely depending on whether the client proceeds with the recommended investments or not. This needs to be understood as contingent charges are often identified to be an issue solely for defined benefit pension transfers.

Contingent charges have become a hot potato and during my writing of this book after the FCA originally backed down from imposing a ban on these for defined benefit pension transfer advice they have since changed their minds. A ban is now being planned.

In respect of pension transfers a contingent charge is where a relatively small fee (or none) is levied for the firm to assess whether a defined benefit transfer is in the best interests of the client. If it is, a much larger percentage fee is levied to implement the transfer and provide the investment advice. If a transfer is not suitable the client walks away having paid just the small fixed fee or nothing.

Whilst I don't give advice on transfers from defined benefit pensions I do occasionally advise on transfers from personal pensions or occupational money purchase pensions without protected benefits. I don't like and never use contingent fees for two reasons. Firstly there is a big financial benefit for the adviser for the transfer to go ahead. Even if the adviser does not talk up the transfer or push the client into the sale when it is not in their best interests there is always the perception of bias. It is no different to the days of commission. If the client went ahead and bought a product the adviser got a handsome payment, if the client didn't, the adviser earned nothing. We know what human nature is like!

The second reason I don't use contingent fees is that I am not prepared to work for nothing or lose money if a client doesn't go ahead. Nor am I prepared to subsidise those who walk away by charging more to clients who proceed with my advice.

I understand the argument that says clients may not choose to get advice if they had to pay a full fee for the initial pension review only to be told they should stick with the original defined benefit pension. Perhaps, but if the adviser explained the value of that decision, i.e. giving up a gold plated defined benefit pension is not in their interests, that a SIPP in drawdown would almost certainly never provide as good a pension and the risks are too great, maybe the client would think paying a £2,000 to £3,000 fee for the pension review is worth it. They were tempted by a six figure pension transfer value, they had taken the step to explore a transfer and can they now finally put the matter to bed. They had avoided a big financial trap and protected what may be their largest financial asset. Surely that has real value.

Fixed Fees

It should be stated that some advisers neither charge by the hour or percentages. Instead they charge a fixed fee. They may even have a menu of services each with a published cost.

Ignoring the fact that a percentage charge is an example of a fixed fee the question that then arises is how is it determined? Unless an adviser can explain the methodology a fixed fee can look like a figure plucked out of thin air. In contrast an hourly charge or percentage fee is easy to explain.

Logically those who charge fixed fees should determine it by estimating the time that is required to complete the work multiplied by the firm's hourly rate, perhaps with a contingency addition of say 10% on top for unforeseen complexities. Alternatively the fixed fee could be determined by the perceived value to the client.

My view is if you charge a fixed fee other than a percentage charge you need to be able to articulate how you have arrived at it.

Timed charges - a regulator of compliance

Finally I think a time charge is a powerful tool to regulate the level of compliance. My views will be controversial and I will write more on this in Chapter 8 but the principle here is that working on a time charge basis means all client specific compliance is charged to the client, whether that is fact finding, suitability reports, risk disclosures, MIFID II reporting or keeping registers. General firm or adviser based compliance tasks such as FCA returns or CPD naturally are not charged to clients.

The point is the greater the regulatory activity the more the client pays and that raises a moral issue for me which I will cover later on.

How I operate timed charges

My starting point is that pretty well everything I do for a client gets charged. It is based on the conviction that my time is one of my most valuable commodities and for the sake of my self-esteem I am not prepared to work for nothing after the initial introductory free meeting. I did plenty of that in the past earning nothing after prospects walked away from my advice despite putting in hours of work. It is about being fair to myself, recognising I am a business not a charity and respecting the years of study, experience and skills my clients benefit from. At the same time I am scrupulous about being fair to clients to ensure they are only charged for necessary work and get good value for the fees they pay.

Once a new client appoints me as their IFA by signing my Client Agreement I create a timesheet. You can see an example at the end of the chapter. You will see I record three things, the date of the work, the work done and the time spent in minutes. I record time using a digital clock counter, the sort of thing you can buy for the kitchen that counts down and bleeps when the target cooking time has been reached. It sits on my desk. At the start of the chargeable work I typically set the clock counter to say one hour and press start. When the work ends or I am interrupted by a phone call I stop the clock. If at the end of the work session the clock says 21 minutes I record 39 minutes on the timesheet. It is not that difficult.

I record true times for very small minor items of work. For example a two minute phone call goes down as two minutes. I don't round up as I understand solicitors and others do to a minimum of six minutes or an inflation busting 15 minutes as recently suggested by a friend. In some cases I waive the charge for certain minor queries or tasks.

On occasions I forget to set the clock or turn it back on when I am interrupted or turn it off when I go to the loo. In these circumstances estimates are required and any benefit of doubt goes to the client. It is not perfect but it has worked very well for me and my clients over many years. Pretty well everything gets charged - generic advice, telephone calls, e-mails, fund and product research, client specific administration, reports and compliance. I don't charge clients for mistakes that product providers or platform make. I bear the cost myself for minor ones but if they are protracted and time consuming I may seek to recoup my costs from the provider.

I don't record long call waiting times getting through to investment or insurance companies. I just put the call on speaker phone, listen to the music, some good some bad and get on with other work. I do however get cross at the repeated inane messages thanking me for my patience (that is an assumption), telling me that my call will be answered as soon as possible (that is blindingly obvious) or their agents know I am waiting (glad they are on the ball). Fortunately most of the product providers that deal with IFAs have quick pick up times.

It is true that clients are aware when they call me the clock start ticking which is not to everyone's taste but it does concentrate the mind. The client typically gets to the point quickly and I will address their issues succinctly but thoroughly to keep the time costs down to a minimum. If the client is a friend and wants to chat socially I'll stop the clock and only record relevant work time.

At the bottom of the timesheet the total number of minutes is totted up using a spreadsheet calculation and the gross charge is recorded. Underneath I add any credits that need to be taken into account. These may be residual commissions received, adviser charge payments, compensation payments or discretionary discounts I have offered. The latter are offered from time to time for selected clients in certain circumstances, for example in recognition that the cost of advice is especially high, they have been a longstanding customer or they have frequently recommended me.

Please note however I never offer clients a financial incentive for recommendations. In fact I never ask clients to recommend me full stop. They do it entirely off their own backs. It is because they have friends or family who need independent financial advice and trust me enough to recommend me.

The bottom line is the net fee and this is what I invoice a client for.

Payment of fees by invoices or adviser charges

Although I have some clients who pay their fees in whole or part by adviser charges, facilitated by product providers, I much prefer pure invoiced fees. The main reason is that an adviser charge coming out of the investment or pension reduces the amount that is invested and hence it reduces the long term returns.

Take a client who comes to me for advice on creating a portfolio of £500,000. Earlier I estimated a time charge of 15-17 hours with a fee of up to £2,720. If this is paid as an adviser charge the amount the client invests is reduced to £497,280. I take the view the client will benefit more in the long term if they invested the full £500,000 and paid my fee from cash savings. After all this is almost certainly earning a very low rate of interest and surplus cash could be better deployed elsewhere. For example if the investments grow by 6% p.a. every year net of charges for 10 years the £2,720 will be worth £4,871. If the £2,720 is retained in cash at a net interest rate of 1.5% p.a. its value will be £3,156, i.e. £1,715 less. Of course other scenarios are possible and there are no guarantees here but if you believe and tell your clients that long term investment in equities is better than cash savings why would you use adviser charges?

Naturally I am flexible and a client with insufficient cash savings may prefer an adviser charge. I am also aware that for pension business an adviser charge may attract tax relief. As an example consider a net pension contribution of £20,000, which grosses up to £25,000 once basic rate tax relief is added. Let us say my fee is estimated to be £500 the client could make a net contribution of £20,400, the gross pension contribution is now £25,500. The product provider facilitates an adviser charge of £500 but the net cost to the client has been £400. In addition if the client is a higher rate taxpayer a further £100 tax relief will be due on the additional £400 paid in to cover the adviser charge.

Another reason why I prefer pure invoiced fees is as mentioned earlier, they feel more professional. They mirror how you pay your solicitor or accountant. In contrast adviser charges look like commissions especially where adviser charges of 3% initial and 0.5% or 0.75% p.a. ongoing apply which as noted is similar to the old commission structure typical of the industry before the RDR.

Charging for advice on pure protection business

I treat pure protection business in the same way as I do for investments or pensions, charging by the hour. However there is a big difference. Commission is still payable from term assurance and non-investment critical illness and income protection policies. These payments are often substantial. The thinking behind allowing commission to continue post the RDR is that people don't normally buy insurance and without it advisers would have no incentive to sell life cover or critical illness insurance. The result would be a bigger protection gap than already exists.

Depending on the size of the premium the initial commission may exceed the fee and in these circumstances I rebate the excess to the client, either as a timesheet credit, an offset against the cost of other work or as a cash payment. The latter is not deemed *"an annual payment,"* for tax purposes as it originates from pure protection commission and is tax free for the client. This is not the case for legacy commissions or adviser charges from investments that are paid in cash to clients.

I suspect my approach is pretty well unique in the industry, working on a time charge basis and rebating all excess commission back to clients. It is not without risk. If a client ceases to pay premiums on the policy in the initial period, typically up to 48 months, commission will be clawed back by the life company. To mitigate this risk I make it clear in these circumstances that I will recall the cash payment in whole or part. Here is what I wrote to one client:

"The excess commission is £620.10 which I plan to pay-out to you shortly

as a cash payment to your bank. Please note cash payments of commissions from pure protection policies are tax free and do not need to be disclosed to HMRC (unlike payments from investments).

The commission rebate is made subject to the condition that you continue to pay premiums on the insurance policy during the initial period of 48 months. If you cease payments during the initial period Scottish Widows will reclaim some of the £1,545.43 initial commission from my firm and I will make a corresponding claim from you. For example if you stop premiums after 12 months the expected clawback will be ¾ x £1,545.43 = £1,159.07. In these circumstances we have:

My fee (as per the timesheet)	£925.33	
Commission retained after clawback	-£233.74	(£1,545.43 - £1,159.07 - £620.10)
Payment from you	£1,159.07	(£925.33 + £233.74)

Finally renewal commissions, paid from year five onwards are not normally rebated to clients."

In some circumstances if the excess commission is very large or the client is new, and I am not sure of their trustworthiness I would pay the client out in yearly instalments.

Finally I have found that foregoing initial commission instead of making a cash rebate to the client only reduces the premium marginally and it does not seem to represent good value for the client.

Ongoing commissions and cash rebates to clients

I do not normally credit renewal commissions from pure protection policies to clients' timesheets. Generally these are very small, typically 2.5% of the premium and often are less than £1 p.m. Monitoring and recording small commissions is fairly onerous for advisers for the relatively small benefit for clients and they are retained on the grounds they are trivial. The concept of triviality was introduced by the FSA, the predecessor to the FCA and is explained below. That said the time I spend handing minor queries or servicing protection policies is not normally charged to client timesheets.

Following depolarisation of the advice market in 2005 there was no requirement to rebate commissions from pure protection policies for IFAs who wished to offer a fee only service. In contrast this was stipulated for investments and pensions plus income protection or life assurance with an investment element. Even so the FSA permitted fee only IFAs to retain trivial commissions. At what level this was set seemingly was up to the individual firm to decide.

In contrast trail commission from investment and pension pots was always much more substantial and if it is still paid, it is usually credited in full to client timesheets. The exceptions are where the commissions are very small or the client is inactive or we have lost contact and therefore he or she does not have a timesheet.

It should also be noted that in no circumstances should a cash rebate from commission or adviser charges arising from a pension plan be made to a client as these are unauthorised payments and could be subject to penalty charges. In addition care needs to be taken when taking an adviser charge from a pension plan. The fee paid should only be used to cover advice on that pension and associated retirement planning. It cannot be used to pay for other work for example a review of an ISA portfolio.

The rules that restrict adviser charges being rebated to clients or being used to cover non-pension advice exist because ordinarily all payments from pensions are taxable. An adviser charge is exempt provided it is used correctly.

Value of advice

The *value* of advice is the other side of the coin to the *cost* of advice. As advisers we should be able to explain to clients the value or potential value of our advice. If they judge that the benefits will outweigh the costs they are likely to willingly accept your charges, providing they are reasonable. In principle therefore whenever you talk to your clients about the cost of your advice you should explain the value of the advice they can reasonably expect to receive.

The benefits of financial advice are both quantitative and qualitative. The former is defined in cash terms in pounds, shillings and pence. It includes paying lower premiums on a life assurance policy, improved investment returns, reduced fund management charges and policy fees or a reduction in an inheritance tax liability.

Moreover as an IFA you may be able to negotiate or secure discounts for your clients from product providers. Recently my representative at a major platform provisionally offered me a discount on their platform charge from 0.25% p.a. to 0.16% p.a. for a large personal pension transfer.

On a similar theme an annuity provider recently offered a potential enhancement on their quote, (it was already the best of all who quoted), after I explained the client had decided against an annuity purchase. Although they could not match my cheeky request the point is you may have the opportunity to add value for clients who do opt for an annuity purchase.

Finally on quantitative value I have frequently got money back for clients from companies due to errors or poor service.

Qualitative benefits are more difficult to define. They are more subjective and are experienced at an emotional level. The value may be that your clients are assured their financial affairs are in good order. It may be confirmation he or she is on track to retire at a certain date or has peace of mind that a competent financial adviser is professionally managing their affairs and guiding them through the complex and confusing array of options. Imagine an inexperienced investor who receives a large inheritance which requires investing. Attempting a DIY process can lead to confusion and anxiety with the sheer number of choices. The internet is full of useful information and potential traps but it is often overwhelming and difficult to filter. What is true? What isn't? What is relevant to me? I don't understand this investment. What are the risks? What are the tax implications? A quote from E O Wilson is apt here:

"We are drowning in information, while starving for wisdom."

Information overload does not always help people make good decisions. It is why people are driven to seek professional help. They feel a need for someone who they can trust to guide them through the complexity and give personal advice that is suitable for them. This is a major reason why I consider the outlook for the advice industry to be bright. DIY investing, low cost robo-advice and guidance services will be suitable for some but not for all or even the majority.

Coming back to the quantitative value of advice it is important to inform clients that improved investment returns cannot be guaranteed in advance. However I can tell a client that there is a very good chance of this, based on sound thinking and experience. Consider these benefits of investment reviews:

1. Retaining large holdings in poor funds for too long is a drag on portfolio returns. Weeding out the laggards which have minimal prospects for recovery in favour of better quality funds with greater investment potential will most likely improve returns in the medium to long term.

I guess it is like inviting an expert in antiques into your house to rummage through your loft and identify what is valuable and what is rubbish. An adviser should be able to review a client's financial arrangements, policies and investments and say "that's good, keep; that's very highly valued, time to cash in or that's junk, ditch." What you end up with should be better quality.

2. Good management of the asset allocation of the portfolio is likely to pay dividends in terms of improved returns. The changes needed may be wholesale or just minor tweaks. I frequently find when I take on new clients a significant revamp to their asset allocation is needed. Invariably their portfolio is unsuitable for current market conditions or it is out of balance, for example it is dominated by a very large amount in a single fund or there is too much cash. Moreover it may not reflect the investor's attitude to risk, capacity for loss or requirement for ethical investment.

At the end of 2018 I took on some new clients. They both held SIPPs valued at £465,000 between them but the whole lot was in a single fund. As it happens it was a good defensive multi-asset fund, one that I have recommended to my clients, but not in truck loads as here! These clients were highly exposed to fund manager risk, i.e. him making bad asset allocation and stock selection calls. The portfolio was crying out for greater asset allocation diversity, a good spread of funds and a greater allocation to equities to take advantage of the sharp sell-off in equity markets from September to December 2018. The clients also wanted some ethical investment. Their pre-existing fund was not ethically managed or a socially responsible investment (SRI). So I recommended a portfolio of funds that included global equities, specialist equities, UK and global smaller companies, property and multi-asset.

When I undertake reviews for existing clients minor changes more than wholesale revamps are usual. However throughout the spring and summer of 2018, fearing a sell-off in equities I recommended profit-taking and risk reduction and a shift from equities to multi-asset and other cautious risk funds. It wasn't a "we are all doomed," message with advice to sell all equities to cash and run for the hills but an asset allocation adjustment. It proved a good call as when the sell-off came in the autumn client portfolios were modestly impacted. In contrast some markets and sectors fell into correction territory, with falls of 10% or into bear country, with losses of 20% or more.

3. Experience that good advisers do deliver good investment returns and can prove that retrospectively. Demonstrating this requires future reviews to see what returns have been achieved.

One way I have done this is to benchmark all a client's funds' returns against the Investment Association (IA) sector average over one and three years, sometimes five years, or I look at quartile rankings. Of course I have recommended plenty of duff investments and made bad calls but I think in all the years I have undertaken investment reviews I have found significantly more of my recommended funds have beaten the average than have underperformed it and the number of first and second quartile funds has exceeded the number of third and fourth quartile ones.

Communicating the value of advice

One way I communicate value is to put the fee into context. Take the £500,000 investment portfolio described earlier. I stated I could advise and arrange this in around 15-17 hours. Taking the upper estimate, a fee of £2,720 will apply. As a percentage that is 0.544% p.a. of the amount invested. In relative terms this is very good value compared to the 1% to 3% fees that the FCA found many advisers typically charge.

What I might say to a client in this situation is that 0.544% is the hurdle rate for the required investment growth to recoup that initial advice fee. It is a very modest target in my view especially as it only needs to be achieved once not year on year. In fact any half decent investment adviser should be able achieve that easily. If the portfolio grows by a modest 4% p.a. return net of platform and fund charges the client will gain much more than the advice costs they have paid, even if a fee for annual reviews equivalent to around 0.5% - 0.6% p.a. is taken into account.

I would also argue that most investment advisers would be reasonably expected to achieve higher portfolio returns over the medium to long term than a client acting on their own using a DIY approach. Moreover the margin of that outperformance should be considerably more than the hurdle rate, in this case 0.544%. The tools advisers have for doing this are knowledge of stock markets and funds, skills in asset allocation and high quality fund selection using research capabilities that we have access to.

My instinct that an adviser outperformance premium exists is backed up by research carried out by Intrinsic, an IFA network in conjunction with consultants Boring Money. They found investing without advice can cost investors dearly in lost returns and risks. According to Intrinsic's chief executive, Andy Thompson:

> *"...unadvised investors suffer an average annual loss of around 5% compared with the sort of risk-based, diversified portfolio an adviser will usually recommend."*[12]

---

[12] Money Marketing (17/1/19)

The annual loss referred to is not absolute in the sense that DIY investors will reduce their capital 5% every year but it is relative i.e. their returns will underperform those of IFAs by 5% p.a.

Here are two communications (both slightly edited to improve the text) from actual client scenarios after I have provided quotes for work that explain the value of advice:

> "It is important to assess the cost of the work in relation to the value of the work. It is axiomatic for me that I am sure the value of the work will exceed its cost. Otherwise why should clients engage me? Initially the value for clients comes from having confidence that high quality and suitable platforms, investment strategies and investments have been selected, pitfalls are avoided, considerable time savings made and anxiety is reduced compared to a DIY solution. Later I expect value to become evident from good investment returns and profit levels that far exceed the cost of advice."

The second focuses on the benefits of switching to a lower charging platform which offers a much greater investment choice and access to the highest quality funds:

> "Advice costs should also be assessed in relation to the value of advice. Lower charges offer an easily quantifiable and certain benefit. For example take platform fees. ATS's (Alliance Trust Savings) charge is £350 p.a. prior to drawdown whereas Aviva's charge of 0.21% p.a. which is £1,186 p.a. based on a pension fund value of £565,000. So there is an immediate saving of £836 in the first year, greater if fund growth is taken into account.
>
> Crucially the benefit accumulates year on year and recoups my fee of £3,336 in four years. However where I think the greater value will arise is from the vastly improved investment choice and access to the fullest range of assets, funds and fund managers. I cannot stress how significant this is. An enhanced portfolio return of just 0.6% p.a. will recoup my fee in the first year and start to add value in year two.
>
> A rather crude analogy might be picking a football team from the best players residing in N16 and E5 (the area of London where my client lives) and putting them against a team picked from the best players in the rest of the country. Whilst the team from Stoke Newington and Clapton

might beat the UK All Stars XI you probably wouldn't bet on it!"

You may have different ways to communicate value but it should be integral to the provision of quotes and discussions on the cost of advice.

Fee estimates

If you operate using a time charge you will not always be able to provide an estimate in advance, for example a telephone call from a client with a query that has to be addressed immediately. You don't know if it will take 10, 20 or 40 minutes so you can't give an estimate, but your client knows the clock will be ticking.

A second example is when undertaking investment reviews. I don't know at outset how many fund switches I will recommend before I have undertaken the initial portfolio and fund assessment. So I can't give a firm quote for the whole review. In these circumstances I normally quote for the initial review with a quote for a second stage of advice provided later when I know what the work entails and what investment changes are needed.

In other cases it should be possible to provide reasonably accurate quotes especially where advice is centred on arranging investments, pensions or life assurance products. The more experience you have the easier it becomes.

Providing estimates for general financial planning for example creating a retirement income plan or inheritance tax planning is more difficult given the work is not well defined, complications may arise and the end point is not clear at the start. Here I provide a best estimate in advance with updates if the cost of work is likely to exceed this.

Website disclosure of fees

I think it is essential that my fee structure is clearly explained on my website. Firstly it is about being transparent from the very start. It is a subliminal message that says I will be transparent throughout all our dealings. Secondly it enables a potential client to understand how my fees are determined without having to get in contact with me. It removes a potential barrier that could deter them from making an enquiry.

I don't know about you but whenever I undertake internet research on professional services whether an accountant or an electrician it drives me nuts trying to find their fee structure or charge out rates. There is plenty of information on what services the business offers and how wonderful they are but I just want to see something about the charges without having to make a direct enquiry. It is invariably a determining factor whether I go further with this company or look elsewhere.

However clearly I am in a minority. Most adviser websites don't state how they charge for their services. They might say we will provide a fixed fee quote for the work before it commences but that's it. Here is an example:

> *"As is typical for financial advisors in ...and across the UK, we will give you a fixed cost for providing our advice and this fee would take into account our time, research, advice, and policy/plan implementation.*
>
> *Once you are happy with this, a fee agreement will be issued giving you complete peace of mind that there will be no unexpected charges to meet."*

All well and good but to find out how a firm's fixed fees are determined and what the cost of work might be means the prospect has to get in touch and engage with the adviser. This barrier may deter the client from making contact and means such firms miss out on attracting potential new clients.

I also wonder if adviser firms are slightly embarrassed by their fees, knowing that a 2% or 3% initial charge for large investment will be a turn off if the figures are published on the website. Of course if the potential client then makes contact and engages with the firm, a fee agreement will be supplied and this information will have to be disclosed, so it is delaying the inevitable. Perhaps though the thinking here is if an adviser gets to talk to or meet the prospect, wins their confidence and trust, impresses them with their service and investment credentials then the 2% or 3% charge might be easier to swallow. So the strategy might be to delay disclosure of fees as late as possible.

A defence for not publishing fee rates on websites that I have heard is that fees are individually determined and can only be communicated in discussion with the client. I think this is a rotten excuse. Whilst individual quotes are of course essential there is nothing to stop firms publishing their fee rates in full in general terms for example their hourly charge out rates or percentage fee structure for investing a lump sum.

My advice to any firm is be fully transparent on your fees from the get go, starting with your shop window, your website. To do so means you will stand out from the crowd. Not to do so is counter-productive in my view and you may miss out on potential clients.

Here is what I write on my website:

> *"If you decide to appoint me as your IFA an hourly fee of £160 per hour applies for all work. An estimate of the total cost will however be provided in advance.*
>
> *When a fee becomes due, normally on conclusion of the work a timesheet is sent with each invoice. This shows the work done, the relevant dates and the time spent in minutes.*
>
> *There are a variety of fee options which will be discussed with you. A pure fee applies when the work is fully chargeable by invoice. However for investment products there is an option of paying for advice through a product fee called an Adviser Charge. This has replaced commission and is an individually agreed fee that is built into the product sale i.e. it is paid for from your investment.*
>
> *Commission may be payable to the firm from arranging pure insurance products. Unlike most advisers initial commissions that are received are fully credited to you, typically by being offset against the cost of my work. This reduces or eliminates a directly invoiced fee. If the commission exceeds a fee, the excess will be rebated to you in some way. It may be re-invested into the insurance product to reduce premiums, used to cover the cost of other work, paid as a cash sum to you or kept on your timesheet as a credit for future use. Please note cash rebates are not made from investments or pensions.*
>
> *Currently VAT is not levied on fees, but this may change in the future."*

I accept there are no indicative examples here but in my Client Agreement which is published on my website there are:

> "For your guidance, to advise and arrange an investment portfolio of £100,000, the time required may total seven hours' work with a fee cost of £1,120. Advising and arranging a regular premium pension plan for £500 p.m. may take fours' work with a fee charge of £640."

The FCA and fee competition

In an article in the Winter 2018 edition of the Personal Finance Professional magazine Rory Percival, a former compliance specialist at the FCA and now an independent compliance consultant states the advice market is not competitive i.e. there is almost no correlation between price and demand. Also he found there is extensive price clustering with firms charging similar amounts.

This will be a concern to the FCA as an uncompetitive market is potentially damaging to consumers. This is because without any likelihood an adviser could lose business to rival firms there is no incentive for advice firms to strive to provide good value for money services and up their game.

I agree with Rory Percival's general point but I think he has missed something about supply and demand and how regulation has contributed to an uncompetitive market. By making the advice process so complex and over-regulated there are fewer firms to service a vast number of people who are looking for advice especially as the banks largely withdrew from the advice market after the RDR.

In other words regulation has contributed to demand exceeding supply. It is only in a market where there are more advisers chasing fewer clients that price competition should become keener.

Conclusion

There is much to be gained by having an attractive fee proposition, one that is crystal clear, fair and stands out from the crowd. I think that mine does.

Others will come to a different conclusion as to what they think is the best fee structure for their firm and their clients. Whatever you decide you will need to believe in it and be able to articulate it clearly to your clients with a sense of conviction. You may need to handle objections. If you are reluctant to put your fee rates on your website perhaps that is a strong indication that your fee structure doesn't stand up to scrutiny on fairness or value for money.

Finally on the question of fees, I am seeing evidence to suggest that there is a trend of increasing fees as adviser firms are asked to cope with the costs from a barrage of new regulations and Professional Indemnity Insurance (PII) costs as explained in Chapter 7. Advisers are increasingly focussing on their wealthier more profitable clients and are willing to let others go.

The starkest example I found came from an article in Money Marketing (23/5/19) from Tony Byrne, managing director at Wealth and Tax Management. He writes:

> "The increasing burden of red tape has left advice firms struggling to service clients with smaller amounts, so they need to draw the line somewhere."

He then highlights the challenges facing advisers including from the RDR, MIFID II, PII and he concludes:

> "What has become apparent is that the ever-increasing burden of red tape is strangling IFAs and making it inevitable that we can only afford to serve high-net-worth clients. It has become literally loss-making to service small clients. Many IFAs are having to sack clients they previously advised because they can't afford to look after them anymore."

His firm's solution is to accept new clients who are willing to pay a minimum fee of £2,500 a year, meaning in effect they must have £250,000 to invest as they charge 1% p.a. They will take on clients with less than £250,000 but the minimum fee will still be £2,500.

For their existing clients they have started to offer them three choices:

- Pay the minimum fee of £2,500 p.a.
- Revert to their robo-advice proposition
- Find a new adviser.

I don't think I could introduce a minimum fee as some of my clients have small investment portfolios or they don't want annual reviews. Instead I will charge an hourly rate for the work done so I am fair on myself and the client. If I do no work for a client in a year, they pay no fees and I don't get paid. If I do 10 hours work I get paid £1,600. If I think the value of the work will not exceed its cost I won't undertake the work, but I won't sack the client.

However what I found incredible about this article was Tony Byrne's firm's intention to increase their minimum fee to £5,000 p.a. within 12 months and £10,000 p.a. within three years. That is a very bold aim. It will only be achievable for the very wealthiest of his clients, perhaps with £1 million of investments. Even for these people he will need to convince his clients the value of the advice exceeds its cost. What advisers cannot do is simply expect to justify their fees on the basis they are worth it!

Moreover Byrne said he has come across a number of firms who are practising this type of fee system. (I also found by chance recently one in south west London with a minimum charge of £3,600). As a result Byrne says that such firms are shedding many of their smaller clients and becoming more profitable as a result.

This approach of ramping up fees clearly runs counter to Paul Armson's observation above that clients are baulking at high advice fees. Just because someone has a very large portfolio and can afford big advice fees it doesn't mean they will be willing to fork out for it unless they think the fee represents good value. Advisers like Tony Byrne are clearly taking a risk.

What is interesting here is if this fee inflation continues, high quality independent financial advice will become restricted to the very well off and those willing to pay jumbo fees, and it will be a dent in the regulators' objective to make advice more widely available to the masses.

Appendix - Timesheet

DATE	ACTIVITY	TIME (minutes)
13.8.19	E-mail correspondence with client on trackers and investment, client notes	5
10.9.19	E-mail correspondence with client on possible ISA investment and UK equities, client notes	14
12.9.19	Fund research on trackers, e-mail to client with recommendation and fund documents, client notes	14
13.9.19	Apply for AJ Bell ISA online, e-mail to client, client notes and new business register	9
16.9.19	Process cheque for sending to AJ Bell. Client notes and filing	8
20.9.19	Place ISA fund purchase instruction, client notes	2
	Letter of recommendation to client, client notes and filing	31
1.10.19	Print contract note, update investment summary, filing, e-mail to client	3
19.12.19	Update investment and pension valuation statements and send to clients, client notes and new file creation	48
20.12.19	Fact find and documents to client, client notes	3
28.12.19	Start investment commentary letter	50
30.12.19	Complete and send investment review, client notes	39
	Review OMW and SW, e-mail to client with advice to re-register, client notes, filing	35
31.12.19	Print, complete and send ISA transfer forms to clients, client notes and filing	31
2.1.20	Respond to client update on financial position, client notes	15
3.1.20	Review BMO UK Real Estate fund, e-mail to client with recommendations and fund documents, client notes and filing	33
6.1.20	Place fund order to buy Liontrust SF DM fund, client notes, fund switch log	3
9.1.20	Read fact find, e-mail to client, client notes and filing	11
28.1.20	E-mail to client about ISA transfers and advice on sale of SW American Growth, client notes	13
29.1.20	US investment fund research, e-mail to client with advice and fund documents, client notes	34
5.2.20	Letter of recommendation for ISA transfers and fund switches, client notes	38
	Minutes	439
	Hours	7.32
	GROSS FEE (@ £160 p.h.)	£1,170.67
6.10.19	Compensation for correction deal on L&G UK Index Trust	£113.95
7.2.20	Fee received	£1,056.72
	NET FEE	(£0.00)

5. Giving financial advice - fact finds and risk

The bad old days

When I first started out in the industry financial advice was delivered by a standard industry method, a well-trodden two stage process. At the first meeting with new clients you conducted a fact find which could be a long and laborious process, taking several hours or the whole evening. You identified clients' financial objectives and needs. Conveniently these would be things that could be fixed from something in your toolbox, i.e. your firm's range of products.

The next meeting was a presentation in which the "adviser" turned up with a stack of product brochures, illustrations and a good sales pitch. The policies you recommended would be a perfect solution to your clients' financial needs. If you were lucky the client would sign up then and there. The following day you came into the office with a big smile on your face, armed with one or more applications for processing, knowing that a big fat commission payment would follow. Your colleagues without recent sales might have been a bit envious whilst your boss would be very pleased.

If the sales presentation went badly or the client was sceptical you would be told, *"I want to think about it."* Advisers were of course trained to handle objections but a third meeting might have been necessary to secure the business. If you were unlucky you would not hear from the prospect again or you would get a polite rejection when you chased them up. You felt despondent.

Looking back I can't believe I ever subscribed to such a rotten process, but I did for a while until I took control and become my own person. Leaving a closeted sales environment, first at Liberty Life and then at the Investment Practice was necessary to be liberated.

Advice by process not event

Over the years I have developed a fairly unique style of working. It is based on the principle that advice is a process not an event, involving short episodes of engagement, discussion, clarification, advice and reviews through a series of conversations, e-mails or letters. The process may take anything from several weeks or months or even longer depending on the complexity of the work and the level of the clients' interest.

I rarely meet clients these days with most contact undertaken by post, phone and e-mail. I have clients in London and the South East, a few further afield, some of whom I have never met. One I have successfully advised at distance for more than 13 years now without us having ever set eyes upon each other. We have built up an excellent rapport through telephone conversations and engaging e-mail correspondence. Mutual trust is sky high.

My occasional face to face meetings are normally at my home office. Typically it is for potential new clients who want put a face to my name, see if they like the look of me and check my home is not a palace with a Rolls Royce parked on the drive. I don't have one by the way...a drive that is... nor a Rolls Royce come to think of it. This is fair enough. For existing clients a get together might be for a review followed by a lunch. Some of my clients are friends or if not best buddies at the very least they are people where there is a mutual enjoyment of each other's company at a social level.

The reason why I request clients come to me is it eliminates the need to charge for my travel time. I come back to my philosophy on valuing my time. Why should I take half a day to travel to and from London for example for a meeting with an existing client and not be paid for my time, even if I am paid for the hour or so for the meeting itself? Over the years however I have made some exceptions and have driven to see a number of vulnerable elderly clients in Kent who were unable to travel to me or who needed me to visit and sort through a mountain of financial paperwork. Latterly, one who I visited until her recent death was happy to pay for my travel time.

Initial meetings with potential new clients

For potential new clients the principal is the same as for existing clients. I will never visit them at their home or their office if they live at distance (outside Eastbourne and its immediate environs). I can't risk that the time cost of a couple of hours in the car on top of an hour long free meeting will not recouped, because the prospect does not become a paying client.

I guess there also is a subliminal message here for potential clients, some of whom may be tempted to think advisers, including myself, are desperate for their business and are there for their convenience. I say this because if the potential client has any sense they should be talking to two or three different advisers before selecting one. Having a stream of potential suitors turning up at their door is nice and convenient for the client but for the unsuccessful advisers the experience will be unproductive and a waste of valuable time especially if they have travelled a fair distance. There may also be a loss of confidence.

So I take the view if I am giving up an hour of free time (often it is more) to meet with the prospective client, I think it is reasonable to expect something in return, that they give up their time and travel to see me.

You may of course take a different view especially if you are at the start of your career or building up your business and your client bank. You are perfectly justified to think the chance to get in front of a potential client to explain what you have to offer and why they should appoint you as their adviser is one that should not be passed over lightly. As it happens I can't recall a single example where there was an impasse, where the potential client has refused to travel to see me. Generally they have been delighted to do so whilst a trip to the seaside has been a pretty good added incentive.

Of course there is an alternative, one that I haven't actually used, that the initial free consultation is conducted by phone whilst Skype or Facetime are options to put a face to a name and make it more personal.

I have been fortunate that my "conversion rate" of prospects to clients after an initial meeting or discussion has been good even in the face of competition. In trying to analyse why that has been so, I can think of various reasons. Firstly I have had a head start if I have come highly recommended by existing clients.

Secondly I enjoy meeting new people. I think I engage well with strangers and find common ground easily. It just seems to come naturally and is not something I have to work hard at. If people come away thinking they like you and this is a relationship that might work, that is a big pull in them choosing you as their adviser. You will recall I said that the initial meeting or discussion is like a blind date. I think the principle of only having one chance to make a good first impression applies here.

A third factor is that I try to understand and communicate that I get what is on the person's mind and what advice they are looking for. This involves listening and commenting relevantly and giving enough in my responses that the person thinks yes I think I can benefit from Mike's advice. It is not trying to impress but it is about getting alongside people and addressing their issues.

In this respect I have found it important to comment on the poor experiences potential new clients may have had with other advisers, bearing in mind that once bitten they are likely to be twice shy. They may be wary when they first meet you and not inclined to trust you. Empathising with them and demonstrating you are different will help win the sceptics over.

As an example I took on a new client in early 2018. He had an IFA who took over from a retiring adviser but he was not happy with the new firm's advice. The new adviser was recommending a transfer of his and his wife's SIPPs to a discretionary fund manager (DFM). I read the report and expressed my concerns about the high charges. Here is selected correspondence:

> **Client** *"For a thousand pounds he has written a report (most of which I could have written myself, as it's mostly a summary of what our investments are at the moment) advising what he's already been saying but now giving precise figures for costs which to me seem eye-watering."*

They did to me too. Initial charges totalling £10,000 would be levied on the couple's pension plans and ISAs valued at around £866,000. It was not stated who would receive that fee but almost certainly it was the IFA. That was an incredibly steep cost for what appeared to be just an introduction to a DFM. But it didn't stop there. The IFA would then be paid 0.75% p.a. and the DFM 1.5% p.a. in ongoing charges.

Me *"There are lots of interesting comments in the pages from the report that you sent me. Firstly the charges on page 9 for the X/Y (IFA/DFM) service are clear and confirm both our assessments - they are unacceptably high and crucially for me are not justified by the actual or claimed benefits. DFM fees normally are subject to VAT although this is not clear from the 1.5% p.a. charge stated in the table whether the 1.5% is inclusive or exclusive of VAT.*

Page 25 - At the bottom of the page it is stated your Fidelity ISAs are paying 0.5% p.a. adviser charge. This is presumably going to X (the IFA) and amounts to around £1,235 p.a. based on the valuations on page 23. This payment should have been providing a commensurate investment review service for your Fidelity ISAs or credited to you in some other way. Judging by the fact you both appear to be invested in a single fund within your Fidelity ISAs I suspect this service has not been provided and if so there are potential grounds for a complaint. I would be inclined to ask how much money have X received from the Fidelity adviser charges since they took over from your former IFA and what services have they provided for these payments."

I also discovered the IFA was also receiving adviser charges on the SIPPs. Had the clients gone ahead and transferred to a DFM these of course would have ceased.

Client *"Your comments below were hugely helpful and of course at times rather alarming. The situation with Standard Life seems awful, and no better with regard to Fidelity. Whether I will formally complain to X I'm not sure; I wouldn't expect to get anything back except excuses, namely the assertion that they have been advising us for at least a year to go down the DFM route and this would have sorted out all the issues with regard to Fidelity and Standard Life.*

I'm glad that my suspicion about all that has held me back from making the final commitment."

Me *"I don't think that (the delay) matters as they have received the adviser charges from Fidelity and they must be used to benefit you, for example to discount the £1,000 fee you paid."*

Client *"Thank you for suggesting that I challenge X (IFA) regarding the £1,000 report fee. They have responded to my complaints very much as I predicted - saying that it was my fault for delaying making decisions - but end by saying that they have 'asked for your ongoing adviser fees to be switched off moving forward and we have agreed to waive the £1,000 report writing fee'. So that is a result!"*

It was one of those satisfying outcomes when a client received tangible benefits, not just saving on the £1,000 report fee but more importantly avoidance of the very high initial costs and ongoing charges his former IFA was set to receive had the transfer to the DFM gone ahead.

Fact finds

Once a client has decided they want me to be their IFA I ask them to sign my Client Agreement and a separate Privacy Notice. At that point my chargeable work begins. I then send a fact find for the client to complete. It is a Word document that they can populate electronically and then e-mail back to me. There are two benefits of a client undertaking this task. Firstly they save on fee costs compared to me spending an hour or two interviewing the client to get all the relevant financial and personal information needed to provide suitable advice.

Secondly it requires clients to engage more with their own finances if they are required to locate investment and policy documents and record key information from these on the fact find. In addition asking them to set out their financial objectives in writing should help clarify their thinking. As a result clients should feel more involved in the advice process.

There are of course disadvantages of my approach in that a face to face or telephone conversation to complete the fact find enables an adviser to pick up on clients' feelings and so called "soft facts." However I am normally able to ascertain these from the initial discussion and subsequent telephone conversations. A lot can be gained from what clients' write especially from the free form sections of the fact find, reading between the lines and asking questions to seek clarification.

Some people complete fact finds well. They provide a lot of detail and useful information, including their own investment summaries and budgets. This demonstrates real interest and engagement. Others clearly put in minimal effort and leave important gaps. However good or bad I normally have to go back to all clients for additional information, to get clarification on points that are not clear or to iron out inconsistencies. This is where the e-mail chains begin.

For existing clients fact finds need updating after a while. Prior to reviews or new advice I ask clients for an update on their financial circumstances, for example changes to their financial objectives, attitude to risk or income requirements. The changes are recorded in my client history notes, explained in the next chapter.

Eventually after two to three years the fact find needs rewriting. Most of my clients are normally OK with this but I have a few for whom it is a real chore or it feels intrusive. It seems as if they would rather go to the dentist to have teeth pulled. I am generally flexible here because these people are good friends and I can demonstrate that I have a good knowledge of their financial affairs. In addition I can normally get the key information I need by requesting an update on the clients' financial circumstances or asking a few simple questions such as, *"Do you have a need for additional income or has your risk profile changed?"*

As you are no doubt aware the regulations require advisers to "know their customers," not specifically to complete a fact find, which is merely a method of collecting information on clients' finances and circumstances. However it is not the only way. Therefore I am not going to allow a refusal to complete a form to be a deal breaker. Relationships are crucial and I am certainly not going to antagonise clients and friends by insisting on something they find disagreeable. Moreover I take the view as advisers we should adapt to our clients, their attitudes and preferences rather than shoehorn them into a strict advice process, even if the regulations suggest otherwise.

Fact finds come in all shapes and sizes. I created my electronic Word document from scratch in 2016 having scrapped a previous paper form. I enclose a copy at the back of the book. You will see it asks for the usual information you'll be familiar with.

I don't ask the client to fill in tons of detail on their policies and investments as I did in the past as copies of plan documents and valuation statements will usually provide me with the relevant information. I also make enquiries direct to providers after submission of letters of authority and they normally send me comprehensive policy information.

Moreover I don't want to bore the client to death with an overly long and complex fact find. So I don't ask the client to provide a detailed expenditure budget. I am not that interested to know they pay £200 p.m. in Council Tax, £30 on gym membership or £100 p.m. in gas and electricity. Instead I ask for consolidated high level information:

> "Total net monthly income:
>
> Total monthly expenditure:
>
> Do you need additional monthly income: Yes or no? If yes how much?
>
> Do you have any major one off expenses in the next six months?"

If the answer to the last question is yes, I ask them to list these items with the amounts and dates required. This is normally sufficient to understand a client's budget although in my experience people tend to underestimate their expenditure. This is not unexpected as knowing about your fixed regular outgoings or direct debits is much easier than keeping track of recurring variable costs such as food shopping or entertainment, or one off larger spending on holidays or work on the house.

One way I try to assess true outgoings is to ask clients to compare their cash savings now with a year ago. If cash savings have risen by say £12,000 it suggests that there is surplus income of around £1,000 p.m. and vice versa. I appreciate this is simplistic as one-off large costs, such as roof replacement or a new car or capital injections, such as an inheritance from granny or a £5,000 premium bond prize must be taken into account. But if cash reserves are consistently going up or down and it can't be explained by one-off factors it is a good indicator there is a normal income surplus or deficit.

Assessing clients' risk profiles

In giving investment advice one of the most important tasks of a financial adviser is to explain the meaning of investment risk and to assess a client's attitude to risk. The concept of risk is complex and nuanced and it is essential clients and advisers are on the same page when discussing risk, to avoid misunderstanding and disappointing clients. It also reduces the potential for complaints.

To explain risk I supply a document to clients when they complete the fact find. It covers the various facets of risk. Taken direct from my document here are some sections and additional commentary:

"Three risk metrics

There are three key risk metrics that all investors need to consider singularly and in combination. These are:

*1. The risk you are **inclined or willing to take** to get a good return from your investments. This is referred to as your attitude to risk.*

*2. The risk you are **able to take** based on your financial circumstances. This is referred to as your capacity for loss.*

*3. The risk you **need to take** to meet your financial objectives.*

The former, your attitude to risk is more of an emotional characteristic and is influenced by your personality, preferences and experiences of investing in the past. The risk you are able to take and need to take are more rooted in objective financial facts and planning needs.

A client's attitude to risk, the risk they are willing to take and their capacity for loss, the risk they are able to take may not match. For example a cautious risk investor will have a large capacity for loss if they hold a very high level of cash savings in addition to their investments. In these circumstances it may be entirely appropriate for a cautious risk investor to invest some money outside of their normal comfort zone in order to generate a higher return or to meet their specific financial objectives or needs (point 3).

The opposite is also true. An adventurous risk investor may be attracted to funds or stocks with the potential to produce very high returns but a low income and lack of cash savings means they cannot afford to lose money. They have a low capacity for loss and inevitably they will need to rein in their enthusiasm to invest adventurously. Another way to illustrate this is to consider a compulsive gambler of modest means who takes risky bets with money he or she dare not afford to lose!

The third element of a personal risk profile i.e. the risk an investor needs to take is assessed in relation to their financial goals. Consider someone with £100,000 of capital who requires a minimum of 5% p.a. income for their essential day to day living expenses. They may be a cautious risk investor and naturally prefer to keep their money in cash or cautious risk investments. However they can't get the income they need from cash savings and it will require them to invest adventurously in equities and bonds beyond their attitude to risk.

Similarly an investor with an absolute requirement for ethical investments may have to accept a higher level of risk than their attitude to risk or capacity for loss might ordinarily dictate. This is because ethical funds carry additional risks due to their relatively high investment in smaller companies and the restrictions on the sectors of the economy they can invest in. For example they will avoid investment in tobacco companies and in some cases pharmaceuticals. These are defensive stocks and tend to perform well in economic downturns.

In general the risk you need to take will trump your capacity for loss and attitude to risk. These three personal metrics will be assessed using this document, in my "fact find" and in discussions with you.

Investment and asset risk

Different asset classes have widely accepted inherent risks. By risk I mean the potential for investments to fall in value and for volatility. This is not strictly the same as a loss. Here it is important to note there is a difference between a crystallised loss and an uncrystallised loss. The latter is a paper valuation. For example if you invest £10,000 into an ISA and six months later your valuation statement shows it is worth £9,000 you have made a paper loss. If you continue to hold the fund, after a further year the value may have risen to £10,500. The paper loss has turned into a paper gain. If *however you sell the investment after six months you will crystallise a real loss.*

Typically on a scale of increasing risk, (potential for volatility) we have the following major asset types:

Cash, Government Bonds, Corporate Bonds, Property, Equities & Commodities.

Cash includes most National Savings & Investments.

Within each asset class there are various types of investment with differing risk profiles. For example corporate bonds include high quality investment grade stocks and high yield bonds with lower credit ratings. The latter have a greater risk of default i.e. failing to make an interest payment or repay the loan and are more prone to price movements. Similarly emerging market equities carry more risk than those from developed markets.

However to describe the risk of each asset class as being fixed, for example that cash is always low risk and equities are always high risk is simplistic in my view. This is explained below.

The nature of investment risk and the meaning of loss

In broad terms there are three risk outcomes:

***1.** You can lose all your money.*

***2.** You can lose more than your money and have a liability in excess of your investment.*

***3.** The value of your investment can fluctuate and can go down as well as up. The risk issue here is one of volatility and getting back less than you invested if you cash out at a low valuation point i.e. crystallise the loss.*

The types of investments recommended by most IFAs are not normally subject to the first two risks. The former applies for example to holding individual stocks and shares, particularly those of smaller companies. If the company collapses your shareholding may become worthless. The second risk applies to direct investment in some derivatives contracts which are complex and speculative. Interestingly many investment funds use derivatives to hedge risk rather than increase risk but most private investors will never encounter or purchase them on an individual basis, nor will their adviser recommend them.

The principle risk outcome for investors as explained is the volatility of value in which investments fluctuate constantly with the movements of the prices of the share or equities held by a fund. For this reason equity funds should be regarded as medium term investments with a minimum holding period of three to five years. Over these periods history shows share prices tend to rise although there is no guarantee of such in the future.

If equities are likely to deliver medium or long term profits what is the problem with volatility? Firstly some people cannot accept the value of their investment should ever be less than the amount invested and take the view that they would have been better off if their money had been kept in the bank! Secondly access to the investments may have to be delayed until valuations recover to avoid crystallising losses. This may create problems if capital is required at a particular time, for example a financial emergency, a mortgage repayment date or retirement date. Thirdly in extreme cases valuations may be depressed for long periods of time for example the Japanese stock market which was in the doldrums for 20 years following a property crash in 1990.

For these reasons all investors, not just very cautious ones should retain sufficient emergency cash to avoid being forced sellers at low valuation points. Very cautious investors are likely to prefer to avoid equity investments altogether given the exposure to stock market variations unless their financial needs require this.

Although generally high returns are associated with high volatility and vice versa good fund managers may be able to achieve high returns with below average volatility. In contrast some funds may have poor medium to long term returns with above average volatility.

Finally in respect of the first risk described above it is highly unlikely a collective investment fund such as an OEIC or unit trust will go bust and you will lose all your money. This is because funds hold a large collection of shares and simultaneous multiple insolvencies are highly unlikely. Further, investor protection for authorised funds is provided by the Financial Services Compensation Scheme in the event of insolvency of the investment manager. This is up to £85,000 per investor per fund manager.

Types of risk, other than volatility of value

So far I have described risk in terms of volatility but to define risk purely in terms of volatility of value is simplistic. Cash does not suffer from volatility of value but carries the risk of low interest rates and returns being eroded by inflation.

There are different types of risk many of which cause the headline risk of volatility. These include systemic risk, inflation risk, default risk, currency risk and counterparty risk. Systemic risks are threats to the whole financial system and impact virtually all investment types. The banking crisis of 2008 and the sovereign debt crisis of 2011 and 2012 are recent examples.

In contrast unsystemic risks are specific to individual stocks or asset classes. For example structured products and many ETFs are exposed to counter party risk, an institution that is contracted to provide the investment returns. If the counterparty does not meet its obligations investors may not receive the income or capital return set out in the contract. Overseas investments are subject to currency fluctuations which can enhance or reduce returns to UK investors. Finally corporate bonds are subject to default risk i.e. that interest payments are missed or capital is not repaid by the bond issuer.

When I advise you, I will explain specific unsystemic risks of particular investments. These are also detailed in documents such as Key Investor Information Documents (KIIDs) and fund fact sheets. I will also document the current market risks of particular investments and asset classes and provide an overall risk rating for each fund recommended. These are however my own assessments and they may differ from those of the fund manager including the 1-7 risk rating provided in the KIID.

Finally it is my view there is no such thing as a risk free or guaranteed investment. Cash deposited with a bank may collapse and an investor could lose some money and although the UK Government underwrites National Savings & Investments (NS&I) and has never failed to repay investors, in *my view one could never say such circumstances could never occur."*

The end stage is an assessment of a client's attitude to risk or their risk profile. Whilst there are some very good investment risk assessment tools on the market I prefer a relatively simple self-assessment. The way I request it is as follows:

> "In general the higher your risk profile the greater the volatility you are prepared to accept to obtain a potentially better return. In this section I describe five investor risk profiles and request that you identify which profile most fits your current attitude to risk.
>
> ### Very Cautious
>
> You will be a very cautious investor if you are unwilling to accept any volatility of value or that your investments could ever be worth less than the amount invested. Capital preservation will be your predominant objective even at the cost of low returns that do not keep pace with inflation.
>
> In this case cash and many National Savings & Investments (NS&I) are likely to be the most suitable investments but not those that invest in equities or even gilts or corporate bonds.
>
> ### Cautious
>
> A cautious investor will accept some volatility in value especially in the short term for a potentially higher return from cash or to beat inflation. A mixture of cash, NS&I and lower risk bond, equity, multi-asset or targeted return funds is likely to be suitable but your portfolio will be weighted towards the lower end of the risk scale. A cautious investor will have to accept some unsystemic risks for example default risk from investment grade corporate bonds for example to receive a higher income than from cash.
>
> ### Balanced
>
> A balanced investor will accept moderate levels of volatility, especially in the short term in order to achieve returns in excess of cash and inflation. This investor will accept some higher risk, higher volatility equity investments for strong capital growth potential if these are balanced by

lower risk holdings. They will also accept moderate levels of unsystemic risks for example currency fluctuations or default risk from corporate bonds.

Adventurous

An adventurous risk investor is attracted to the potential of higher returns and is willing to accept a fairly high level of volatility within their portfolio. They will also accept other unsystemic risks for example currency fluctuations or default risk. However they will include some low risk investments in their portfolio to moderate volatility and provide diversity.

Aggressive

An aggressive or high risk investor considers high potential returns of utmost importance and is willing to accept high levels of volatility and unsystemic risks. They are unlikely to be attracted to cautious risk investments.

It is important to note that an investor's risk profile may change over time. For example younger people in their 20s and 30s may be more willing to accept risk given the long investment period to retirement and the risk reducing features of monthly savings. As people approach retirement the priority may be to protect capital values, lock in gains and reduce risk.

Similarly in periods after sharp stock market falls many investors will become more cautious if they see losses in their portfolios whilst others will be happy to take more risk. This is because they see opportunities to buy stocks and funds cheaply. Perceptions of risk are very personal based on both objective and subjective factors.

Please note the risk descriptions above are my own definitions and may differ from other IFAs' assessments.

I would be grateful if you could please let me know or write on the fact find in the relevant section your own assessment of your risk profiles for both investments and insurances separately using the stated profiles described above. You and your partner may have different risk profiles; therefore please ensure individual profiles are noted."

Now I am sure some readers will be concerned that I ask clients to self-identify their risk profile. Surely that is the adviser's responsibility you may think. However remember what I said earlier, that a client's attitude to risk or risk profile is the risk an investor is inclined or willing to take to get a good return from their investments. I suggested that their attitude to risk is an emotional characteristic and is influenced by their personality, preferences and experiences of investing in the past. That is intensely personal and I do not want that decision taken away from the client. In contrast as stated the risk an investor is able to take (capacity for loss) and the risk they are required to take (in order to meet their financial needs) are more rooted in objective financial facts and planning needs. Consequently I feel as a financial adviser I have more reason to assess these risk measures.

In some cases I may query a client's assessment if other facts seem to contradict their chosen risk profile. For example I may find a new client says they are cautious risk, but discover when I read the fact find they hold a lot of equity funds or direct stocks and shares. In other words there is a mismatch between what risk profile they ascribe to themselves and what they are invested in.

Naturally it is important to ask how those investments were acquired. Were they self-bought, acquired from a demutualisation, inherited or recommended by another adviser? Self-bought funds would suggest a client has more appetite for risk than first appears. In addition the length of time they have held the investments is telling. If it has been for a very long time through many cycles and stock market sell-offs that is a fair indication that they are reasonably comfortable with the volatility they have experienced, assuming of course they have been aware of the fluctuating valuations of their investments.

In consideration of all the facts, hard and soft I may suggest a different risk profile may be appropriate for the investments being advised on. In some cases I may recommend two risk profiles are adopted! As an example if a client has a large lump sum or a sizeable personal pension cash transfer to invest but they also wish to save on a monthly basis for retirement, many years away, I may recommend for a cautious risk investor that the lump sum or transfer is invested defensively but a balanced or even balanced/adventurous risk strategy is adopted for the regular investments.

This differentiation is based on the view that regular investment of small sums carries significantly less risk than lump sum investment, especially when markets are high. The danger here is if you invest a single lump sum at a high valuation point and markets fall shortly afterwards, the whole investment slumps in value. For example if a £10,000 investment falls by 20% its value drops to £8,000. If instead you start a £500 p.m. investment plan a loss of 20% i.e. £100 is less significant in cash terms. Moreover if the fund remains at the lower price for a period of time, each additional investment of £500 in months' two, three, four etc. results in the investor buying more units than they would have acquired before the 20% price fall. When markets and prices recover an investor gains from the greater number of units they have bought.

With regular savings you have multiple investment dates with some contributions being made at high and some at low valuation points. Slumps mean the impact of stock market crashes is not uniform. For example let us say units are bought at 50p, 60p, 70p, 80p and 90p over a period of time. The fund price then reaches a high of say £1 and then there is a stock market crash of 30%. The units bought 90p are now worth 70p. The units bought for 50p are also worth 70p but unlike those bought for 90p they are still in profit.

Of course at low valuation points and in steadily rising markets it works the other way, a lump sum will generate a higher return than investing the same amount of money on a monthly basis. This is because with the latter rising prices means fewer units are bought for each fixed monthly contribution. Understanding market conditions and valuations and the different characteristics of investing single contributions and small monthly sums is a crucial element in giving investment advice.

Regular investors may also benefit from the volatility of fund value from "pound cost averaging." This is a mathematical phenomenon where the average cost of buying units is less than the average price of those units over the same investment period. Moreover this benefit increases the greater the volatility. I suggest this is a topic you undertake some personal study on. Opinion is however divided and some people consider pound cost averaging to be a myth!

The addition of balanced or adventurous funds to a predominantly cautious risk portfolio through regular savings increases diversity which counter-intuitively may have a risk reducing benefit, similar to the efficient frontier hypothesis for blending equities and bonds. In contrast a portfolio of all cautious risk funds may be too correlated or fail to capture the upside when equity markets rally.

Clients are normally comfortable with a higher risk profile when the benefits of regular investing are explained. Moreover long timescales reduce the risks of equity investment. There is no reason why a cautious risk investor saving for retirement in 25-30 years' time should be scared of investing in adventurous risk equity funds. Your clients however should be encouraged to discount short term volatility and not panic when they see paper losses in the early years.

In my view regular monthly investment is underused outside of pension savings. Many clients use their annual ISA allowance in full to invest in stocks and shares, funded from cash savings. For those that don't have the resources to do this, an ISA savings plan is the next best thing and for those who fully use their ISA allowance each year a long term regular monthly savings into a dealing or general investment account that all good platforms offer is highly recommended.

Risk is not fixed

I take the view that the risk profiles of different asset types are not fixed, both in absolute terms nor relative to other asset classes. Although in general equities are higher risk and more volatile than fixed interest or bonds, risk is variable, depending on valuations and market conditions. For example with loose monetary policy and vast amounts of Quantitative Easing (QE) since the global financial crisis, bond prices soared and yields fell to historic lows. Initially fixed interest was a great investment. However in recent years with very low yields bonds have carried an asymmetric risk, plenty of downside interest rate or duration risk and measly upside potential. The point is that at the time of writing in early to mid 2019 investing in bonds (especially developed market government debt and high quality corporate bonds) with their ultra-low interest rates carries substantial risk, arguably greater than equities.

Whilst a bond price collapse has yet to materialise and has become less likely with a recent dramatic change of policy by the US Federal Reserve who flipped in 2019 from aggressive tightening of monetary policy to easing, if it does occur investors will face significant capital losses. Even if they don't, negative real yields on government bonds are common. This means interest rates are less than inflation and investors are guaranteed to lose money in purchasing power terms. In some cases prices are so high that yields to maturity mean investors face losses not only in real terms but in cash terms too.

The other side of the argument on the relative risk of bonds and equities relates to equity prices. There was a sharp sell-off in global equity markets between September and December 2018, caused by US interest rate rises, quantitative tightening, the US/China trade war, a slowing Chinese economy, Brexit and a shutdown in the US government. The value of equities was attractive at the end of 2018 given much of the bad news was priced in. In other words the risk of investing in equities was significantly reduced compared to earlier highs in the year and in my view it became a buying opportunity in January 2019.

The changing nature of risk is also affected by the time an investor is in the market and how they invest. The longer an investment is held, the greater the chance of profitable returns and the lower the downside risk. I remember reviewing a client's portfolio a few years ago. She had invested £3,000 into a high quality European equity fund twenty years earlier, before becoming my client. The value of the holding was about £21,000. It had increased seven fold and dividends had been paid out. However the key point here is that a 10%, 20% or 25% fall in the unit price although would have dented the value of the holding but the investment it would have still been highly profitable. The shorter the investment period the greater the chance that fund values will be less than the sums invested. Time in the market is crucial and a buy and hold strategy normally delivers very strong long term returns from equities. What this means is investment in a specific fund carries a different risk potential over one, five or 10 years.

As noted there is also a marked difference between investing a lump sum and regular contributions. You can invest in the same fund in these two ways with different degrees of risk. As mentioned earlier, large single investments means there is a greater sum at risk. Investing multiple small amounts in the same fund monthly dramatically reduces the risk profile of the investment.

The point is I don't subscribe to the idea that investments have fixed risk profiles. For this reason I dislike and avoid centralised investment propositions (CIPs) where investors are categorised by a risk profile and then a set off the shelf asset allocation is brought out and used to determine what a client should invest in. It may be considered appropriate that all cautious risk investors should have for example 60% in fixed interest or bonds, 25% in equities and 10% in property and 5% in cash, or with minor variations around this asset allocation. Well that may be suitable in certain market conditions but surely not all. As I write I wouldn't touch that asset allocation with a 10 foot barge pole for a cautious risk client looking for capital growth in the medium to long term. The fixed interest allocation is far too high in my opinion and is too risky whilst the equity exposure is far too low.

Eschewing CIPs I take the view that client portfolios should be entirely bespoke. The result would mean three different cautious risk clients of mine would probably end up having different asset allocations unlike with a CIP. I don't ignore a client's risk profile but I tailor investments to a variety of factors in addition to their risk profile, including their capacity for loss, personal circumstances, financial objectives, need for income, requirement for ethical investment and timescales.

Portfolios for cautious risk clients will naturally differ from those for adventurous risk clients. The latter will invariably have a higher allocation to equities and will include more in emerging markets, commodities and specialist funds. Cautious risk clients' equity exposure will be more focussed on developed markets of the UK, US and Europe and Japan.

Cash and insurance risk

Finally on the subject of risk I also document cash and insurance risk as follows:

> "**Cash risk**
>
> *This has already been alluded to. It is important to realise a very cautious investor who invests in cash is still subject to risk i.e. that the interest*

received taking does not keep pace with inflation.

Cash is attractive if there is a real rate of return in excess of inflation. However at the date of writing many cash accounts pay very low rates of interest.

Another risk from investing in cash are periods when interest rates fall. Through the 1990s as interest rates fell many investors dependent on bank or building society interest found themselves with insufficient income.

A further problem with cash is that the underlying capital deposits are eroded by inflation as there is no scope for capital growth except where interest is re-invested and the amount of interest is higher than inflation. This is in contrast to equities where an investor receiving dividends can also expect capital growth in the medium to long term. This in turn often results in income growth.

In conclusion a risk adverse investor runs a risk of poor returns from cash and insufficient income by not being more adventurous. This highlights the fact there is no such thing as a "no risk" investment.

Insurance risk

In financial planning people should consider their attitude to insurance risk as well as to investment risk. Here I use three risk profiles:

A low risk person will insure against all or most risks, death or critical or long term illness.

A high risk individual will be willing to take the chance of not having insurance.

A medium risk person will insure some but not all risks.

It is possible that your risk profile for insurance is different to that for investment e.g. a cautious risk investor in respect of investment may be high risk when it comes to insurance."

First stage of advice

Once a client has completed the fact find and I have obtained any missing information and resolved any queries, the next step for me is to identify and set out the work that is required. This is normally clear from the initial request for advice and the client objectives that are stated on the fact find. In addition as noted I may identify financial needs that the client has not spotted. In these circumstances I set out what I think their needs are, why they are important to address and if they should take a priority over other financial planning requirements including potentially the clients' own objectives.

Most of my work these days is creating and reviewing investment and pension portfolios, mainly for existing clients. Most of my clients have retired or are close to retirement. They tend to be asset rich and have no debt. Those in their 50s and 60s who are still working are high earners. I do advise new investments but product advice is only part of my work these days. General holistic, pension and tax planning also features in what I do. Answering queries and addressing investment concerns, which come in all shapes and sizes, is also very important for me and my clients.

I no longer give advice on mortgages or loans and only rarely advise on protection. This is because my generally very well-off and greying clients have paid off their mortgages, their children have flown the nest and they have no need for life assurance except perhaps to cover an anticipated inheritance tax bill. If they are single they have no financial dependents. If they are retired they have no need for income protection. Of course when I first started out in the industry my clients were younger, in work, indebted and had financial dependents and my business mix was much more protection oriented. This will be the market that most new advisers will start out in.

Once the work is agreed I will provide estimates for the cost of my work and if the client agrees off we go.

6. Giving financial and investment advice - dynamics and processes

When I take on a new client invariably a whole host of financial issues that need to be addressed will become evident once the fact find has been completed. The client's various financial needs and objectives will be prioritised and tackled in stages. In contrast for existing clients the work is more likely to be limited advice to a single financial issue. It might be an investment portfolio review, advice on making new ISA or pension contributions or inheritance planning.

As stated my advice is typically supplied in multiple bite sized communications in which I highlight financial problems or planning opportunities for example misbalanced asset allocations, investment portfolios which are out of sync with market conditions, poor quality funds, taxation issues or opportunities for additional investment or pension contributions. Subsequently I make recommendations to rectify the problems, first generic and then specific.

Throughout the advice process I will set out the reasons why changes are required so clients understand there are things that need to be addressed. However I want more than this. I try to gauge how convinced they are with my observations and if they are on board with my advice. This is where asking for feedback from clients is essential.

Client to product not product to client

I start from the position that I am an adviser not a salesman and that identifying client needs and meeting them is central to all I do, whether it involves advising a product or not. Holistic advice, financial and investment reviews, and tax planning with no product sales are as important, or more so than shifting investments, pensions or insurance policies.

New business is a relatively minor part of my work. When I first started out it was very different. If however an adviser's or firm's income is derived principally from adviser charges there will be a natural focus on selling - advising and arranging products. In my view true independence is not just about advising on the full range of Retail Investment Products (RIPs) from the whole market of product providers but it is general and holistic advice that is independent of any product advice and sales.

Naturally I do recommend products as solutions to clients' financial needs but this is undergirded by another principle here, that I go from client to product not product to client. What I mean by this is that I start with clients' financial objectives and needs and then determine what might be a suitable product, if indeed a product is required. The final stage is to recommend a high quality provider.

Where I think a problem arises is if we start with the product and then work out who we can sell it to. That was the old sales model that was the industry norm when I was learning my trade in the 1990s. Whilst there has been a clear shift away from this approach over the years with the RDR, firms dependent on adviser charges and targets will invariably still be driven by product sales. A firm charging 2% for investment advice on £500,000 i.e. £10,000 will not be paid if the client does not agree to go ahead with the investments recommended. The fee is contingent on product sales, which is why I think it is a rotten way to operate.

The other culprit constantly pushing advisers into a product to client way of operating are investment and insurance companies and their broker representatives. I frequently get approaches from company representatives wanting to meet up to run by their great new investment or multi-asset range. Some suggest it can be done in 20 minutes. I am not sure who they are kidding. My meetings with broker reps rarely last less than 45 minutes to an hour.

Then there is the constant stream of e-mails from product providers promoting their wares. I read the most interesting and relevant ones. Sometimes I am impressed and really like the fund or product, or think it could potentially fit into client portfolios but that's all. The e-mail gets filed, the information moves to the back of my mind but I don't think who can I sell that to? If when advising a client later I decide the product could be suitable for meeting their needs I'll then take a second look.

To conclude I frequently tell broker representatives that I go from client to product not product to client i.e. I will not be looking to sell it, no matter how impressive it is. I think they understand. In my experience it seems to work as they are not too pushy.

Giving investment advice

Over the years I have gradually focussed on advising investments and investment portfolios. This is what interests me most and I am fortunate that I have a sizeable group of high net worth individuals and couples who came to me looking for this sort of advice. They have cash to invest and pre-existing investments and large pension pots to review and manage. They are dream clients.

I pretty well manage all portfolios in house, recommending suitable platforms, asset allocations and funds. I advise on the full range of RIPs but I don't give advice on individual stocks. I leave that to DFMs and fund managers who have the skills to analyse balance sheets and companies' fundamentals. I see my role as creating and maintaining bespoke collective investment portfolios to meet clients' financial objectives and needs and which are suitable for their risk profiles and capacity for loss.

I eat, drink and sleep economics, stock markets and the fund management business. I constantly read and listen to fund managers and economists. I take it in and then develop my own investment convictions and strategies. These views are typically expressed in my investment blog which has been successfully running since 2012. Putting my thoughts in writing on the economy, markets and investment strategies helps clarify and sharpen my understanding, making me a better investment adviser. In addition my muses provide an interesting and hopefully useful commentary for my clients. They are also intended to provide a context to the specific investment advice I give them. For example if I have written a blog about the case for investment in Japan my clients will understand my thinking and reasons if I subsequently recommend a Japanese equity fund to them.

In my blogs I have covered the passives v actives debate and why I favour active fund management. I have explained why I like smaller companies and why I thought profit-taking and risk reduction was important in the first part of 2018. I could go on.

Strategic v tactical investment

In general I am an advocate of a buy and hold investment strategy. Most advisers realise how difficult it is to time the market correctly. To know when it has peaked, have the courage to sell equities (when perhaps no-one else is) and then spot the bottom of a slump and buy back in at the right time takes a genius, a crystal ball or exceptional luck. I am not gifted with any of these qualities so a buy and hold strategy is entirely sensible. It is a key plank of Terry Smith's investment philosophy. Smith is manager of the Fundsmith Equity fund and he advocates buying good companies and then doing nothing. This is a key plank of a quality growth investment style.

This view is supported by the startling analysis that various investment companies publish to encourage a buy and hold strategy. For example Fidelity used data from Datastream to show that £1,000 fully invested from 31/12/04 to 31/12/19 in the FTSE All Share index would have returned 7.6% p.a. If the 10 best days were missed the return fell to 3.3% p.a. If the 20 best days were missed the return was just 0.8% p.a. and for the 40 best days the return was -3.2% p.a. The reason given for these outcomes was that the biggest price movements occur over short periods and are clustered together.

Despite my support for buy and hold strategies I think some tactical overlays are worth trying, for example investing cash at low valuation points as explained above or if clients' circumstances warrants changes. An example here might be gradual risk reduction as retirement approaches. Incidentally I don't think this is a universal given requirement or always beneficial. The subject of life-styling retirement investment strategies is discussed in Chapter 13.

In recent years in my regular investment reviews I recommended selected tactical profit-taking and risk reduction as equity markets rose inexorably from 2016 through to mid-2018. This involved switches from equity funds to cautious risk investments, notably targeted absolute return, volatility managed and other multi-asset funds. I did not recommend wholesale dumping of equities. It was a case of trimming large fund holdings and switching profits to funds with more defensive qualities but leaving equity exposure intact, albeit at lower levels.

It proved to be a good call with the sharp equity market sell-off in the last four months of 2018. The actions did not protect client portfolios fully, only cash would have done that but it limited the downside losses. That is a key element of investment portfolio management. You aim to reduce volatility and by capping losses it means there is less of a hill to climb when the recovery comes. John Husselbee, head of multi-asset investment at Liontrust describes this as winning by not losing.

Investment managers and IFAs may try and be too clever. Tactical investment requires not only getting your call on market moves right, for example knowing a stock market crash is coming but also it requires getting the timings precisely right, not only once but twice, when to sell and when to buy back in. It is fraught with danger. For example there is evidence that some of the best market gains occur prior to a downturn or recession, so selling too soon means you may miss some of these late bull market returns.

In conclusion the difficulties of tactical investment have led some, notably quality growth investors to adopt a simple but effective model of fund management, to ignore the global macro-economic and political noise and just concentrate on stock selection, buying the best companies and holding them long term. Terry Smith believes you should concentrate on what you can control, not speculate on or worry about what you cannot. Even if you can predict the global economy - inflation, the timing of interest rate rises, if and when recession will strike he asks, what can you do about it? I think that is a good philosophy and applicable to life in general.

Having decided on a suitable asset allocation for the client's needs the next task is to pick suitable funds. This is covered in Chapter 11.

Investment reviews

I recommend regular investment reviews are undertaken. For some clients these are typically done on an annual basis although I am very flexible here. A change in clients' circumstances and financial needs may trigger the requirement for one-off reviews as might stock market conditions, so they may be more frequent than annually.

I don't insist on annual investment reviews. Many of my clients don't feel they need one or they are unwilling to pay the additional fees each year. They may instead prefer *ad hoc* reviews. If alarm bells start to ring here and you are thinking what about MIFID II requirements, you'll find out what I have to say about this in the next two chapters.

It is important to explain to clients the case for investment reviews. In general over time adventurous funds will grow capital faster than cautious risk ones. The former will increasingly dominate the portfolio and if left unattended it will drift up the risk scale as a consequence. Portfolios need rebalancing from time to time. Risk can be reduced and profits can be protected by switching to defensive funds with the potential for significant, if not complete, capital protection. Only cash can do that although as noted inflation is the enemy of cash, so it is never risk free.

Reviews should also ensure portfolios are best aligned to current market conditions and the asset allocation is still suited to these conditions. It may require reducing exposure to overvalued assets or sectors and switching to undervalued ones with more upside potential. Finally regular reviews will ensure poor funds are spotted early and weeded out. Retaining these for too long, especially large holdings, will be detrimental to portfolio returns.

In January and February 2019 I initiated reviews for clients holding significant cash within their investments. I recommended tactical investment into high quality equity or multi-asset funds. The thinking was these should benefit from the relatively low prices resulting from the stock market sell-off at the end of 2018. Although markets rebounded in 2019, typically a three to five year investment period is required to assess the success of an investment strategy.

During 2018 a key focus of my investment reviews was to assess the performance of various cautious risk funds in client portfolios. Some funds had been held for several years. What became evident was that many funds in the targeted absolute return space were performing very poorly. They were failing to capture the upside whilst not always providing protection on the downside.

I took the view that as a very minimum all cautious risk funds whatever Investment Association (IA) sector they were located, be that the IA Targeted Absolute Return, the IA Mixed Investment (0-35% Shares) or the IA Volatility Managed should have delivered net returns in excess of RPI inflation in the last three years. In virtually all cases if the fund had failed to beat inflation it was replaced. There is little point in continuing to invest in such funds if you have lost money in real terms after inflation is taken into account.

I write more about investment reviews in Chapter 11.

Communications

Naturally I aim to put all my thinking, analysis and advice to clients in writing, both e-mails and letters.

All my e-mails for each client including their responses are stored in an individual Outlook folder. There are literally dozens and dozens and probably hundreds of e-mails for some clients. In order to help locate a specific e-mail amongst a very long list, at a later stage, I will normally change the subject when replying to an e-mail if the subject under discussion changes. For example a chain may begin with a subject heading of *"Pension contribution."* As you know if you hit reply the subject will become *"Re: Pension contribution."* Let's say at the end of the e-mail chain about making a pension contribution the client makes an enquiry about something else e.g. Brexit concerns or whether gold is a good investment I will delete the *"Re: Pension contribution"* and insert *"Brexit"* or *"Gold."* It is a simple thing but it will save you time looking for a specific e-mail, the proverbial needle in a haystack, six months or a year later when you may need to refresh yourself on what exactly you wrote on the subject.

I normally send final suitability reports by post or by e-mail as PDF attachments. A PDF is a format which the FCA regards as "durable" unlike e-mails themselves. I am not quite sure what they consider the risk to be here. I suppose the concern is that it is possible to modify the original text when replying in order to cover up bad advice or an omission but quite frankly I think the durable format requirement is a solution to a problem that does not exist. That is because unless I am mistaken the text of the original e-mail in the client's inbox cannot be amended and the date and time of that e-mail is fixed.

When delivering my investment advice to clients the use of e-mail may become impractical if I need to attach too many documents. Typically I will send two documents per fund - the fund fact sheet and the KIID (a KID is required for investment trusts). So if I recommend 10 funds, a covering letter and a fund proposals document, that adds up to 22 PDFs. It is simply too much data to send all this by e-mail. It is also unfair on the client if there is too much to open and view on screen. Personally I find it easier to read and take in the content of long documents if they are in paper form than scroll through the equivalent file on my PC or iPad. So it all goes by post.

Files

I keep paper files in addition to electronic ones. The paper files will typically contain copies of letters and selected e-mails, investment research, copies of fund documents, contract notes, application forms and other paper based documentation.

My electronic files consist of Outlook folders to store e-mails and PDF attachments and I also have a variety of client specific spreadsheet and word processor files, notably investment valuation statements and letters. My son is convinced he has dinosaur ancestry as I still use Microsoft Works. Yes you hear me right. On the evolutionary scale it is technology one up from an abacus or a slide rule! In all fairness it is software that has served me well for more than 20 years, it is very simple to use and as they say, if it isn't broke don't fix it. I do however occasionally use Microsoft Word and Excel.

I am not entirely happy with my filing system having records in two places. It evolved out of my experience when I left my first network, Burns-Anderson in late 2010. I had to give up all my paper files. There were around 300 of them and they were very comprehensive and included paper copies of all e-mails. I have no idea where they are now, I assume when Honister Capital the parent company went bust they fell under the control of the administrator. When I joined Financial Ltd I decided I would not print out everything for my paper files to avoid a repeat of data loss. Electronic data storage then became more important and the dual filing system evolved.

Although my dual filing system works well for me I realise when it comes to selling my business it may require considerable amalgamation to get all my files in good order, depending on what an acquirer wants.

Client history notes

On this word processor document I record a summary of my dealings and advice to clients including documents I have supplied, telephone conversations had, e-mails sent etc. with the relevant dates. An example of a document is included at the end of the chapter. It is for the client I mentioned earlier who wanted to cash in his pension. You will recall I advised against this and recommended inheritance tax planning was his most important financial need.

To ensure the record keeping works well and is up to date when I conclude a meeting, come off the phone to a client or finish sending an e-mail I immediately record the main points whilst they are fresh in my mind. It is about being disciplined but after a while it becomes second nature and it no longer feel like a chore. Having these records will become your friend very quickly.

You will see that the notes are brief and to the point. I don't normally include much detail about the advice given in my client history notes if it is delivered in an e-mail or a letter. I can dig these out if necessary to see what I wrote. If however I have an extended telephone conversation or face to face meeting with a client which is not subsequently detailed in writing my client notes will be more substantial.

The value of keeping these notes is they are a clear written record of what work I undertook, what advice I gave and when. The principle here is summarised by an old Chinese proverb:

"*The faintest ink is more powerful than the strongest memory.*"

The lesson is clear.

For me client history notes are highly useful documents that serve as an aide memoire to review the advice I have given. They may also come in handy if there is a complaint.

Whatever method you employ make sure you keep accurate and complete notes of your dealings with clients.

You will see from the appendix that the compliance notes at the top of my document serve as a prompt that a new Client Agreement may need to be issued or a fact find needs to be updated.

Suitability reports

I suppose I am old school because I still refer to these as letters of recommendation. I think the old term makes more sense to a client. They are getting a written report on what I have recommended and why. I think they get that the why bit will include my reasoning on the suitability of the advice to them. However I suggest you play it by the book and call them suitability reports, and to avoid passing onto you a "bad" habit I'll call them by the term the FCA require.

My suitability reports vary in length. They can be as short as three or four pages. They are very rarely in excess of eight or nine. I try to keep them short on the principle that more is less. There is more chance clients will read your letters and reports and grasp the key elements of the advice if they are short. A long report full of general technical information is more likely to result in the key points getting lost.

As noted the FCA have made it clear that there are only three key things that need to go into a report, as articulated to me by compliance consultant, Rory Percival, when he was at the FCA.

These are:

- The client's objectives
- Why the recommendation is suitable
- Potential disadvantages.

During my years at Burns-Anderson and Financial Ltd the list of things that their compliance departments mandated had to be included in the suitability reports got longer and longer. After Rory Percival's response I wrote back and listed all the things I had been including in my suitability reports. I asked which were not necessary. Here is his reply from January 2015:

> "The topics that clearly do not fall into these areas are:
>
> - Client agreement
>
> - Client circumstances other than objectives
>
> - Investment strategy: you need to cover why suitable and disadvantages but not repeat what has been covered in previous reports but if the overall advice is a prolonged process then it may make sense to bring it together in a single report or at least cross-refer to previous reports. It doesn't need to cover the detail of the products (other than the disadvantages) as these are covered in the product disclosure material
>
> - Fund platform recommended - yes, but not products/services not being recommended
>
> - Charges are covered by product disclosure but a summary in the SR would be good practice, particularly when replacement business is concerned where we would expect to see a cost comparison.
>
> - References to KFDs etc. - not mandatory but good practice
>
> - Taxation except where this is a disadvantage. However some aspects such as implications to clients would be good practice
>
> - Limited or full advice disclosure (although this should be clear by some means e.g. letter of engagement)
>
> - Adviser charge disclosure (although this should be clear by some means e.g. letter of engagement)."

The message was very clear. There is no requirement to overload clients with unnecessary information and trivia, such as repeating what is in a fact find especially statements of the blindingly obvious, for example:

"You are 42, married with three children and work as a doctor..."

Suitability reports need to be brief and to the point and cover the essentials. They don't need to be full of pages of general financial information. That can be covered in separate guides or appendices. For example I have written short papers on various subjects such as investment trusts, ethical investment and income protection which I pass on to relevant clients during the advice process.

I understand why reports have become unnecessarily bloated. Compliance departments insist on them to cover their own backs. To reduce the potential for complaints or claims of compensation they insist on throwing everything plus the kitchen sink at clients. I was told if it wasn't written down it did not happen. A fair point you might think but I was pulled up for not repeating something that was in the fact find in the suitability report as well. The fair point morphed into one that effectively said if it was not written twice it did not happen!

I also wonder if another reason for very long reports is that advisers think if a high fee will be more acceptable to clients. I am not sure that always washes with clients. You will recall what a new client told me about a report he had received from his previous IFA:

> *"For a thousand pounds he has written a report (most of which I could have written myself, as it's mostly a summary of what our investments are at the moment) advising what he's already been saying but now giving precise figures for costs which to me seem eye-watering."*

Intelligent clients will see through waffle and padding.

The issue of the length of suitability reports has also been covered in the financial press. An article in Money Marketing on 13/10/17 stated:

> *"Advisers and the regulator have reached agreement that many suitability reports are too lengthy.*
>
> *The longer the reports, the less enthusiastic clients become. In its suitability review earlier this year, the FCA found many suitability reports were too complex. But is it possible to make them shorter?*

The FCA has provided a number of examples where suitability reports included superfluous information. However, it has been reluctant to say how long they should be.

The fear, as the regulator expressed at the Money Marketing Interactive conference last month, is that putting a minimum or optimum number of pages would give advisers a licence to produce reports to exactly this standard, regardless of the client's circumstances.

That means advisers lean towards caution, including too much information rather than too little. According to the FCA's rules, reports only have to include three things: clients' demands and needs, why the solution is suitable to meet the objective, and the potential disadvantages. But at what point are each of these points satisfied?

Former FCA technical specialist Rory Percival says some stock sections can be removed and reports would still meet these requirements.

He says: "A lot of advisers have templated objectives, which don't work for the client, regulator or ombudsman because they are so obviously templated. We see too many that say things like 'you are looking to have your money managed by a discretionary manager' in the objectives and then 'I have recommended this discretionary manager' in the recommendations. This is never a client's objective."

The disadvantages also need to be personalised, he says. "Instead of 'the new solution may be more expensive, and investment performance may not offset costs', it is better to say 'the new solution is 0.5 per cent more expensive, but I believe it is still suitable because....'"

Percival says information on status and scope of service can also be stripped out, is better confined to the terms of engagement letter and does not need to be repeated in the suitability document. He says

"Often we find that advisers have a lengthy paragraph repeating a lot of the fact find information. You are 52 years old, work as a civil engineer and have a wife and two children. Clients know that. There may be some client information you want to have because it gives more colour to the client objectives but you don't need to repeat the fact find. There is also a tendency to include everything that the adviser hasn't recommended. With the exception of stakeholder pensions, that isn't necessary. Some advisers want to replicate their whole research process in the suitability report and that isn't necessary."

Similarly, Percival says,

"advisers can create guides to investments, defined benefit versus defined contribution, retirement income or inheritance tax planning and hand these to clients, rather than giving repeated disclosures in every suitability document..."[13]

I was quite interested in the subtle change to one of the three essentials for suitability reports that Percival articulated to me a few years ago, from "client objectives" to "client demands and needs." This better reflects my own view that clients' financial needs are more important than their financial objectives.

As for the word *demands* that seems somewhat odd and I don't like it. I see it in general insurance documents I receive, informing me of demands I supposedly have, although have not made. It conjures up an image of an assertive client coming into an adviser's office and fist bashing the table demanding action or results.

Another specific issue with suitability reports arises from my e-mail chains. The suitability report is the final piece of correspondence in the advice process but a lot of important content has been communicated earlier. I reference or quote these key communications in the suitability report with the relevant dates. The benefits of this are firstly covering earlier material serves as an audit trail to explain how we arrived at the final outcomes, concluding what might have been a lengthy advice process. Secondly having the key elements summarised in a single document is useful for the client when the advice is given and when it is reviewed in the future. They don't have to search through lots of e-mail correspondence on their PC or tablet to refresh themselves on the background material.

---

[13] www.moneymarketing.co.uk/suitability-document-short-report/

Despite the repeated content I manage to keep my suitability reports short whilst cutting and pasting sections from e-mails keeps my additional time costs to a minimum. I also use italics for repeated content which gives the client the opportunity to skip reading sections of the report if the advice is fresh in their minds and they feel they do not need to go over it again.

CLIENT HISTORY NOTES

Client (s):	^&*(%$^
Client No:	76
Client Agreement Sent:	26.5.18 (DA7)
Signed:	26.6.18
Fact Find Completed:	26.6.18
Fact Find Updated:	
Proof of Identity:	Online check - Smart Search - 3/4/18
Proof of Address:	Online check - Smart Search - 3/4/18

23.3.18

Letter to client after request for advice. X is husband of my deceased client Y. Outlined potential work, the cost and value.

31.3.18

E-mail to client about transfer forms for wife's former Fidelity investments following probate and the additional permitted ISA subscriptions. Explained funds could be sold to cash though not advised without a review.

E-mail from client to confirm transfer option is required.

3.4.18

Doing business with Fidelity and Key Facts document to client.

25.5.18

Confirmed completion of transfer of Fidelity investments from Y to X. E-mail correspondence with client on taxation of inherited annuity. Explained it was tax free.

26.5.18

Fact find and documents on risk and ethical investment to client.

1.7.18

Completed fact find received from client.

2.7.18

E-mail to client with request for further information on fact find gaps with comments on financial planning needs that I see. I don't think he should draw benefits from his personal pension. This is however X's primary objective.

5.7.18

Additional e-mail correspondence on why I advise not vesting personal pension and on IHT planning being the most important planning issue.

10.7.18

Further e-mail correspondence yesterday and today about tax free cash post 75 and pension, IHT and CGT issues, latter in relation to sale of Z (the name of the property).

11.7.18

Final advice to client about Friends Life pension after clarification that benefits including tax free cash must be taken by the day before the client's 76th birthday. Presented options including plan transfer and covered investment reviews.

19.7.18

E-mail to client with IHT calculations and comments.

24.7.18

Letter to client with options for IHT mitigation.

22.8.18

Meeting here to discuss IHT planning options. Some discounted, others of interest to client. See letter of 23/8/18 for summary.

24.8.18

Letter to client with summary of discussions and recommendations.

Note

Client did not take matters further but I was fully paid for my work.

7. Regulation - a 30 year personal review

Regulation is neither all good nor all bad. There are bucket loads of both. An adviser's job is to embrace the good and manage the bad so that the outcomes for clients are beneficial and advisers avoid complaints and falling foul of the regulator.

Over the years I have been a financial adviser there have been enormous changes in the regulatory landscape. Much has been very necessary and commendable. It has largely driven out the sharks from the industry, lowered product charges and has vastly improved transparency and outcomes for clients.

When I first started out working with Liberty Life there was no requirement to put advice in writing. You simply relied on verbal presentations. What was provided to clients in writing was the brochure for the product you were selling, with fetching titles such as Plan D or Plan M backed up with Heath Robinson style quotes. You punched in the figures into a small desk top machine and out rolled a long narrow strip of paper a bit like a till receipt from the supermarket. It contained all the relevant figures and it was stuck into the correct position on a pre-printed quote card to fill in the various figures and projections in the blank spaces.

Today we have compulsory suitability reports and rightly so. It struck me early in my career that it was important to put my advice in writing and I recall writing occasional hand written letters, a bit like I used to do for pen pal friends, before I got my first computer. I can't recall any access to letterheads or letter writing facilities at Liberty Life.

In the old days life companies could provide quotes that did not take account of their actual policy charges. They typically used generalised costs that could be less than the true figures. Clients ended up with illustrations that showed higher projected investment sums than had the true charges been used. About 20 years ago the rules changed and illustrations were required to use the company's own charges. This change was entirely appropriate.

Commission disclosure in cash terms to clients prior to a sale was also made compulsory. It wasn't when I first started out. Over the years, charges and commission disclosure has become crystal clear and commission itself was banned from new investment and pension sales with the RDR, which came into effect on 31/12/12.

With MIFID II (the EU's second Markets in Financial Instruments Directive) was introduced on 3/1/18 fund transaction costs had to be disclosed in illustrations and when advisers recommend funds. Previously these figures were buried in bulky annual reports and accounts. Investors now know pretty well everything about fund costs and charges apart from the salaries of fund managers, office rents and the money spent on departmental paperclips.

Financial products themselves have changed beyond all recognition in the last 30 years with a relentless driving down of charges from regulation, competition and pressure from an often hostile financial press and the consumer lobby. Mis-selling scandals gave them plenty of ammunition.

When I first became an IFA in 1992 unit trusts typically had initial charges of 5% or 5.25% and bid-offer spreads on top. Annual charges were typically 1.5% p.a. These costs included commission payable to IFAs, typically 3% initial and 0.5% p.a. trail, but even before the RDR initial charges had fallen to 3%, squeezing investment company margins. In the post RDR world, funds typically have no initial charges and many dual priced unit trusts have either converted to OEICs or have moved to single pricing thereby eliminating the bid-offer spread, if not the actual costs of dealing which are now charged to the fund as a whole rather than to individual investors.

Pension and savings plans including endowments used to have very high upfront costs with no investment or a reduced investment allocation in the first two years. A policy might have had 70% to 100% of the premiums taken in charges. Alternatively many policies had capital units, bought in the first few years. These had huge annual management charges, as much as 4.5% p.a. Then there were bid-offer spreads of 5% and policy fees, for example £2.50 or £3 p.m. With hindsight the charges were outrageous.

The upfront charges were justified as legitimate setup costs, which included commissions, although they undoubtedly made a big contribution to profits as well. It might have taken 7-10 years for a plan to recover these charges and the investment to go into profit whilst exit fees could be exceptionally high for plans with capital units. These were structured to collect the set up fees and commissions over the lifetime of the contract which meant the sting in the tail was a large penalty was applied if the client transferred out. Recent regulations have capped very high exit fees on old pensions to a maximum of 1%, effectively tearing up the original contracts on products that the regulators at the time were perfectly happy to be distributed.

The first regulation of product charges was the introduction of Stakeholder pensions in 2001. The FSA set a maximum all in fee of 1% p.a. No charges could be levied for starting and stopping contributions.

Modern pensions typically have no initial costs unless there is an adviser charge and no exit fees. The client gets 100% invested at outset. Nil investment periods and capital units have gone. Of course there is a platform or account charge, typically from 0.20% to 0.45% p.a. and some SIPPs have one-off set up fees.

Costs and charges have been slashed in the last 30 years whilst transparency and disclosures are now crystal clear. It is a totally different world to when I first became an IFA.

When I joined the industry anyone could become a financial adviser. If you could count to 100 you were in, even if you answered in the job interview, *"One, two, miss a few 99,100."*

At the end of November 2017 data from the FCA showed there were 25,951 registered advisers, very slightly up from December 2016. However at the end of 2011, a year prior to the RDR the FSA estimated numbers to be 40,566. That decrease however pales into insignificance in the context of adviser numbers in the late 1980s and 1990s.

A report, *"Polarisation and Financial Services Intermediary Regulation,"* from London Economics in July 2000 undertaken for the Financial Services Authority (FSA) makes interesting reading on adviser numbers.

Polarisation was introduced in 1987. This required advisers to be either independent or tied to selling the products of a single company. Back in 1987 it was believed there were over 200,000 tied agents although an article in Professional Adviser dated 9/4/18 suggested in 1988 there were 250,000 advisers. This higher number almost certainly included IFAs.

By July 2000 the number of tied agents had fallen from 200,000 to 60,000. In 1999 there were around 25,000 IFAs as well. Although the London Economics report says the fall in numbers partly reflected a reduction in the number of registered backroom staff, it is clear adviser numbers have plummeted since the introduction of the Financial Services Act (1986) and since the London Economics report in 2000, a reduction from about 85,000 to 25,951 in November 2017 has occurred.

Back in the 1990s most advisers were tied agents - salesmen of pensions, life assurance and savings plans. There were armies of them working for life assurance companies and banks. Multiple providers were out there selling, Allied Dunbar, Abbey Life and Legal & General to name a few. The man from the Pru was still alive and well. These worked as industrial branch advisers, not just with Prudential but Pearl, the Co-op and others. They visited people at home, selling policies and collecting very small premiums. The products were high charging but at least penetration was strong and advice was accessible. Working class families bought life cover and saved for their future.

Advisers now must pass exams, gain qualifications, undertake CPD and are strictly monitored. We are one of the most highly regulated industries. The level of professionalism is incomparable to my early years and whilst the focus on product sales is arguably still too high in my opinion there is much more holistic financial planning advice being provided today than previously. Financial products are better quality and have much lower charges. Fee disclosure and transparency is infinitely better, conflicts of interest are managed well and commission from new product sales is banned.

In conclusion regulation has worked very well. It has transformed the industry, made it more professional and significantly improved client outcomes. So what's not to like about it? Plenty!

At its root I am troubled by the underlying belief system of the authorities that has driven and still undergirds regulation and its ceaseless output, from bureaucrats in Brussels, or the Treasury and the FCA (and their predecessor the FSA) here in the UK. Between them they have been responsible for the avalanche of new regulations over the years.

Whilst it not a stated principle, it is my opinion that the regulators have a world view that essentially thinks customers lack common sense and should bear little or no personal responsibility for the actions they take. The regulators believe the public are vulnerable and have to be protected from their own stupidity and from an industry that would otherwise rip them off, if it were not for their very noble interventions.

The regulators in essence consider customers to be victims, advisers and product providers to be perpetrators and the regulators to be white knights in shining armour, there to save the public. You might consider this view to be extreme and whilst it is clearly not the whole picture, poor regulation has had a damaging effect. The actions of the regulators have decimated the financial advice industry and have perversely led to bad outcomes for those they ostensibly are there to protect. Worse I don't think they get what they have done.

I perhaps first got wind of the patronising attitude that the regulations engendered when I first joined Burns-Anderson in 1996. I remember on a training course we were told when handing out a business card to a prospective client that it was a requirement we had to tell them that the telephone number on the card was the number they had to call to contact me! Yes you have read me correct. Precisely who or what the client might think the number on the card would get them through to takes some guessing - the local Chinese takeaway was one possibility of course. Needless to say I ignored this "rule." Even if it was an urban myth and just idiocy dreamt up by a very zealous network compliance department it shows the mindset of those who job it was to interpret the regulations.

The mindset of the regulators that treats the public as stupid of course is not unique to the financial services industry. It has affected much of our day to day lives whether it is the BBC telling us other chocolate bars are available, if a guest inadvertently happens to mention on air a Mars bar or Milky Way. The belief here is if the BBC presenter doesn't put out this caveat we'll all think they are promoting a brand. Similarly when any celebrity is accused of a sexual assault or any other crime the news report always concludes with the caveat that he or she denies all the allegations. Failure to say this presumably means we'll all conclude they are guilty as if we are not intelligent enough to know the accusations may not be true and will only be proved if the case goes to court.

At Wembley Stadium back in 2018 I was amused by signs on TV screens at the refreshment counters that said, *"All hot drinks contain hot liquid,"* whilst at a cricket club where I used to play regularly there was a sign on the tea hut that said, *"Children are the responsibility of their parents not the cricket club."* Well they were things I never knew. An absurd health and safety culture is alive and well in the UK and warnings of the blindingly obvious abound.

At work people are sent on training courses to use step ladders or are forbidden to change lightbulbs. Schools close at the slightest bit of snow due to fears of accidents.

One of the most ridiculous examples of health and safety gone mad I heard was a call to a council about a supermarket trolley dumped in a tiny brook, by all accounts just a few inches deep. The council concerned said they could not retrieve it at this time as they had no-one available who was qualified to wear wellington boots! This training course must be on everyone's bucket list. No doubt you have your own stories but this mad health and safety culture is everywhere.

Of course we know that much of this patronising rubbish has nothing to do with health and safety but it is about a fear of being sued, avoiding compensation claims and covering the backs of organisations. The point is our out of touch judicial system has failed to squash frivolous claims for compensation. Courts should be throwing out cases where someone did not exercise common sense and personal responsibility, with all costs paid by the litigant. If they did Wembley Stadium would not need signs like they have. Idiocy seems to be protected by the law.

It seems to me entirely reasonable to conclude the same patronising culture has infiltrated the regulators of the investment and advice industries. What are the equivalents? It might be inane and repeated risk warnings such as *"past performance is not necessarily a guide to the future,"* and *"the value of investments can go down as well as up,"* as if the public lacking a modicum of common sense don't get this.

My clients have had these risk warnings set out in multiple suitability letters over many years and the message now must wash over them. But no doubt if I had a client who complained they had lost money on the back of my investment advice and it was shown I failed to repeat these risk warnings in the latest suitability report I would no doubt be held liable for mis-selling, despite the fact I had issued the same risk warnings umpteen times previously.

The problem with an over protective risk adverse society is we do not teach people to be critical thinkers and assess risk for themselves. The lack of questioning and scepticism by investors when being advised (not by any decent IFA) to invest their pension money in unregulated investment schemes such as Cape Verde holiday complexes, Brazilian teak plantations or UCIS schemes is amazing.

Why are people not naturally sceptical? Why are they not getting second opinions, checking whether their advisers are authorised and regulated by the FCA and undertaking research on the investments they have been advised to buy? Is it because they think there will be someone else to blame if it goes pear shaped? Compensation after all is a human right, isn't it?

One reason for this state of affairs is that general financial education, including in schools, is very poor, despite efforts by the government's Money Advice Service, widely thought to be a failed project. It has now merged with The Pension Advice Service in a new quango. People are unprepared and are seemingly unable to identify financial scams, bad investments and dishonest or dangerous advice.

A second reason why the public are not critical thinkers is a consequence of what I have described above. They have been molly coddled by an elite group of superior beings who have set themselves up as their protectors. All the blame for bad financial outcomes is due to product provider or adviser failures, none is attributable to the public for the actions they take or fail to take. Effectively the attitude is you can be stupid but don't worry we'll find a way to blame someone else and get your money back. The FOS and the FSCS are on your side and if they can't help you the claims industry is there for you. Also bear in mind common law does not apply to financial advisers and the 15 year long stop for making a complaint and gaining compensation is unavailable to them.

Financial regulation has been driven by a continuous process of identifying real or perceived injustices inflicted on the public by the investment and advice industries, whether it is bad advice, mis-selling, opaque fees or high costs. So those in charge undertake investigations and thematic reviews and then formulate and introduce new rules and regulations. They then identify more injustices and poor practice and repeat the process.

There have also been the wholesale changes to the regulatory framework, depolarisation in 2005, the RDR in 2012 and MIFID II in 2018. The busy bodies dump the old regimes and replace them with something new that they think will fix all the ills of the investment and advice industries. However after a few years, despite warnings of bad outcomes and unintended consequences that were patently obvious and predictable in advance the regulators undertake more market reviews and set about making more changes. It is never ending. New regimes are not given time to bed in before the next wave of consultations, policy documents and regulations comes in. The bureaucrats and regulators naturally have to justify their existence and their fat pay packets. To stop meddling, tinkering and overhauling is not in a regulator's DNA. It could mean they would be out of a job.

So what are the bad outcomes from over-regulation of the investment and advice industries?

Over-regulation has restricted access to advice

In the past access to financial advice was much more widely available especially for lower income households. Small premium policies were available and industrial branch and bank advisers serviced the masses. However incessant regulation has driven up costs and resulted in death of this market by a thousand cuts. Now financial advice is seen as a privilege only affordable by the well-off.

As noted above the number of financial advisers has plummeted since the 1990s and the RDR with its ban on commission was widely predicted to further exacerbate this trend. It is only set to get worse as advisers are an aging bunch and there will be a wave of retirements in the next 5-10 years. The Heath Report 3 (THR3) published in January 2019 is a comprehensive survey on the availability and future of professional financial advice. It was published by Libertatem, an independent trade body set up to support advisers (now the Impartial Financial Advisers Association or IFAA). Its survey showed 45% of advisers surveyed are over age 56, 21% wish to retire within five years, with a quarter of those wanting to retire immediately.

Moreover there is a dearth of new entrants. Over regulation plus a highly critical press has indirectly contributed to making financial advice seem an unattractive career option. Why should you for example take the risk of becoming an IFA when you could face hefty compensation claims and they can come after you for mis-selling claims long into retirement.

The earlier Heath Report 2 was researched at the end of 2014 to examine the effects of the RDR. It showed high street banking financial advice had all but been withdrawn from the market, removing advice for six million consumers. Moreover 6,500 IFAs had left the sector since June 2005 and the number of clients each serviced more than halved on average.

Another example of restricting access to advice came from the EU's MIFID regulations which were first implemented in 2004. MIFID II was a later addition. Here's a question. Given all the supposed benefits of free trade and the single market during our membership of the EU, do you think if a British citizen living in France had contacted me for investment advice on his stocks and shares ISA that I could have advised him? Logically any sane person would think yes, it should be a given. Well it wasn't. It depended on where the client was physically located when I advised him. If he was in Dover I could give advice but if he was in Calais I couldn't. If I sent him an advisory e-mail to a French e-mail address and he was in Dover that was OK but if he was in Calais well I would be breaking the rules. That is unless I had a passport to give advice to people living in France.

Here is how the FCA put it on their website (this is prior to us leaving the EU):

> *"If your UK-authorised firm wants to provide financial advice, set up a base or run permitted activities in an EEA state, you can apply for a 'passport' to do this. The EEA states are: Austria, Belgium, Bulgaria, Croatia, Cyprus (Republic of), Czech Republic, Denmark, Estonia, Finland, France, Germany, Greece, Hungary, Iceland, Ireland, Italy, Latvia, Liechtenstein, Lithuania, Luxembourg, Malta, Netherlands, Norway, Poland, Portugal, Romania, Slovakia, Slovenia, Spain, Sweden.*
>
> *You may need a different passport to be able to give advice on different products – even if you are advising the same client on a range of products, or a small number of clients.*
>
> *You may also need a domestic authorisation in the EEA state in question for a business you run that is outside a passport's remit."*[14]

To obtain a passport for any EEA member there was bureaucracy and cost, although application fees if charged were small. The biggest cost however was instead of mandatory bi-annual compliance reports that regulated firms had to make to the FCA, called GABRIEL[15], a MIFID firm who had a passport to give advice in a EEA country had to undertake these returns four times a year. Mine take three or four hours to complete and I have to pay my accountant to prepare financial statements that GABRIEL requires. Moreover the amount of capital my firm would have had to hold would have been 50,000 Euros, instead of £20,000 without a passport. The bottom line is if I had applied for a passport I would have needed to raise my fee rates for overseas clients.

The absurdity of it all is that if a Brit contacted me for advice on their UK investments and he or she lived in Spain I would have needed a separate

---

[14] www.fca.org.uk/firms/passporting
[15] GABRIEL is *"gathering better regulatory information electronically."* It is clunky and cumbersome. It is angelic in name if not in nature.

Spanish licence. That is more cost, more bureaucracy.

These people retain British citizenship, they have British passports and have UK investments and yet I couldn't advise them. It was a dystopian outcome reducing access to independent advice. Whilst there were firms who are able to advise expatriate Brits, customer choice is highly restricted and hence so is the competition.

Incidentally there were two main passports an adviser would need if they wanted to advise on the full range of products. One covers MIFID investments such as ISAs and collective investments such as unit trusts and the other pensions and insurance based products such as investment bonds. The second falls under the Insurance Disclosure Directive (IDD) and does not require the enhanced GABRIEL reporting and capital adequacy.

With the UK having left the EU on 31/1/20 albeit we are in a transition period I understand the passporting arrangements will come to an end. How that affects UK advisers dealing with their UK clients in the EEA remains to be seen.

Over-regulation has driven up the cost of advice

Additional regulation increases the amount of non-productive time firms and advisers must allocate, reducing the time available to give advice to clients and hence limiting their ability to generate revenue. This drives up fee rates.

In March 2016 the final report of the Financial Advice Market Review (FAMR) was published jointly by HM Treasury and the FCA. Here are some interesting statements from the report:

> *"The Financial Advice Market Review (FAMR) was launched in August 2015 in light of concerns that the market for financial advice in the UK was not working well for all consumers."*

> *"We believe that the RDR has brought about a positive step change in the quality of advice available to those with larger amounts to invest. However, steps need to be taken to make the provision of advice and guidance to the mass market more cost-effective."*

> *"A number of factors combine to mean that not all consumers can currently afford to access the advice they need at a price they are willing or able to pay. The market currently delivers high-quality solutions to those who can afford advice."*

> *"... many consumers with lower incomes or investible amounts are unable to pay for advice. Part of this is attributable to the fact that those with less wealth find advice less cost-effective than those with greater wealth, as the cost of advice proportionate to the investible amount is more significant."*

Bad outcomes from the RDR were predicted in advance but I am not sure the authors of the FAMR attributed any responsibility for the lack of affordability of advice for the masses to over-regulation. After all they were marking their own homework and it would be an admission they got it wrong.

THR3 reckons that professional financial advisers deliver over 75% of all financial advice across the UK, worth £7.6 billion to the UK economy. According to the THR3 of the 1,456,396 complaints to the FOS in 2018 only 1,678 were against advisers. The IFA sector has 5.3 million consumers so this level of complaints is very small.

Against this minute level of complaints advisory firms are expected to fund £80 million, which is their share of the large regulatory system's £543 million. Advisory firms also fund around £400 million of FSCS fees, before a proposed 25% reduction. Of course these costs are ultimately borne by the paying public.

THR3 suggest that the hard regulatory costs per client per annum are set to rise substantially in the next five years with a drop in adviser numbers and a fall in the number of clients each firm services. The RDR has resulted in advisers ditching clients with small investment sums and concentrating on the wealthier, those who can afford to pay their fees.

Then there are the burgeoning costs of Professional Indemnity Insurance (PII) and a limited market. THR3 quotes a leading PII broker which makes interesting if depressing reading:

> *"The market for IFAs remains limited when compared with that for, say*

solicitors and accountants..."

"...they are not the mainstream commercial liability insurers...frankly, it no longer makes any commercial sense to write IFAs."

"The reason for this is primarily unpredictability - the unpredictability of regulation itself: FOS decisions, government pensions strategy..."

"Both the FCA and FOS appear (in the eyes of the insurance market at least) to have taken the concept of consumer protection to illogical extremes whereby insurers are expected to blindly reimburse the cynical investor who knows his/her way through the complaints system.

It is estimated that of claims for sums of more than £35,000 over 80% involve claimants who fully understood what they were doing and/or made investment decisions based on greed.

Such facts/motivations are often exposed in the course of conventional litigation...but the FOS has decided all claims must be inherently valid, even when evidence exists to the contrary and they bend over backwards to find for the claimant.

Whereas there is no doubt that in the past a section of the financial adviser community has abused the trust placed in it, the correctional pendulum has swung too far in the opposite direction resulting in disillusioned advisers, disillusioned PI insurers and a growing base of consumers with an over-developed sense of entitlement to compensation, irrespective of their own contribution to the problem.

The FCA continues to carry the taint of being a reactionary only regulator - unable to nip individual or systemic problems in the bud - even when potential scandals are brought to it in a parcel, with a bow on top.

Whether this is due to apathy, ignorance or even a perverse doctrine of anticipated self-justification is hard to divine but it continues to fundamentally fail in doing its job - to stop bad financial things happening - and instead expect PI insurer pay for that failure.

Insurers are not a convenient repository into which an unwelcome financial burden can be off-loaded as seems to be the raison d'etre for the FSCS who, in turn, just ratchet up their levy the next year.

You only have to spend 10 minutes on the comments section of the financial press to see the exasperation of those advisers who do a 'proper job' but onto whom the fallout from the crooked or incompetent is foisted.

If the PI market is to survive beyond the next few years (and there is a distinct danger it won't) and instead possibly develop and even thrive, then the FCA must introduce a 'long-stop' on liability plus a mechanism by which FOS decisions and dare I say, the FCA's own 'reviews' can be quickly and professionally sanity-checked."

This is a damning indictment of the regulatory regime from a PII professional which I agree with. Fundamental change is needed.

Since I read this comment two events have highlighted the problem caused by the FCA even further. Firstly there was a major scandal with the collapse of London Capital & Finance who issued risky fixed rate mini-bonds. It went into administration in January 2019. Around £236 million is owed to around 14,000 investors. The shocking thing is that a well-known IFA, Neil Liversidge wrote to the FCA in November 2015 with his concerns about the marketing of the bond and the interconnections between the LC&F and the companies they were lending money to. Suffice it to say the FCA did nothing allowing the company to continue to take investors' money. It took until January 2020 for the FCA to ban the promotion of risky mini-bonds.

The second event was a rise in the maximum Financial Ombudsman Scheme (FOS) award from £150,000 to £350,000 on 1/4/19 increasing the risk to advisers and PI insurers.

Over-regulation has reduced competition

The FCA on the *"About Us"* section of their website state:

"Our strategic objective is to ensure that the relevant markets function well and our operational objectives are to:

- *protect consumers – we secure an appropriate degree of protection for consumers*

- *protect financial markets – we protect and enhance the integrity of the UK financial system*

- *promote competition – we promote effective competition in the interests of consumers."*[16]

In my view the FCA has over-focussed on the first objective to the detriment of the other two. The consumer is king in the eyes of the FCA and nothing else seems to matter. They don't appear to get the fact that if they over-regulate the advice industry they will decimate it, to the detriment of the consumers they are so keen to protect. Geese and golden eggs comes to mind here.

Financial advisers will become an endangered species and the high costs of advice will prohibit the public from getting it except for the very well off. If these trends as highlighted earlier continue the problems identified by the FAMR will only get worse. In my view the FCA must view the advice community as an integral part of protecting and enhancing the integrity of the UK financial system. If they don't, the consumer will suffer. It is already happening.

In this section I want to highlight the issue of competition. In my view over-regulation has had a damaging effect on competition in respect of product providers and advisers.

When I first started out as an IFA in 1992 I discovered a wonderful world of provider choices existed. I was freed from the constraints of only being able to advise Liberty Life products. There was a huge variety of offerings, mainstream and niche. The choice of life assurance companies offering diverse savings, pensions and investment products was enormous.

Here is a list of companies that I did business with in my first few years at the Investment Practice:

- Equity & Law

---

[16] https://www.fca.org.uk/about © Financial Conduct Authority

- Fidelity
- Prolific
- Commercial Union
- National Mutual Life
- Permanent Insurance
- Norwich Union
- Pegasus
- Life Insurance Company of India
- Gartmore
- Sun Life
- Abbey Life
- M&G
- Perpetual
- Skandia
- Clerical Medical
- Scottish Amicable
- Scottish Life
- General Accident
- Prudential
- Guinness Flight
- Friends Provident

- Scottish Equitable
- Eagle Star
- Allied Dunbar
- Provident Mutual
- National Provident Institution.
- Save & Prosper
- Sun Alliance.

Anyone who has been in the industry will remember these companies with a certain amount of nostalgia. New entrants may never have heard of many of them. Virtually all of these were independent companies and between them they offered a fantastic range of products and product features. Diversity, choice and competition was enormous and this list of providers did not include a multitude of other life companies that had direct sales forces and which did not operate in the IFA market, including Medical Sickness Society, Pearl, Liberty Life, Cannon Assurance, Sun Life of Canada, General Portfolio and Equitable Life.

Today they have virtually all disappeared from the face of the earth. They have either closed to new business, merged with other life companies, were taken over or were sold to firms to manage closed book business. With their demise went choice, innovation and competition.

No doubt there are various reasons why there has been such a dramatic decline in provider choice in the last 25 years. Some smaller life assurers were simply unable to survive on their own in the face of competition but that doesn't explain how the exotic and heady mix of multiple life offices and investment companies came to market in the first place. The environment of the 1980s and 1990s allowed them to be born, become established and thrive, at least for a while.

What changed was the exorable driving down of charges, with pressure from the regulators and the consumer lobby, and increasing costs were principally to blame. They were regulated out of existence.

Many of these smaller life assurance companies have been gobbled up by companies that have become behemoths. Take Aviva. It used to be called Norwich Union. Mergers and acquisitions over many years resulted in Axa Equity & Law, PPP Lifetime, Commercial Union, General Accident, Provident Mutual and Friends Provident all falling under the Aviva banner.

What has also resulted in the last 25 years is the concentration of new business going to a few mega providers such as Prudential, Aviva, Standard Life and L&G, whilst closed book acquirers such as Resolution and Phoenix have gobbled up lots of existing closed book businesses.

Whilst some new entrants notably online life assurers and overseas companies have come to market and the asset management business is healthy with a plethora of boutique fund managers and DFMs, I am in no doubt that over-regulation has significantly reduced competition in the life and pension market, one which served the mass market very well for many years.

Finally it is obvious that if over-regulation drives out advisers, competition will decline. The FCA's operational objective to promote competition has been a failure.

Over-regulation has confused the customer

I take the view that more is less. The more paperwork an adviser issues to their clients - long suitability reports, complex charge disclosures, illustrations and bulky terms and conditions documents the more likely the key messages i.e. the really important things consumers need to grasp will be lost in the detail.

The concept of transparency has become a quasi-religious belief for the regulators of investment companies and advice industry. It has foisted upon us increasingly complex and wide ranging requirements to dump more and more information and disclosure documents on our clients. It is stuff they generally don't want, don't need and don't read.

What I find interesting is that the regulators are double minded and confused when it comes to charge disclosures. Worshipping at the altar of transparency, the RDR led to the demise of bundled or dirty share classes and the creation of unbundled or clean share classes. Bundled shares classes typically had an annual management charge (AMC) of 1.5% p.a. It was divided up with 0.75% p.a. going to the fund manager, 0.5% p.a. trail commission to the adviser and 0.25% p.a. to the platform holding the investment.

The RDR stripped away adviser and platform fees requiring these costs to be charged and disclosed separately to the client. What was left was the raw AMC i.e. an unbundled or clean share class. To complicate matters however, discounts on standard AMCs were negotiated between investment companies and platforms. This led to the fund rebates being credited to client accounts as cash payments meaning you could buy the XYZ (I Accumulation) fund with different net AMCs once the discount was taken into account. Later cash rebates were banned in favour of credits consisting of additional units. In addition super clean shares classes were created with lower than standard AMCs depending on what platform you used.

The proliferation of share classes of the same fund on a platform with different charges adds to advice costs as more research time and hence cost is required to find the cheapest and to avoid falling into a trap of picking the wrong one.

Whilst I think the unbundling of costs was logical, transparent and broadly in investors' best interests, concern was expressed that the AMC was an inaccurate measure of fund management costs, because it did not include additional fund expenses such as auditor, regulator fees and custodian charges.

It became a requirement following EU legislation to disclose the total fund costs as the ongoing charges figure (OCF). The OCF must be displayed on the Key Investor Information Document (KIID), a standard regulatory disclosure document which had to be issued in advance to investors in from July 2012. The paradox is the OCF is a bundled charge. So we have a situation where the AMC has been unbundled from platform and adviser fees but then packaged up with other stuff into the OCF. So which is best - unbundled or bundled charges? Logically for consistency everything should be unbundled for maximum transparency, but it isn't. I don't think the regulators are clear in their own minds on what is best.

Subsequently MIFID II introduced in January 2018 required the estimated transaction costs when the fund manager buys and sells stocks to be disclosed. So first the AMC was not good enough as it did not include miscellaneous fund expenses. That resulted in the requirement to disclose the OCF. Then the OCF was found wanting as it does not account for estimated transaction costs.

That said I think it is helpful to disclose transaction costs as it does provide investors with a total cost of fund ownership. I'll call this the TCO. It is the most useful thing to come from MIFID II, everything else is pretty well useless or worse downright unhelpful.

So here are the equations:

TCO = OCF + transaction costs

OCF = AMC + additional fund expenses.

If you add in performance fees that some funds levy we can further add complexity to these equations.

If you worship the god of transparency you could argue all the transaction costs should be separated out, stamp duty and broker commissions and figures for all the additional fund expenses individually listed, auditor fees, regulatory costs and custodian charges. In fact we may as well throw in the fund manager's coffee bill and taxi fares to business meetings around London while we are at it.

What is missing from all this is a simple question, yet to be asked. What do clients actually want? In my experience the benefits of unbundling and transparency are over-rated and I think the OCF and an overall total cost of fund ownership (TCO) would suffice as complete, fair and transparent disclosure of fund charges. Yes these are a bundled charge but it is all in and simple to understand for investors.

I don't think clients want a detailed breakdown of all the constituent elements of investment costs. You will recall for example how the public objected to the Ryanair model of charges, a base cost with lots of extras added on. They just wanted to see the final all in price they would pay for their flights.

Similarly when we had new carpets fitted at home at the end of 2018 we opted to buy from a local firm that had an all in charge in the price per square metre - the carpet, the underlay, the fitting and fixtures in contrast to a national carpet retailer with individually disclosed costs for each element. It was much clearer what we would be paying and we did not need a calculator or degree in maths to work out the total cost.

Also can you imagine if the same level of transparency on costs was applied to food sold in supermarkets? For example if you pick up a packet of chicken breasts all the individual costs are broken down on the label so you can see how the final price is divided up - how much goes to the farmer, how much the abattoir is paid, the costs of transport and finally the amount for the supermarket. And what if the Food Standard Agency insisted the supermarket's cut should be further broken down into the amount attributed to costs, money paid in remuneration to the board of directors, staff salaries and shareholder dividends. After all shouldn't we have the right to know Tesco's profit margins and how overpaid the board is? Transparency is king isn't it? Quite frankly no-one cares and it would be far too complex and costly to do, pushing up the price of food.

The problem with transparency is that it is endless and drills down into complexity and irrelevance. If we carry on with a quest for perfection we'll be getting down to disclosing the gender pay gap at the investment company on the fund fact sheet and details of share options for their staff. Herein lies the problem. It reminds me of something in physics, the Heisenberg Uncertainty Principle.

> *"The Heisenberg Uncertainty Principle is a law in quantum mechanics that limits how accurately you can measure two related variables. Specifically, it says that the more accurately you measure the momentum (or velocity) of a particle, the less accurately you can know its position, and vice versa."* [17]

The way I have understood it is the more accurately you try to measure

---

[17] Google. Other search engines are available.

or define something the more wobble or uncertainty you create in the process and it results in less accurate and unsatisfactory outcomes. A classic example of this is with MIFID II. In an attempt to get more transparency on costs, the rules proscribe methods for calculating fund transaction costs and for not an insignificant minority of them the figures turn out to be negative. Yes negative!

The implication here is that the fund buys and sells stocks through the year and ends up paying no costs for these transactions. In fact it ends up getting a credit; money is paid to the fund. How on earth does that work? Last time I checked there was no such thing as magic money trees. Clearly it doesn't reflect reality. Negative transaction costs is all down to something called "slippage" but the requirement to report negative figures is a nonsense. So would someone from the EU, the FCA or Gina Miller, a cheerleader for MIFID II as well as a stickler for due process with Brexit, please explain the logic to me. Or perhaps Werner Heisenberg has an opinion on it.

On the question of fund charges I often tell my clients that the values of their investments are net of all fund and platform charges and costs. Pre-MIFID II, transaction costs were always reflected in valuations, they are not new costs. It is just now they have to be disclosed separately.

In summary I think clients should be given the OCF and TCO and that's about it. With a bit of simple maths they can work out that transaction costs can be calculated as the TCO minus the OCF. They can then compare fund costs on a fair basis. Yet what I find amazing is that more than two years after MIFID II was introduced the regulations have not required transaction costs to be disclosed on fund KIIDs. Pick one up and you will only find the OCF. Incredible!

It is about time the FCA and EU regulators wake up to the mess they have created. They need to see they are bound by a flawed ideology that says transparency is always beneficial. They fail to see that the more transparency you have more complexity, inaccuracy and confusion is created. The FCA will preach about the virtues of outcomes for consumers but don't seem to get the negative outcomes from their actions. No wonder many of my fellow advisers think they are out of touch.

Other problems with MIFID II & its sidekick PRIIPs

Aside from the issues highlighted above with fund transaction costs, MIFID II has caused no end of problems for the investment and advice industries. Firstly there is the requirement for DFMs (discretionary fund managers) to write to clients when their portfolios fall 10% or more since the last reporting date. At the end of 2018 several of these letters were issued for a number of my clients who hold managed portfolios of AIM (Alternative Investment Market) shares for inheritance tax planning purposes. UK smaller companies were especially hard hit in the global stock market sell-off.

You have to ask what is the point of these crash reports? Investment is for the long term and investors know that the value of shares go down as well as up on a daily basis. Some investors however will panic and be tempted to sell, the worst thing they can do in most circumstances, as they will crystallise losses or lower values at the very least. Why cause unnecessary anxiety or put a temptation in front of them to sell?

In my view if DFMs are required to disclose 10% falls they should also be required to report 10% rises. If these were mandated the 10% declines would then be understood in context and their impact softened. Take my clients for example. Had the rules been in place from 2016 they would have regularly received letters informing them of 10% rises in their portfolios, quite possibly every six months. A 10% fall would then be judged in the context of multiple 10% rises and upbeat reports and hence the downturn would be viewed as relatively insignificant.

Then there is the absurdity of misleading projections on Key Information Documents (KIDs), not to be confused with KIIDs. KIDs arose from the EU's PRIIPs regulation which came into force on 1/1/18 a couple of days before MIFID II. The alphabet soup gets thicker year by year. PRIIPs are Packaged Retail and Insurance based Investment Products and includes investment bonds and investment trusts. Although KIDs have similarities to KIIDs, the former must include the potential loss of capital under a stress scenario and other performance scenarios of the product.

KIDs have been universally derided since launch. Pretty well everyone in the industry thinks they are misleading, confusing and unfit for purpose. Firstly there is the same issue of absurd negative transaction costs that I described for retail funds above. Secondly projections are based on past performance and are considered unrealistic and misleading. In one case an optimistic assessment of returns was based on a 30% p.a. rise. No wonder one investment trust manager advised the first thing you should do when you get a KID is to tear it up.

An article in International Adviser from 26/7/18 highlighted how out of touch the FCA has been:

> "The AIC joins the European Fund and Asset Management Association (Efama) and leading international adviser associations in condemnation of the requirements. Welcoming the publication of the FCA's call for input: PRIIPS Regulation – initial experiences with the new requirement, Ian Sayers, AIC chief executive said: 'The FCA's review must put consumers at the centre of the process.
>
> The FCA seems more interested in defending the regulations than accepting what is obvious to everyone else, that KIDs are confusing and misleading.
>
> Arguing that negative transaction costs are not inaccurate epitomises this problem. There may be a technical basis for arguing this, but for a consumer it simply does not make sense.
>
> The argument that performance scenarios are not forecasts, but illustrative, is just semantics. If they are not intended to give investors an idea of what they might get back, what is the point of them?'"[18]

The AIC is the Association of Investment Companies, a trade body for UK investment trusts. They refuse to publish them on their website.

Another issue with MIFID II are the complex ex-ante and ex-post disclosure requirements which detail all advice and investment costs and consolidated figures in cash and percentage terms. Whilst platforms have the technology to produce the relevant data, what if a client has investments with several platforms plus direct holdings with investment companies? They will get multiple reports through the year. If so should all this information be amalgamated by their advisers and at what cost

---

[18] https://international-adviser.com/uk-regulator-must-see-danger-in-the-priip-kid/ (26/7/18)

to produce it? According to a compliance consultant I spoke to the rules don't require amalgamation but what is the value of multiple ex-post reports and how do I split up and incorporate my invoiced fees when I have a single charge for advice on investments held on several platforms?

Then there is the different treatment for pensions which are not MIFID products and therefore are not subject to ex-ante and ex-post cost disclosures. So we have a situation that a client may have the same OEICs and unit trusts in both their ISA and their SIPP but cost disclosures only apply to the ISA. What is the logic and consistency of that? To clients the differential treatment must be confusing and unsatisfactory.

I have to wonder if ex-ante and ex-post fee disclosure is a solution to a problem that does not exist. Advocates of total transparency see a problem because they think investors can never get enough of knowing how much those greedy bastards are charging for managing their investments. However none of my clients have ever asked for consolidated charges in cash or percentage terms for all the investments they hold. As explained earlier I am crystal clear on disclosure of my own fees with each minute of my time accounted for. In addition I will often calculate an estimated percentage for my charges when I provide quotes. For example if a client has £100,000 to invest and I estimate 10 hours of work then my fee will be £1,600 or 1.6% of the amount the client has to invest.

Another problem I have with MIFID II is the rules mandate annual reviews for clients where there is an ongoing relationship with a firm or adviser. At the review the adviser must undertake an assessment to ensure the financial arrangements put in place are still suitable. The client then must receive a report in writing.

I have clients who value and want annual reviews but the majority don't. They prefer *ad hoc* reviews which are invariably less frequent. In general I recommend annual reviews for clients with investment portfolios to ensure the asset allocation is still appropriate, bad funds are weeded out, risk is reduced, profits are banked, tactical re-investment is undertaken and portfolios are rebalanced. But not everyone wants this.

They may prefer reviews when their circumstances changes rather than reviews determined by the calendar. These flexible *ad hoc* reviews could be triggered by stock market or economic ructions or changes to clients' circumstances or financial objectives. They typically happen at unpredictable times, not at a set yearly date.

To finish my review of regulation I have a question for the FCA. If clients don't want consolidated charge disclosures or set annual reviews why should they be foisted on them and moreover be forced to pay for the privilege? That is a question I tackle in the next chapter.

8. An adviser's response to regulation

Don't say why

In Chapter 2 I set out what I believe makes a good financial adviser. The first quality I suggested, and arguably one of the most important is that advisers must be client focussed. That should not only apply to the advice we give but it should also apply to the burden of regulation we foist on our clients. Good outcomes are the goal we must keep in mind when thinking about regulation.

In Chapter 7 I explained why I think that not all regulation is good and why care is needed to ensure compliance works well for customers. In my view this requires a personal and tailored application. Regulation should result in meaningful benefits and genuine protections for customers. Moreover the fees clients pay for compliance should represent good value to them.

The rules should not be a burden for our clients and the adviser is the best person to judge what a client can handle and to decide what they need or don't need. Bespoke is best. However this view is in conflict with what the regulators mandate, leading to bad outcomes. They simply expect the rule book, plus the kitchen sink to be thrown at all clients without any individual flexibility as to what they can cope with, need or want. So typically they get too much mandated information, which they don't read or understand if they do.

Delivering measured and client focussed regulation is difficult because historically the regulators' attitude to the investment and advice industries has been, *"When I say jump don't say why, say how high?"* The message is clear, *"don't question the rules, don't interpret them, don't apply them with any degree of personalisation or common sense. Just follow them to the letter."*

Investment professionals have typically danced to the tune of the FCA and the EU with blind obedience to the rules irrespective of the bad outcomes for clients. However more recently with the requirement to issue KIDs to investors in investment trusts and investment bonds mandated by PRIIPs regulations, there has been a lot of criticism from the industry about negative transaction costs and unrealistic investment projections. There are signs professional advisers and fund managers are beginning to question meaningless bureaucracy. Quite right too.

Who are you kidding?

To illustrate let's consider KIDs again. On the KID for a well-known investment trust I looked at, under a favourable scenario it is stated that the average annual returns could be expected to be 37.38% over one year, 25.96% p.a. over three years and 22.63% p.a. over five years. For the latter a £10,000 investment would grow to £27,732.

The use of these figures is harmful in my view even if the projections prove to be true in the next five years. Is it responsible to put them out to the investing public? Will they expect too much from their investment and end up being disappointed?

KIDs also provide projections in three other scenarios - moderate, unfavourable and stress. For the latter over five years investors are told to expect a 17.48% fall each year reducing their £10,000 investment to £3,826.

Aside from what are likely to be unrealistic and potentially misleading projections I have five other concerns, just five!

Firstly how are investors expected to assess which scenario is most likely? Do they have to come to their own assessment or will they expect advice here and with what potential liability if the advice proves wrong? You can imagine a complaint in 2024. *"You told me in 2019 the next five years will be favourable and I have just read an article that said the stock market has boomed since 2019. However I only got a 10% p.a. return from this investment trust whereas I expected 22.63% p.a. in the favourable scenario based on a KID you gave me."*

Secondly investors could be tempted to make a misjudgement. In the example above the worst case scenario is that their investment will fall by 17.48% p.a. but the best case is they can expect a return of 22.63% p.a. Since the upside figure is more than 5% p.a. higher than the downside one there is a favourable balance of probabilities that could sway them to invest in something that may be unsuitable for them.

Thirdly the KIDs make it clear that investors can compare the figures with the scenarios of other products. I printed off a KID for another popular investment trust and under the favourable scenario the average return over five years was cited as 32.97% p.a. This was more than 10% p.a. greater than the first investment trust! By chasing the highest potential returns investors could invest in trusts that are too high risk and again unsuitable for them.

Fourthly five years is an entirely arbitrary investment period. The KID says it is the recommended holding period. It should say it is the recommended *minimum* holding period in my view. By investing for a longer period of time and choosing the best time to sell the downside risks can be mitigated and the chance of good investment outcomes is increased.

Fifthly these projections have blown a big hole through the regulations governing the way investments and life and pension products are illustrated. Maximum growth rates have been mandated and have been the norm for many years. Illustrations carried low, mid and high growth rates that were identical for all companies offering the same product.

I remember way back in the 1990s with gilt yields in double digit figures pensions could be illustrated with a maximum growth rate of 13% p.a. Life policies had lower growth rates due to life company taxation. As investment returns fell with declining interest rates the high pensions' growth rate was reduced to 10% p.a. By 2014 the permitted rates had fallen to 2% p.a. (low), 5% p.a. (mid) and 8% p.a. (high). These apply to ISAs today.

Currently pension projections can be varied by the product provider but they need to take account for inflation. This can result in negative growth rates.

Aegon explain this on their website:

> *"Each provider decides the rates of return they believe are suitable for different types of investments. Some may be more or less optimistic.*

Different providers might use different rounding conventions to arrive at the mid-rate. Charges, deductions and any investment guarantees will also vary."[19]

For example a document I have seen from Standard Life shows that for most pension funds they use -0.5% p.a. as lower rate, 2.5% p.a. as the intermediate rate and 5.5% p.a. as the higher rate but for selected funds the rates are tweaked depending on what assets they invest in. Please note these are real rates of return after 2.5% p.a. inflation. This is why the lower rate is negative. A 2% p.a. nominal return will translate into a -0.5% p.a. real return once inflation of 2.5% p.a. is taken into account.

The point is we have a regulatory regime that strictly limits growth rates on ISAs and pension investments to 8% p.a. nominal, 5.5% p.a. real, yet permits investment trusts and other investments that are subject to PRIIPs' rules to illustrate at 20% or 25% p.a. It is inconsistent and confusing to clients. I would like to know how that is a good outcome. Quite frankly KIDs are not fit for purpose and pretty well everyone accepts this apart from perhaps the FCA who has been slow to react to industry concerns.

When problems were first raised about misleading projections the FCA advised that companies could provide caveats and statements alongside the KID that made things clearer for investors, which is a *de facto* admission the information in them was flawed. This is classic Heisenberg wobble, the more you try to perfect transparency the more inaccuracy is created.

KIDs should be scrapped or rewritten but unfortunately it is set to get worse if no action is taken. They are coming in for retail investment funds which are subject to UCITS regulations i.e. unit trusts and OEICs. They were due to start issuing KIDs instead of KIIDs at the start of 2020 although their implementation has been delayed for two years. Let's hope the regulators finally wake up and make wholesale changes before 2022. There have been encouraging signs this may be happening. An

---

[19] https://www.aegon.co.uk/support/faq/how-do-i/documentation/personal-documents/how-can-I-find-out-more-about-projection-rates.html See under "Why are your growth rates different from other providers?"

article from Investment Week (28/2/19) reported an FCA review of the PRIIPs regulations:

> "Scope, transaction costs calculations, "performance scenarios" and "summary risk indicators" (SRI) are part of a plethora of issues the FCA believes the European regulators and politicians must address in a review, which is expected to be completed by the end of 2019.
>
> However, in response to its consultations on the controversial regulation, published on Thursday (28 February), the FCA warned that the asset management industry itself must work harder to address concerns about transaction cost methodology. The regulator warned that further evidence of "poor application" of the methodology could result in it undertaking "more detailed investigations."
>
> The FCA said responses "did not provide credible evidence to support claims that the methodology is not working as intended," and that "unrepresentative transaction costs in KIDs are a result of poor application of the PRIIPs methodology."
>
> Chief executive of the FCA Andrew Bailey said: 'While awareness of the rules appears good, we found that firms take inconsistent approaches, risking confusion for customers, who may be misled about how much they are being charged.'"

So whilst the FCA have finally taken notice of the problem and are seeking change from EU regulators they still managed to take a sideways swipe at the investment industry. Fortunately I am not involved in transaction cost calculations but by all accounts they are very complex and I have seen many examples of negative figures. I can't believe all these fund managers are independently getting the calculations wrong due to their own fault. The underlying principles and methodology must be flawed.

In conclusion on KIDs, I will issue them when giving advice on investment trusts or investment bonds but I will tell clients the projections are unrealistic and should be ignored.

Miffed too

When the MIFID II came into being 3/1/18 a hard won concession was that non-MIFID advisers (those not advising clients in other EEA states) were not required to record telephone conversations with clients when taking investment instructions as was originally planned. The details could be recorded in other ways. The principle is sound and this is where my client history notes come into play. However 2018 was never going to be easy for advisers with a wave of new regulations - MIFID II, PRIIPs and GDPR (General Data Protection Regulation) with the SM&CR (Senior Managers and Certification Regime) hitting the industry in December 2019.

MIFID II raised several immediate issues for me in respect of consolidated charges disclosures, annual suitability reporting and advice to stick with existing investments. Apart from concerns these were not things my clients wanted I was also worried by the cost to deliver what I thought was the unnecessary to the unwilling.

The point here is that I charge purely by the hour. If it takes me an hour to collate and calculate all the charges in a single document my client will pay £160 for the privilege and if a mandated annual suitability assessment and report takes two hours my fee is £320.

Let's say in addition I undertake a brief investment review and conclude all funds are good and should be retained, MIFID II requires me to write a full suitability report. Previously I would undertake the review and advise clients to hold their investments, in a few sentences. This has now has been converted to a full fat suitability report so that is another hour of work costing the client £160 at least.

My question is who should pay for these additional MIFID II requirements? Perhaps the regulators think financial advisers should simply absorb the costs. Well I don't and I won't. I work on the principle my clients pay for all the specific work relating to my advice to them including regulatory requirements. If the time taken to implement regulations increases, my fees will do so as well. It seems that the FCA and EU regulators exist in a parallel universe. Does it not occur to them the customer will always pay and that driving up fee costs due to more and more regulation makes access to advice even less affordable except for the very well off?

This is where charging by the hour comes to the fore for an adviser. You are justified in passing onto clients the costs of all necessary work including compliance. Extra work means extra time and equates to extra fees. However with a percentage charging structure say 2% p.a. initial and 0.75% p.a. ongoing, it is an all in fee and the work is potentially boundless. So if the regulatory requirements increase the work has to be delivered for that fee. It is after all a fixed charge. Of course next year an adviser could raise their percentage fees in response to increased regulation, but that might go down with their clients as well as a lead balloon. Also it is much harder to determine how the extra work should reflect itself in increased charges. With a timed charge it is easy and exact.

You could be tempted to think that is the end of the matter. The regulations keep coming, I keep charging my extra costs to clients, they keep paying and everyone is happy (or not). The process is then repeated with the next round of bureaucracy, except it doesn't. This is where treating customers fairly comes in.

Treating customers fairly (TCF)

The FCA's legislation on treating customers fairly is in my mind the single best piece of regulation in the financial services industry, although it pre-dates the FCA. On the FCA website the page is headlined:

> "All firms must be able to show consistently that fair treatment of customers is at the heart of their business model."

Underneath it says:

> "Above all, customers expect financial services and products that meet their needs from firms they trust."[20]

The phrase above all suggests to me that meeting customer needs is primary, not secondary or even, dare I say it, it is not subservient to

---

[20] https://www.fca.org.uk/firms/fair-treatment-customers © Financial Conduct Authority

fulfilling the requirements of the regulators.

I looked up the definition of fair. The online Cambridge Dictionary says:

> "...treating someone in a way that is right or reasonable...
>
> If something is fair, it is reasonable and is what you expect or deserve."[21]

The term reasonable suggests to me fair is measured, appropriate and right. Being fair means delivery on what customers expect. Moreover I suggest the recipient is the best judge of what is fair especially if they are the bill payer. By definition if customers think what they are receiving is unreasonable and inappropriate it is unlikely to pass the test of being fair. You can't say to clients, it doesn't matter that you think such and such is fair or unfair, the regulators decide that and that is the end of the matter.

I am also certain fair requires providing tailored advice to the individual, that which is appropriate to their needs. Surely that cannot mean standard packages of advice and procedures for everyone. One of my clients died recently. She was a widow in her 80s with multiple health problems but she was very well off and needed a lot of investment advice and financial management as her affairs were complex. However with a failing memory and a lot of stress in her life she could not cope with a full blown three course regulatory meal.

Long technical explanations and reams of paperwork including fund fact sheets, KIIDs and complex investment reports would largely go unread and would cause confusion and anxiety. I was not prepared to inflict that on her. She needed the essentials in a simple and digestible format. So we agreed a light touch advice process would be best, one that was tailored to her needs.

In my assessment I needed to be flexible on the rules in order to be rigid on fairness and this is axiomatic in all my dealings with clients. I can't see how advisers can be truly client focussed or be compliant with TCF in any other way.

---

[21] https://dictionary.cambridge.org/dictionary/english/fair (14/1/20)

The FCA list six outcomes for TCF:

> *Outcome 1: Consumers can be confident they are dealing with firms where the fair treatment of customers is central to the corporate culture.*
>
> *Outcome 2: Products and services marketed and sold in the retail market are designed to meet the needs of identified consumer groups and are targeted accordingly.*
>
> *Outcome 3: Consumers are provided with clear information and are kept appropriately informed before, during and after the point of sale.*
>
> *Outcome 4: Where consumers receive advice, the advice is suitable and takes account of their circumstances.*
>
> *Outcome 5: Consumers are provided with products that perform as firms have led them to expect, and the associated service is of an acceptable standard and as they have been led to expect.*
>
> *Outcome 6: Consumers do not face unreasonable post-sale barriers imposed by firms to change product, switch provider, submit a claim or make a complaint.*[22]

Outcome 3 say consumers should be "appropriately informed." This strongly suggests communications should be relevant and appropriate to their needs, i.e. bespoke.

Notice outcome 4 refers to advice that is suitable and takes account of consumer circumstances. This will differ from client to client. In addition outcome 5 refers to products and services that are acceptable and as clients expect. The concept of products and services they "expect," something that defines fairness comes up again.

I like the FCA's TCF requirements. Unlike other regulations TCF is principles based. It is less defined and prescriptive than rules based regulation. It is about doing the right thing. Moreover fairness is all encompassing. An adviser can't hide behind a defence that what they

---

[22] https://www.fca.org.uk/firms/fair-treatment-customers © Financial Conduct Authority

did or failed to do did not break a specific rule. There are no technical get out of jail cards with TCF. If it does not pass the reasonable and fairness test it is a breach.

Let us now consider the FCA's principles for businesses as stated on their website:

1. *Integrity:* A firm must conduct its business with integrity.

2. *Skill, care and diligence:* A firm must conduct its business with due skill, care and diligence.

3. *Management and control:* A firm must take reasonable care to organise and control its affairs responsibly and effectively, with adequate risk management systems.

4. *Financial prudence:* A firm must maintain adequate financial resources.

5. *Market conduct:* A firm must observe proper standards of market conduct.

6. *Customers' interests:* A firm must pay due regard to the interests of its customers and treat them fairly.

7. *Communications with clients:* A firm must pay due regard to the information needs of its clients, and communicate information to them in a way which is clear, fair and not misleading.

8. *Conflicts of interest:* A firm must manage conflicts of interest fairly, both between itself and its customers and between a customer and another client.

9. *Customers: relationships of trust:* A firm must take reasonable care to ensure the suitability of its advice and discretionary decisions for any customer who is entitled to rely upon its judgment

10. *Clients' assets:* A firm must arrange adequate protection for clients' assets when it is responsible for them.

11. *Relations with regulators: A firm must deal with its regulators in an open and cooperative way, and must disclose to the appropriate regulator appropriately anything relating to the firm of which that regulator would reasonably expect notice.*[23]

Again it is worth highlighting some key points from these principles. In principle 6 a firm must pay due attention to the interests of its customers i.e. what is appropriate for their needs and treat them fairly.

Principle 7 says a firm must pay due regard to the information needs of its clients. By definition these should be individually determined otherwise we run the risk of shoehorning clients into one size fits all regulatory solutions. Shoehorning is something the FCA has made clear they do not like, yet regulatory shoehorning, a one size fits all would appear to be acceptable.

Principle 8 is an interesting one. Conflicts of interest can arise in various ways. Surely one which I don't think the FCA have considered is a conflict of interest between what the rules mandate and what clients need, want, are capable of digesting or are willing to pay for.

Customer feedback

The FCA encourages firms to get customer feedback as part of the TCF process. They state:

"Customer feedback can help you identify where you are treating customers fairly and where improvements are needed."[24]

I agree feedback is very important. Often I get uninvited feedback and fortunately it is usually positive. At other times I have asked for it. On one occasion I was taken aback after a survey, when a couple of clients said I did not charge enough!

At the end of 2017 and throughout 2018 I wrote extensively to clients about MIFID II highlighting the good (not very much) and explaining

---

[23] https://www.fca.org.uk/about/principles-good-regulation © Financial Conduct Authority
[24] © Financial Conduct Authority

the bad (most of it).

Here are some of the responses I received about the new consolidated charges disclosure rules and requirements for annual reviews:

> "What a lot of extra work is being required of IFAs! I agree, it is galling that the MIFID is forced on you by the FCA. I do not want all this extra information, which will generate more work for you and therefore more cost to both of us." JF

> "Wouldn't it be great if there was some sort of test a client could take and then they'd be excused from the worst of these tick box exercises?!?" TR

> "You're a star! You provide great honest service, and I applaud your rebellion against cumbersome and needless bureaucracy." DH

> "We'd want to opt out - sounds like a total waste of money." FH

> "We would like to confirm that: 1)We do not require annual reviews of our investments. Any review should be on ad hoc basis as the need arises. 2) We do not wish to receive enhanced charge disclosure as defined in MIFID 2."GB

> "J and I are happy to opt out of the MIFID II requirements where appropriate and avoid the need for you to provide us with excessive time-consuming details on the various transaction charges. We have every confidence in you to do what is fair, transparent and necessary and to continue advising us as you have done so well in the past." BD

> "Thanks for your explanations on this heavy topic - hope you don't sink under the weight of it...we have it easy compared to you!" RF

> "I would of course go with 'opting-out' (in the spirit of TCF) of anything that is in your opinion inessential." HR

> "I want to opt out as I do NOT want full disclosure." JF

> "You're quite right. I don't need more info. Even Fidelity's clear summaries are more than I need when given several times a year." AR

The bottom line is none of my clients want to pay for MIFID II consolidated charge disclosures. None of my clients who have historically opted for *ad hoc* reviews have asked for annual ones. You would think that if damsels in distress needed rescuing by white knights in shining armour they should be shouting "help," from the roof tops. The silence is deafening. The FCA, please take note.

So what is the justification for imposing fee cost on clients for stuff they don't want? None, whatsoever in my opinion.

I can further illustrate this with an example. I recently wrote to a client of mine who I had not had much contact with in the last two years and recommended that I undertake an investment review. His response was as follows:

> *"I have wondered about an investment review a few times but took the view that with this much uncertainty in all directions and with a portfolio split between equities and bonds, etc, here and overseas, churn might just add costs as we try to hedge each twist and turn."*

I responded:

> *"A review does not necessarily mean tactical adjustments to the asset allocation although some selected profit-taking from pure equity funds could be considered for risk reduction purposes. Looking at your portfolio I can see there are some underperformers which I would recommend replacing. Holding on to poor funds for too long, especially larger holdings is a drag on portfolio returns. This would be the focus of a review."*

It didn't change his mind. The question here is, does the FCA seriously expect me to say to this client the regulator doesn't care what your opinion is, you must have a review, like it or not? Does the FCA reckon I should impose an annual review on this and other clients, who don't want them and then require them to pay my fee? It would be a fast track to losing clients. If the FCA will pay my costs I'll happily oblige. Until then they can dream on.

Tailored compliance - putting it all together

The FCA's approach to regulation is not unique. Pretty well in all industries compliance with the rules is highly legalistic and inflexible. The rules are expected to be actioned without questioning and without exception. Investment companies and advisers are merely expected to be executives for the FCA, implementing their diktats without due regard to the needs and requirements of their clients and what it costs them.

In my view the regulator's thinking is muddled. Rules are invented and put in place ostensibly to protect consumers and to lead to good outcomes for them, yet the FCA seem to be incapable of recognising their actions sometimes have the opposite effect. Take the question of the impact of MIFID II on costs to consumers. An article in Money Marketing (28/2/19) was headlined:

> "FCA: Mifid II rules will save investors £1bn."[25]

The then FCA's chief executive Andrew Bailey claimed investors should save around £1bn in charges over the next five years due to MIFID II. Specifically he was referring to the impact of the rules for fund managers that require the costs of stock research to be unbundled from broking and dealing commissions. Some asset managers have borne the costs of research direct without passing them onto investors whilst dealing commissions have fallen as research is no longer bundled in.

All very well and good but if the goal is to reduce costs for investors where is the consistency? Why is the FCA not taking into consideration MIFID II requirements that add to clients' costs? These require me to undertake an annual suitability review, ex-post charge disclosures each year and full suitability reports where the investment or other advice is to do nothing. Adding all these up could take an extra four hours of work costing each client £640 p.a.

Not only is the regulator's thinking muddled it is grossly unfair and quite frankly unacceptable in my opinion. What the regulator expects is blind obedience to the rules by advisers, with no due consideration to the individual needs and wants of their clients. This requires ignoring their individual capacity to handle all the information and disclosures thrown at them and disregards their ability or willingness to pay for full

---

[25] Money Marketing (28/2/19)

fat regulation.

What this boils down to is the regulator believes they know what is best for our clients despite the fact they know nothing about them! Moreover they think they can simply disregard out of hand what we know from many years of advising our customers. The patronising arrogance of the regulator is outrageous. How can top down imposition meet individual client needs and be fair for them when those who imposing are so detached from those they claim to serve?

Given these observations and consideration of what TCF means I have concluded that compliance should be bespoke, tailored to individual needs and requirements. The alternative is to foist the rules on all clients, indiscriminately, irrespective of what it costs them and whether they want it or not. For advisers to be truly client focussed we have to take a view that we are best placed to understand their regulatory needs and what is suitable for them. It is not just being a rebel or contrarian and disregarding the rules but doing the right thing for those we advise and who pay for our services.

There is of course the danger that taken to an extreme, tailored compliance becomes bad practice and an excuse for laziness and sloppiness. No what I am suggesting is there is good compliance and bad compliance. MIFID II is mostly the latter in my view. However the long established fundamental elements in giving advice - gathering relevant financial information from clients (fact finding to use the jargon), undertaking research and assessing the suitability of potential investments, putting advice in writing, issuing KIIDs and selected other disclosure documents, explaining the potential downsides of the advice and record keeping are good compliance tasks. These are fundamental to best practice and the time spent will constitute chargeable work and justifiably so. There is no excuse not to undertake these compliance tasks.

PROD – An exercise in shoehorning

To conclude this section I want to briefly cover yet another regulatory acronym, PROD that has hit the industry since the beginning of 2018. According to an article in New Model Adviser, Citywire Financial Publishers:

> "Prod, shortened from Product Intervention and Product Governance Sourcebook, came into action on 3 January this year at the same time as Mifid II (sic). The regulation originates from the FCA and exists to implement the Mifid II product governance requirements.
>
> The rules set out that all firms should ensure they offer 'good product governance'. This means products should: meet the needs of one or more identifiable target markets; be 'sold to clients in the target markets by the appropriate distribution channels'; and deliver 'appropriate client outcomes."[26]

In the article in October 2018 Rory Percival, a leading compliance consultant and a former leading FCA executive estimated that fewer than 1% of advice firms are compliant on PROD and quite frankly need one to get going! The rules have been received by the industry with as much enthusiasm as a trip to the dentist to have teeth pulled. I can't see any benefit of segmenting my 75 or so clients into boxes when my advice is entirely bespoke and I don't use centralised investment propositions (CIPs) or centralised retirement propositions (CRPs). I think many of my fellow advisers will like me regard PROD as yet another meaningless tick box exercise. In contrast bespoke advice leads to better outcomes.

The idea behind the regulations is you should match appropriate products and services to segmented groups of clients, for example young accumulators, those approaching retirement and those newly retired moving from accumulation to decumulation. However if you agree the FCA's premise that PROD segmentation will deliver appropriate products and services and good outcomes for the clients placed in each segment, then surely you have to concede that an entirely individual and bespoke service will be better still.

In addition if you believe in PROD for products and services then logically regulation and its application should be also segmented. In other words groups of clients could be segmented with regulation adapted to their needs. I wonder what the FCA would say about this.

---

[26] https://citywire.co.uk/new-model-adviser/news/fewer-than-1-of-advisers-are-complying-with-prod-rules-percival-warns/a1166338

I do agree of course with the view that one size does not fit all. For example the use of a single platform for all clients is unlikely to be in the best interests of all. The charging structure of platforms will suit different clients as I explain in Chapter 10 and I guess like me most IFAs were already segmenting our clients long before PROD.

Finally I wonder how the FCA justify PROD given their stance on so called "shoehorning," squeezing clients into pre-prepared packages and solutions for examples CIPs. Does not PROD do the same? Where is the consistency of thought and application? So I conclude that PROD is best described as piffle, rubbish, obsolete and dreadful.

Ministry for the Blindingly Obvious

To finish the chapter on compliance I must tell you about an important institution in the UK that is an undervalued contributor to the country's welfare, the local pub. It might be called the Crown & Anchor or the Eight Bells and mainly it is a place to have a drink and meet with friends. However they are also local offices of the *"Ministry for the Blindingly Obvious."* Inside every pub up and down the land you'll find several old geezers who are regulars, sitting on the same stools at the bar. They are part of the furniture. Some may think they are just meddling busybodies but in fact they are representatives of the Ministry for the Blindingly Obvious, dispensing their pearls of wisdom.

One day an IFA's client called John learns his Premium Bond numbers have come up and he has won £1 million. He goes to his local pub to celebrate. Sitting at his usual spot is Fred. He is long retired and has plenty of time and money to enjoy a comfortable lifestyle. He is joined by John. The conversation goes like this:

"Hiya Fred. Fancy a pint? I've just come into a fair bit of money unexpectedly."

John does not say how much.

"Thanks. A pint of best. What are you going to do with it?"

"I am not sure yet. I need to make an appointment to talk to my IFA. What do you think? I don't know much about investments? Do you?"

> "Well the first thing I would do is pay off your credit cards. You told me a few months back you and your missus had racked up quite a bit of debt and you were paying 17% per annum interest on it. That's a no brainer. You don't need to pay your IFA to tell you that!"
>
> "That's a good idea. I didn't think of that. My first thought was investment or getting a holiday let in Cornwall. Anything else?"
>
> "Pay off your mortgage may also be a good idea if there are no penalties. After that you can look at investing. My IFA handles all that for me."
>
> "Cheers Fred. It is good to get sound advice!"

They toast to the future and the conversation then turns to football. The pub has given the Money & Pensions Service a run for its money today.

A week later, John has sat down to talk to his IFA. Let's call him Mike. (Any resemblance to people in real life is purely coincidental!). John has never had a lot of money. He and his wife are relatively low earners and with a lot of their income going on paying the mortgage and minimum payments on credit cards they have never been able to save or invest much. Mike took him on as a client about five years ago to start a personal pension plan.

> "Congratulations, John. That is the first time I have ever come across a £1 million winner."
>
> "Quite a shock really when I have had so little money in my life. What do you advise I do with it?"

Like all good IFAs Mike got a full update on John's personal and financial affairs. He frowns when he learns that there is £15,000 on credit cards and a £175,000 mortgage. He is currently on a standard variable rate paying 4.99% p.a.

> "You look worried, Mike. What's the problem?"
>
> "I am not allowed to tell you something."
>
> "You are not allowed to tell me something! What do you mean?"

"Do you remember when I first advised you five years ago, you were buying a house and needed a mortgage. I told you I don't give advice on mortgages anymore and I recommended you to an independent mortgage broker in town. For many years I used to advise and arrange mortgages but I stopped about 10 years ago. You may recall I told you I was increasingly specialising in investments and getting so few mortgages enquiries I decided to stop. I then cancelled my consumer credit licence. The thing is I am no longer authorised to give advice on debt without a consumer credit licence. To obtain one will cost me an application fee of £500 and around £340 p.a. thereafter. I can't justify this as it is yet another expensive business cost which I would have to pass on to my clients."

"Oh. I see. But what is it you are not allowed to tell me?"

"OK. For the record we need to get something clear. What I am about to say is not advice. It is just what I am not allowed to say. Do you get it?"

"Yes. I think so. By the way I have already had a chat to Fred down the Rose and Crown."

"So what I am not allowed to tell you is that you should pay off your credit cards in full before thinking about investment."

"Is that it?"

"Yes plus the fact that I can't tell you it may be worth paying off your mortgage as well."

"That's stupid! You are an authorised and regulated financial adviser and you can't tell me that. But Fred can."

"I agree. I could advise you legally but since I probably only get one client a year with debt I would have to charge you £340 for my advice, assuming I don't charge you for a portion of the Consumer Credit Licence application fee as well."

"I see. OK. I'll get my debt counselling from Fred and investment advice from you. And if the bean counters from the FCA come along and challenge you I'll tell them you didn't me give advice."

"Great. Let's start thinking about investment."

9. Marketing and finding clients

This is a vitally important subject as if you don't have clients, you don't have a business and you cannot be a financial adviser.

Satisfied clients will recommend you

Your best source of new clients is satisfied customers. Most of my best clients have come by recommendation. Do a very good job for your customers and prove you are honest, fair and trustworthy and they will recommend you and will do so without prompting. In time you will not need to look for new clients, they will come looking for you.

I can trace generations of such recommendations starting with an old friend. Other clients have come from friends and family, via my website, several from an accountant and the old IFAP, Independent Financial Adviser Promotions, now called Unbiased, and not nearly half as good. Over the years I also continued to service clients from my days at Liberty Life and the Investment Practice.

I never ask clients to recommend me. I want them to do so entirely voluntarily without any influence or pressure from me. When I did ask for referrals many years ago at the start of my career I found it embarrassing and awkward. In the past advisers were taught to ask for referrals from existing clients, in some cases asking for 10 names and numbers. It is cringe worthy and unacceptable.

In respect of recommendations I think I do something different to pretty well everyone else. You may think it makes no sense but I think it is logical even if it seems counterintuitive. Over the years I have been asked by existing clients to contact a friend, colleague or member of their family who is looking for financial advice. My client has recommended me and their buddy is apparently interested to talk to me. Done deal you may think. It may surprise you however but I won't initiate contact. Instead I tell my client to get their friend to contact me.

The reason for this request is that if the prospect is really keen to get advice from me they will make the effort to initiate contact with me. If they do I'll know they are genuinely interested because they have had to overcome a barrier and approach someone they don't know. The reason why I do this is that I suspect my clients sometimes over sell me and push their friends in my direction. Their buddies may however be more hesitant than my client thinks. I want to try and avoid talking to people like this as there is a good likelihood they will not become clients and engagement may prove to be a waste of time.

Evidence for over selling me has come from occasions where existing clients have enthusiastically told me they have recommended me to a friend who will be in contact. Invariably I never hear from them because they weren't as keen as my client had assumed. In contrast the best recommendations come from unexpected calls or e-mails out of the blue from someone a client has recommended. I suspect a softer recommendation has been made in these circumstances.

In conclusion I think there is something to be said for playing hard to get! The quality of your clients is likely to be much better than trying to pick up every Tom, Dick or Harry.

You could of course think I am nuts. If I called those referrals whose details my clients had passed on I might be able to turn someone who is lukewarm into a good client. With a 20 minute chat I might be able to overcome their reluctance. You may be correct. I am not suggesting my hesitant approach is suitable for everyone especially for new advisers building up their client bank. I am in a fortunate position of only needing to take on a few new clients each year and I am happy to take on the red hot few who make the first move and approach me.

A good website is your shop window

A good website is essential for an adviser firm. It is your shop window for potential clients. Consequently it is worth spending money on a good design - ensuring the content is appropriate, that it is visually attractive and it is easy to navigate.

My observation is that adviser websites are packed with general information about financial products, calculators and market data but not enough about the unique services that the firm offers, their values and specialisms and crucially how they charge for their work. In part I suspect this is because many websites are bought off the shelf and these are padded with general bumf that the content designer knows will be applicable to most of their customers. They are a bit like the general financial planning magazines that are marketed to advisers shortly after Chancellors' budgets. The idea is you order a couple of hundred, they are topped and tailed with the firm's details and then sent out to clients or professional contacts with a hope they will generate leads.

The other reason I suspect websites are loaded with general stuff is that firms don't have a unique selling point or if they do they don't have the ability or confidence to articulate it.

My view is that websites should be bespoke, created from scratch and should reflect who you are as an adviser, what your values are and the individual services you offer. Your website should stand out from the herd and should demonstrate why your service proposition is attractive and deserves a closer look.

Unless you have online functionality for existing clients to log in and view their portfolios, mine doesn't, your website is primarily there to attract new clients. Before the RDR I used to get a lot of enquiries from my website by marketing myself as a fee only adviser rebating all initial commission and investment trail to clients. In the past if you googled *"fee only IFAs"* my website often appeared on the first page of the search results. Now of course all adviser firms are fee only.

In the post RDR world your website will stand out if you have clear information on your firm's charges. In fact a link is needed in the top menu visible on the home and every other page. Bear in mind few adviser websites set out their firm's charges. Of course specific quotes or estimates are needed when dealing with individual clients but that is not an excuse for not detailing online your fee structure including your hourly charge out rate or your percentage fees, unless of course you are embarrassed by your charges.

You can check out my website, *www.montgo.co.uk* . It is simple but I think fairly effective. You will see it is not overloaded with content and there is very little about products. Instead I focus on my business ethos, how I give advice and charge for it and how I differ from the crowd. It is very specific about my business without lots of general financial information you can find on a hundred other websites.

Potential clients can download a copy of my Client Agreement from the Contact page. This document is much more meaty, containing the dry legalese that the FCA require and that is essential to avoid potential complaints.

Another key element to my website is my investment blog. My articles add new content to what would otherwise be a very static website. It gives existing clients a reason to revisit and provides a clear and detailed insight into my thinking and convictions on investment planning and portfolio management. This has value for both new and existing clients. For the latter as mentioned earlier, an understanding of my investment thinking provides a context for my specific advice to them.

For potential clients if they like what they read about my investment philosophy and the way I communicate and conclude I have a level of investment competency and nous that could benefit them, it will be a positive incentive for them to approach me for advice.

I write one or two blogs a month depending if I have anything relevant to say. They cover my thoughts on the global economy, global stock markets and investment analysis and strategies. The articles are often prompted from something interesting I have read or listened to from a fund manager or chief investment officer but readers will be left in no doubt what my opinions and conclusions are. They will learn I strongly favour equities for the long term and that I am a big fan of active fund management. In my blogs you will find articles on gold, Premium Bonds, the outlook for the global economy, equity investment and index tracking.

Finally having testimonials from existing clients on your website is very useful. Clearly no firm will include reviews from clients who are unhappy with their service and I think prospective enquirers will understand you have cherry picked your best ones. That said providing your clients have been given free rein to express what they feel, highly complimentary comments about you are worth their weight in gold. Two testimonials on my website highlight this for me:

"Mike has been my IFA for a number of years. I find him admirable – a combination of deep knowledge of UK financial services, customer understanding, intelligence and flexibility means that he provides excellent and effective advice. His strong sense of personal integrity and ethics mean that I can be sure that his advice is given solely with my interests in mind. The proof of the pudding is in the eating – my personal financial portfolio is in significantly better shape than it would have been without Mike!" TR

"Mike has now been our IFA for over 12 years after we had been badly let down by another organisation, and during this period my wife and I have built up a very close working relationship with him on all matters affecting our family finances. He is extremely approachable, taking whatever time and effort are required to explain complex issues; throughout the period of our relationship we have found him absolutely competent and diligent, with not even the smallest detail left unattended. We consider Mike a "one-off" in his profession and would have no hesitation in recommending him." RK

Being described as having a strong sense of personal integrity and ethics and being a one-off are comments to be treasured.

We'll find clients for you

Starting out as an adviser you are likely to be desperate to get clients unless you are lucky enough to be given a client bank to service. As a result it is easy to be tempted to pay for marketing support that will prove ineffective. About 10-15 years ago I bought a year's advertising in Yellow Pages. That was during the days when the directory left on your doorstep was as thick as a house brick. I paid about £500 for a year, either for a quarter or an eighth of a page advert. I might as well as have flushed my cash down the toilet. It was useless. In 12 months I had a single call and that was from a company trying to sell me something.

Over the years I have also had lots of people approaching me with their search engine optimisation (SEO) services or wanting to sell me leads. I have taken some advice from my technology savvy son on my website but to be honest I don't know whether any of the SEO services are really effective in generating good quality leads. Besides I am happy with my website and generally as stated I only look to attract a few new clients each year, providing they are high quality.

In respect of lead generator firms there is a fundamental flaw in their business proposition in my view. The idea is you buy leads for say up to £50. The lead generating company gets *certainty* of income, £50 per go, but the adviser only gets a *potential* income. There is no guarantee that the lead is not a time waster or a poor quality prospect. There is no guarantee the adviser will earn anything from the lead and recoup his or her costs. It is very similar in principle to providing personal details to a business, marketing something or the other with the promise you will be entered into a prize draw. The data gatherer gets certainty of benefit, your personal details while you only have a possible but unlikely benefit.

With this model there is no fair sharing of risk or good outcomes. It is skewed deal in favour of the lead generators. I have often said to them, let's do it a different way. I'll pay nothing for each lead but on conclusion of my dealings with each potential client you introduce, I'll pay you an agreed percentage of the fees I earn, say 30%. If the quality of the leads are that good you'll earn more money per lead that way than me paying you a fixed fee per lead. If I earn nothing so do you, so risk and reward is equally shared. Have any lead generators agreed to that suggestion? No of course not. It suggests to me that there are not as confident of the quality of their leads as they would like to make out.

Social marketing

When I first started out as an adviser I saw all social occasions as an opportunity to market myself. After all, the person I got talking in the pub, at the cricket club or at a party was a potential client. I was keen to sell myself and get conversations around to the subject of money. As time went by I did not need more clients and quite frankly when I was out socialising I didn't want to talk about what I did or hand out general financial advice in casual conversations. I wanted a break from all that. It was about having a good life work balance. Of course if at a social event people ask me what I do I'll tell them but I have no incentive or desire for them to become clients.

It is much harder if you are new in the industry and lack clients. My only advice would be don't be pushy in these social occasions and try to gauge if those you talk to are really interested or are just making polite conversation. This means letting them take the initiative for it to go further. About two years ago a guy I play football with found out what I did and then subsequently asked for pension advice. He became a good client and also introduced me to a former work colleague who proved equally as good. These outcomes are bonuses. I didn't go looking for the business, it found me.

Finally remember to give yourself a break on occasions. You need to relax and not feel you are constantly on duty. You can always suggest to someone you meet at a party who wants to talk money that you arrange to do so later.

For a while I was a member of a breakfast club in Eastbourne attended by other business owners. Each person stood up and gave a minute's talk on what they did. It was interesting but fruitless and I dropped out. I am not saying don't try these networking events but don't waste too much time with them. In my experience marketing promises a lot but delivers very little.

Finally I cannot comment on social media marketing, how to do it and whether it is effective. You'll need to find someone else to advise you on that. Don't ask Fred though. He is much too old and technophobic for that sort of thing.

Professional connections

I have had one accountant who referred good clients to me in the past. He has now retired and that source of business has dried up.

I did try marketing to accountants in Eastbourne some years ago. I wrote to them with a view of gauging interest in attending a seminar on tax efficient investments that might be of value to their clients. It proved fruitless. I suspect that accountants and solicitors do have concerns about financial advisers and still don't see us as true professionals. Moreover as noted in Chapter 3 if you are a restricted adviser as opposed to an IFA you are unlikely to get introductions from solicitors and accountants.

At various times in your dealings with clients you may need to introduce them to solicitors and accountants or you will have contact with them when a client dies. Normally this involves supplying full investment details to a solicitor in their role as executor of a client's will. Ensuring you are professional in the way you co-operate and communicate could potentially lead to a business relationship in which you receive introductions. This is another example where good English is crucial. Sloppy grammar and spelling will damage your credibility.

10. Dealing with platforms and providers

On the whole I find most platform and provider service standards are good or excellent, although less so with some of the bigger life assurance companies. Like them or not product providers are your friends. You need them to place business and manage it in the future on behalf of your clients, so you'll need to get on well with them.

These days the vast majority of investment business is placed on platforms rather than direct with investment companies. When I started out as an IFA we placed business direct with the investment companies running the funds. Skandia Life who later became Old Mutual Wealth then pioneered the concept of fund supermarkets, enabling IFAs to buy and hold funds from multiple investment companies. The Skandia concept was revolutionary and of real administrative benefit to both advisers and clients. Over the years other companies launched fund supermarkets and wraps evolved from these. Today we have modern platforms. Wraps extended the concept of fund supermarkets by allowing investors to buy, hold and manage a broader range of assets including shares and cash. The term wrap however has been dropped in favour of platform.

I use a variety of platforms for my clients. In the past I used Skandia Life and Fidelity FundsNetwork, today it is mainly the latter plus AJ Bell Investcentre and Alliance Trust Savings (ATS). The regulator takes the view that the use of a single platform by an adviser or firm is unlikely to be in all their clients' best interests and I agree. For example ATS uniquely in the adviser market levied a flat fee as opposed to a percentage charge. As a result ATS were very competitive for large portfolios. For example take a pension pot of £500,000. ATS charged £350 for a SIPP not yet in drawdown. This was for their "Inclusive" option which gave investors 35 free trades in the year.

In contrast all other adviser platforms have percentage fees. Fidelity for example levy a charge of 0.25% p.a. across the board plus an investor fee of £45 p.a. With a pension fund of £500,000 their platform charge is £1,250, £900 more than ATS's. This excludes the investor fee. Not surprisingly all my clients with ATS have large portfolios. In contrast I wouldn't have dreamt about putting a client with a £30,000 pension fund with ATS where a flat fee of £350 represents a charge of 1.16% p.a. This is much higher than Fidelity whose charge adds up to £120 p.a. for a constant £30,000 pension pot.

Since writing the first draft of this chapter the Embark Group acquired the advised clients of ATS. The direct to consumer side (D2C) of the business was bought by Interactive Investor, the only other flat fee platform I am aware of. However be aware that Interactive Investor does not accept adviser business and remains a D2C platform. Moreover ATS's advised clients are being migrated onto the Embark platform in the second half of 2020. Whilst they have promised fee protection for pre-existing ATS clients any new customers advisers put on the platform will be subject to Embark's normal percentage fee structure. Although it is very competitive I think the market will be poorer in not having a flat fee platform for adviser clients.

Each adviser will have their own favourite platforms, but our choices must be undergirded by due diligence. Whilst this should be based on research, facts and analysis, personal likes and dislikes comes into play. For example I have never used Cofunds (now Aegon), Aviva, Transact, Ascentric or Nucleus. Lots of other advisers do. Am I the only adviser not to recognise their qualities? I doubt it. Even if I was, would it mean I am using significantly inferior platforms? Not necessarily.

You could argue my due diligence is faulty because I have never used these platforms. In fact I have to admit I have never even considered them or if I have it was just a cursory look! Is that a crime? I don't think so.

Firstly I have very good reasons for using the platforms I do and if challenged I think I can defend my choices.

Secondly it is not possible to undertake entirely objective research on all available platforms, focusing on facts and technical analysis and rank them objectively - the best, second best etc. with no grounds for anyone to dispute the results. It is not like the Premier League table where the positions of the 20 clubs are determined purely by points won and goal differences and there is no arguing against it.

Check the due diligence of 10 adviser firms on platform choice and you are likely to get 10 different sets of results. This is because platforms are not funds which you can rank by performance over any period of time. There are too many variables, moving parts and subjective assessments in play. The significance advisers attribute to the same set of facts will vary and personal preferences and experiences clearly influence our final choices.

Aside from very wide investment choice and competitive charges, good online functionality, financial strength and service standards are very important qualities I look for in a platform. Sometimes however there may be conflicts between these five qualities. For example I first started using ATS in the autumn of 2016 for a number of clients with very large pension plans, given their very low platform charge as explained. However the service at ATS was terrible. They made a lot of errors which created all sorts of problems. This extended to their handling of subsequent complaints. I ended up wasting a lot of my time, some of which I successfully invoiced ATS for.

Fortunately I had an excellent broker representative and eventually the issues were resolved. However it got so bad on occasions I felt I could no longer place new business with ATS. It was not only me as ATS received a lot of complaints and flak from advisers. However to their credit they began to address the problems and through 2018 I began to see real improvements. The problem I think was ATS simply lacked the resources to deal with the volume of business that came their way due to their unique and compelling charging structure.

The point I am trying to make here is that ideally a platform should be excellent in all five key areas - investment choice, charges, online functionality, financial strength and service but the reality may be that one of those qualities is below par. As advisers we have to live with realities not perfections.

That said I think as advisers we have an important role to highlight problems we encounter with platforms and providers, especially in discussion with your broker representative or someone else that has the clout to drive change. If enough advisers make a noise the problems will be taken seriously by the platform and improvements are more likely.

As an example I reported a lot of issues with Fidelity's online services after a major replatforming exercise. In my experience placing business, dealing and transaction reporting got worse. My very personable rep at FundsNetwork at that time must have thought I am a reincarnation of Victor Mildrew based on the frequency of my gripes. She was however patient and understanding and was willing to take on board and feedback my criticisms. However I suggested practical improvements rather than just have a moan.

Once you have been around for a while you will come on the radar of most financial service companies - pension providers, insurance companies and investment houses advertising their wares. You will get bombarded with marketing e-mails, investment commentaries and requests for meetings with broker representatives. The worst are e-mails. If I go away for a week I'll come home to find 300+ messages in my inbox. Most are irrelevant but filtering them is still required to identify the truly important ones.

Broker reps will contact you - they happen to be in your area next week and they would to come and see you for "20 minutes," to talk to you about their new multi-asset fund range or latest VCT offering. Who are you kidding? I have never done a 20 minute meeting. By the time you have made them a cup of coffee and exchanged pleasantries you are almost done. Unless you are rude and kick them out you should expect a 45-60 minute meeting. Most financial advisers simply don't have that time and you will need to decline many of these requests, prioritising the most important.

I may be inclined to see a representative or talk to them on the phone if I need an update or information on one or more of their funds that I have clients invested in. If they don't know the answer they'll talk to a fund manager or analyst and come back with an answer. Some I will see for coffee or a bite to eat but generally phone calls and e-mails suffice and it is less time consuming.

Of course broker consultants and their marketing people have a clear agenda. They exist to promote their funds or products and hope you will sell them. That is why intermediaries are so important to them. But you don't work for them and are not there to meet their sale targets. As mentioned previously in Chapter 6, I tell broker reps that I go from client to product not product to client which is not only the truth but a way of fending off overly enthusiastic broker consultants.

Aside from broker consultants you know you will have calls on your time from a host of cold callers. The worst are the constant requests from market research companies often on behalf of product providers to take part in a survey. Invariably the time they take is more than they say it will be. I rarely accept these invitations, firstly I don't have the time or interest, secondly I can't be bothered and thirdly I often don't have any definite answers to the questions they pose. They are often too detailed and focussed on trivia and I end up having to guess or say I don't know.

On a similar theme have you noticed how many requests you get from all sorts of businesses to find out how well they did when you have had contact with them. You can't make a call to your gas company, mobile phone network or a pension provider without being asked for feedback. It consists of a series of rather inane questions like:

> *"On a scale of 1-5 where five is very satisfied and one is very dissatisfied*
>
> *How well did the customer services representative understand the nature of your query?*
>
> *How well did they do in resolving your query?*
>
> *Based on your experience today would you recommend us to a friend?"*

You get the drift, annoying as it is!

I can only assume the reason for all these requests is not actually to understand whether customers approve of their products and services with a view to improve them but to harvest responses for marketing purposes, for example so the company is able to claim 90% of our customers expressed they were very satisfied.

My issue with these surveys is that they address trivial matters and miss asking about the really important things that could really improve customer experience - for example the costs and quality of the products, call waiting times and other key service standards. Directed questions should be replaced with open questions which allow free form answers. For example, what do you think about the Smelly Gas Company or how can we improve?

Tips from Victor Mildrew

Whilst having a great proposition, good products, low competitive charges, comprehensive investment choice and high service standards are crucial elements of a top notch provider, I thought it would be helpful to provide a list of observations and tips that could help financial product providers and other companies improve their service standards and stop irritating me and I suspect lots of other advisers too. They may help you in your own dealings with them. You need to be firm as well as polite.

Communications & contact

- If I call your customer services department don't ask me how I am. Fidelity please take note. I am not your friend and I have not rung you to have a personal conversation about how the weather is getting me down, that I am having problems with my rear axle or to discuss some other personal problem. If I need counselling I'll talk to a therapist, not call you. I know you are just being polite but it is much more professional and certainly less irritating if you just introduce yourself and ask how can I help you today?

- If you cold-call, don't ask to speak to the person who deals with the utility bills or is chief buyer of paper clips, just state your name, your company and the purpose in contacting me. Preferably though don't cold call me. If you do I'll probably give you short shrift.

- If you leave a voicemail don't instruct me to call you back. Just state the nature of your call. If I am interested to find out more I'll be in touch.

- If you e-mail me please do not use an unmonitored *do not reply* e-mail address and tell me to call or go online to respond. If an e-mail is good enough for you to contact me it should be good enough and made available for me to reply. Otherwise if I need to respond you are putting barriers in my way, including a potentially long call waiting time for you to answer the phone or navigate through the jungle that is your website.

  Make sure your website has clear and easy to find telephone numbers and e-mail addresses. I dislike it when direct contact is made as difficult as possible, directing you to find what you are looking online or under the FAQs. It is clear you want to keep the number of people you employ dealing with customer queries as small as possible. That tells me something about your corporate culture.

- Employ enough people to answer phone calls. Don't tell me, *"lots of people are calling us today,"* i.e. blame the long call waiting times on everyone else who is trying to get through, especially when I heard the same message the last 10 times I called. The delays are not one-off events, with unusually high demand. It is a permanent state of affairs. Take the blame yourself for not having enough staff and recruit more, or improve your service so that fewer advisers will need to call you in the first place.

- Don't thank me for my patience when I am waiting for my call to be answered. That is an assumption and steam is coming out of my ears!

- Don't give me multiple options to press, as if somehow it is for my benefit, that I am being redirected to a specific department or a specialist. It is annoying as often my queries don't match any of the choices. Instead just answer my call by the first person. He or she should deal with my query or pass me to someone who can. Cut out button pressing requirements, my finger is aching from repetitive strain injury. If First Direct can answer the phone after one or two rings without these annoying button presses so can you.

- If you have to use multiple button presses before your customers get to speak to a human being don't bombard me with complex, long and irrelevant instructions and lectures about something e.g:

    "If you are calling about a mailing we sent you about the change of the objectives of the XYZ fund range please note our customer services representatives can only give you information not advice. No responsibility will be held for any actions you take or refrain from taking. If you need advice on whether the changes to the fund objectives are suitable for you, please go the FCA website to find a financial adviser. Alternatively go to our website www.XYZ.com click link at the top called funds, then changes to funds. If any of the terminology is not clear stay on the line and press option 89, alternatively go to Investopedia, and register for their online services. Please note other investment education tools are available. To hear this message again press option 999 and ask for the men in the white coats."

    All this verbiage is useless. All I want is a valuation or to deal with a specific query so cut it out and the just answer the darn phone.

- Don't employ avatars to answer the phone and then ask me lots of questions. "Why are you calling us today? Are you the customer or someone else? Please state your plan number? What is your favourite football team?"

    Just put me through to a human being. You may think I am robotphobic but it annoys me. Here's is a tip for advisers. Depending on how grumpy I am I have found answering "Arsenal" to every question quickly confuses the avatar and you are rapidly put through to a customer services representative, quite possibly a Tottenham Hotspur supporter.

- If I write to you with a specific query when you write back, firstly make sure the letter is signed by an identifiable person, specifically the one writing the reply, not "customer services" or the titular head of department, who has not come within a mile of the case. The person who writes the response should provide their specific e-mail address or direct dial telephone number if I need to go back to them.

Whatever you do please don't say if I have any further queries I should call the customer services department. That is so annoying having to go through and explain the situation all over again from scratch to someone new especially as the story gets longer and more complex each time there is further contact or new correspondence.

I have had at least one occasion when a response was from one person. After writing back the reply came from someone else and then subsequently a third individual. It was a game of pass the parcel. Someone at the company should take full ownership of the case and see it through from start to finish.

- If you phone me and leave a voicemail message with a telephone number to call you back on, please say the number slowly and repeat it. It is annoying when it is said so fast, like the terms and conditions for a product advert on the radio that it requires me having to play back the message three times before I can correctly write down the full number.

Technology

A major issue in the industry are problems arising from replatforming where wholesale online system changes have created headaches for advisers and their clients. An article in Professional Adviser by Tom Ellis in March 2019 was titled, *"Cofunds and Aviva see Ombudsman complaints rocket after re-platforming."*

Of course navigating around a new site is always difficult. The familiar paths you have gone down for years are no longer there and each new step or process can be a puzzle. Eventually like anything else, do it a few times it gets easier. None the less I have some tips on improving platform and provider technology.

- Don't get advisers to play a game I call, *"guess the mind of the programmer."* This applies not just with financial services company websites. You know the sort of thing. If you don't enter the information in the format the system requires what is perfectly good data is rejected. I might enter my business telephone number as 01323 735303 but it is rejected with a red error message, for example because I left a gap between the two sets of numbers. In my view technology should be smart enough to recognise valid data and convert it automatically to the format that is required.

Some of the worst examples where I am required to guess the mind of the programmer are when undertaking fund searches, for the purposes of investment research or when I place a deal. I frequently experience this when looking for a fund on platforms. If I don't type in the name of the fund in the exact wording or format the programme requires I draw a blank. For example a Standard Life Investment fund, prior to its merger with Aberdeen Asset Management, might have to be entered as SLI or a JP Morgan fund as JPM.

Some systems are unable to interpret what has been entered as a valid alternative and make an educated conclusion on what fund you are looking for. So I end up wasting time having to guess the correct secret code needed to call up the fund and share class I am looking for. On one occasion I tried to find an L&G fund on a platform but it failed to appear because I should have entered L & G, i.e. with spaces between the letters and the ampersand.

A tip for advisers is to use the SEDOL code when searching for a fund and specific share class on a platform search engine. This assumes you can find the codes and the search functions will accept them. SEDOLs are normally shown on fund fact sheets and KIIDs.

- One of the difficulties advisers face when placing fund buy or switch instructions is being presented with multiple share classes available for each fund. In the past it was very simple, retail investors either bought an accumulation or an income share class. Both were dirty or bundled. Although lower charging clean or unbundled institutional (I) share classes existed before the RDR, these were unavailable for most investors as the minimum amount to access them could be as high as £500,000.

Once the RDR banned the sale of dirty or bundled share classes and mandated the use of clean or unbundled share classes for new investments institutional fund charging structures now became available.

However the RDR also led to the creation of "super clean" share classes. These provide discounts on the annual management charges (and hence the OCF) of the standard I or other clean share classes. The result is you can find share classes of funds labelled A, B, C, D, I, P, R, X, Y or Z, though not necessarily all of these for the same fund. These will have differing annual management charges.

Moreover the RDR did not eliminate the old dirty bundled share classes altogether. It just stopped investors buying or switching into them. However you will still find them aplenty in old style ISA and investment accounts run by fund management groups.

Consequently if a bundled pre-RDR fund is re-registered from an investment provider to a platform, the platform may still permit holdings in old retail share classes to be retained whilst Fidelity FundsNetwork at least immediately switch the holding after re-registration from the retail bundled share class to the lower charging unbundled one. The point is your clients may be holding higher charging pre-RDR share classes when cheaper unbundled ones are available.

The problem with having multiple share classes on a platform is the confusion for customers and it is a trap for advisers. If you pick the wrong share class your client will end up paying a higher fund charge (the OCF) than necessary. When faced with a choice of share classes for a particular fund, advisers must check the OCFs for them all to find the cheapest. However on one or two occasions I have accidentally picked a higher charging one which has led to additional work to correct and cost to compensate the client if they lost out by my error.

So what I would like platforms to do is to only permit trades into the cheapest share classes of each fund. Interestingly on the Hargreaves Lansdown website they show all alternative share classes and their costs making finding the least expensive one very easy. Be aware though that Hargreaves Lansdown is a direct to consumer platform that does not accept adviser business and has a high 0.45% p.a. platform fee for investment sums up to £250,000. It is however an all in platform with discounts on the OCFs of many funds.

- Ensure you get transaction reporting right. Fidelity used to have a facility to search and view the transaction history of any particular fund. I found this very useful in seeing what investments were made on which dates, what platform charges were taken from the fund, if any, and what dividends were re-invested for income share class funds to buy more shares.

When Fidelity undertook their replatforming exercise this facility to drill down into the transactions for a specific fund was lost. They replaced transaction reporting with a horrendously complex system with far too many and vaguely worded filters. You can filter by date and account which is logical, simple and useful but it is when you get to filtering by transaction categories and transaction types the problems begin. The first is advisers are expected to know the difference between a category and a type. Secondly on one occasion I counted 62 transaction types. Large numbers of these are vague and repetitive. It is clear as mud. Here are some examples:

> *Adjustment, deal adjustment buy, Int. admn. adj. only, ex wts: sell shares, sell for switch* (two identical filter boxes), *reinvested income, dividend reinvestment...*

The list goes on.

To be fair this is the worst thing about the Fidelity FundsNetwork platform and they are aware of the issues that advisers have with transaction reporting. However change has been slow coming.

Viewing and tracking cash transactions are also important to get right and again Fidelity are poor whilst AJ Bell Investcentre and Alliance Trust Savings have simple but very effective cash reporting.

- Allow a reasonable amount of inactivity time before you log an adviser out. Most platforms are OK but Alliance Trust Savings are far too quick. I seem to get logged out after just 5-10 minutes. Tip for advisers - don't go to the loo and make yourself a cup of coffee during a session on the ATS website.

- A good platform should be able to automatically generate personal illustrations with fund specific information when placing buy orders or fund switches. Fidelity does this very well. Other platforms require advisers to manually create illustrations and that is a turn off.

- A good platform will provide unrealised and realised capital gains calculations for clients with general investment accounts. Again Fidelity is excellent for this. Without these manual capital gains tax calculations can be very difficult especially where there have been previous partial encashments, investment has been funded by regular contributions and dividends have been reinvested.

- I don't do much protection business these days as many of my clients are retired or have no financial dependents but I dislike online applications and avoid them if a paper based option is available, even if it means a smaller commission payment. Online applications may be processed quicker but I suspect they are designed to reduce costs for the insurer, especially if the application can be handled automatically without reference to an underwriter.

  I get frustrated in trying to accurately and comprehensively enter clients' medical details where the drop down choices of answers does not fit or there is no option of entering free form text. I find this especially concerning given the potential for non-disclosure if you are unable to record full information.

So my tip to all insurers - always have the option for a paper based application.

11. Principles of investment advice

As an IFA who specialises in investments I have to include a chapter on this subject although it is worthy of a book in its own right.

In Chapter 5 I covered the concept of investment risk and risk profiling whilst in Chapter 6 I wrote about how I research funds, the difference between strategic and tactical investment and the importance of investment reviews. In this chapter I want to cover additional principles of investment advice and tackle hot potato issues such as active versus passive investment.

Independent v Restricted

As you will gather if you have read the earlier chapters I take the view that the best advice is delivered if you are an independent adviser, meaning you can recommend investments from the full range of retail investment products (RIPs), including investment trusts, VCTs, structured products and National Savings & Investments (NS&I).

If you are a restricted adviser you simply don't have all the tools in your box to do the best job in all cases. Of course if you conclude that investment bonds, OEICs and unit trusts alone are suitable for your clients' financial needs and their risk profiles and they do not require consideration of more esoteric RIPs then that is fine. However invariably this will not be the case for all your clients. Can you honestly say you don't have a single client for whom an investment trust might be suitable?

I have heard the argument that advisers have written them off completely because they are too risky for their client bank. Frankly I think this is an excuse to avoid the inconvenience of restricted advisers having to put in the effort to understand, assess and explain investment trusts to their clients. Outright dismissal also avoids the problem that investment trust business placed direct does not pay adviser charges in the same way they never paid commission. Having to levy a direct fee for advice on investment trusts may be uncomfortable for advisers. However platforms can facilitate adviser charges so this is less of a barrier than it was pre-RDR.

Of course split capital investment trusts have their complexities and risks but plain vanilla UK and global trusts with single ordinary share classes are not significantly more risky in my view than the equivalent unit trusts and OEICs especially if the trust has a low level of borrowing and it trades close to its net asset value.

Investment trusts with their closed end structure have several benefits over open ended funds. Firstly their managers are not forced to sell assets in a market downturn when lots of investors are cashing in their investments. In contrast unless there is sufficient cash in an OEIC or unit trust or ample inflows of new money the fund manager will have to sell stocks or other assets to pay out investors. In a falling stock market invariably poor prices will be achieved, meaning losses for all investors in the fund, including those that are sticking with their holdings.

For property funds it is worse. During the global financial crisis and after the 2016 EU referendum various open ended property funds were forced to close to trading as they could not meet requests for redemptions without having to sell illiquid commercial property assets. There were no buyers, sales could not be completed in a timely fashion or could only be achieved at knock down prices. In contrast closed end property investment trusts were not forced sellers of assets as the shares in investment trusts are traded separately to the underlying assets. This may be something for your private study or CPD!

A second benefit of investment trusts is that uniquely they can retain up to 15% of the income they receive in reserve and pay this out to shareholders in subsequent years. This permits trusts to smooth dividend pay outs and crucially increase the dividend each year. This has led to the concept of dividend heroes. It applies to the shares of individual companies as well as to investment trusts, bearing in mind their legal structures are fundamentally similar and various investment trusts are listed FTSE 100 or FTSE 250 companies. The main difference is their business is to deal in the shares of other companies as opposed to oil production, banking and widget manufacture.

The Association of Investment Companies (AIC) a trade body for UK trusts and a very useful source of information announced in March 2019 a list of dividend hero trusts.[27]

Topping the list were three trusts with 52 consecutive years of dividend increases, the City of London, Alliance Trust and Bankers. The first is a UK equity income trust, the other two are global funds. Seventeen other trusts were listed which had racked up more than 20 years of dividend rises, most in the 30s and 40s.

Whilst yields varied many of the UK equity income trusts were paying more than 4% p.a. These trusts are excellent for income and income growth with long term capital growth potential thrown in for good measure. What is not to like about them?

Of course an adviser will need to understand the concept of discounts and premiums to net asset value and the implications for investors but in reality the complexity of investment trusts is rather overstated.

Bespoke v Centralised Investment Propositions

I also operate on the principle that entirely bespoke investment advice is best.

As with my charging structure I am pretty unique in the industry as I don't like and use centralised investment propositions (CIPs). Mark Polson, of the Lang Cat succinctly defined a CIP in an article in Money Marketing in January 2019 as follows:

> "To create consistent outcomes, advisers today use technology and judgement to put clients in a risk-banded box, which drives volatility limits, which drives asset allocation, which drives portfolio construction. You know all this."[28]

According to Polson, a Lang Cat survey showed 90% of advisers use a CIP.

---

[27] https://www.theaic.co.uk/aic/news/press-releases/investment-company-dividend-heroes
[28] https://www.moneymarketing.co.uk/528250-2/

To fill in a bit more detail, CIPs work something like this. You classify or segment clients according to their risk profile and financial needs, for example a cautious risk investor requiring income or a balanced risk investor seeking capital growth. Investor risk is determined by a risk profiling tool, your own or an off the shelf one, such as Dynamic Planner or FinaMetrica.

You then link the various segmented client groups to pre-set asset allocations. For example for cautious risk investors the ideal asset allocation might be 55% fixed interest, 30% equities, 10% property and alternatives and 5% cash. These are typically rigid allocations, although there is some flexibility to permit small plus or minus increments, for example in the order of 5-10%. This allows adjustments for tactical investment purposes depending on stock market conditions. Adventurous risk clients in contrast will have an asset allocation that is much more dominated by equities, with much lower holdings in fixed interest and cash.

Finally the adviser has access to a range of model portfolios, a list of funds that will reflect the chosen asset allocations. As an example Money Observer have 12 model portfolios for their readers to use on a non-advised basis.[29] For growth investors who are medium or higher risk there are six portfolios, two for short term, two for medium and two for long term investing.

Take a medium risk long term investor. The model portfolio is called Charlie. At the time of writing in the spring of 2019 it consisted of seven funds, a mixture of funds and investment trusts for example the Fidelity Emerging Markets, the F&C Investment Trust and the Lindsell Train UK Equity. All funds are equity investments apart from the Capital Gearing Investment Trust which mainly invests in bonds and has an absolute return focus.

What CIPs do therefore is to put clients into categories or boxes and attempt to meet their investment needs from off the shelf model portfolios. Clients with the same risk profile, financial requirements i.e. growth or income and timescales are likely to end up with virtually the

---

[29] https://www.moneyobserver.com/money-observer-portfolios

same portfolio.

Subsequently with portfolio reviews the adviser will rebalance all portfolios simultaneously or may recommend a specific fund is ditched and replaced with a new investment. To effect the change on a platform a bulk switching instruction will be placed. This avoids manually switching all clients on an individual basis.

Advocates of CIPs argue they offer a clear and consistent investment process. Iboss Asset Management state on their website:

> *"The benefits of a Centralised Investment Proposition (CIP) have been felt by advisers and planners for a few years now. Having a coherent, well-researched and documented approach to advice is undoubtedly beneficial for the firm and client. Invaluable in maintaining consistency across the business, it enables economies of scale to be exploited, mitigates business risk and could even reduce PI premiums. For clients, the consistency offers security and peace of mind."*[30]

I wouldn't necessarily dispute these benefits but my problem with CIPs is I see a conflict of interest for advisers. A CIP is an off the shelf solution which significantly reduces the amount of work required compared to constructing and advising entirely bespoke portfolios. This is because a group of clients can efficiently be advised through the same process and the work done takes less time. A CIP combined with percentage fees increases the profitability of the firm's income. They fit hand in glove. Synchronised portfolio construction and ongoing management for all clients is nice and convenient for the adviser firm. Therefore you have to ask if a CIP is for the benefit of clients or for the benefit of the financial adviser.

Back in the days of the FSA the regulator expressed concern that clients would be shoehorned into model portfolios. I am not sure much has changed.

Polson highlighted other issues with CIPs, for example advisers using

---

[30] https://www.ibossam.com/six-things-to-consider-when-reviewing-your-centralised-investment-proposition/

just one type of CIP and inconsistent asset allocations. The FCA for example found that portfolios labelled as moderate or balanced had bond allocations of less than 5% and up to 60%! That can't be right you might think. However I have a different perspective which I explain below.

In addition Polson found some adviser firms have exceeded their regulatory permissions when rebalancing portfolios. This is because most adviser firms do not have discretionary investment powers and therefore CIP fund switches can only be undertaken after advice is given to clients and they have agreed to it. If such advisers undertake rebalancing and fund switches without reference to their clients, that would be a breach of the rules. Polson logically concludes it is difficult to run model portfolios without discretionary permissions.

I have two other major problems with CIPs. Firstly I take the view that every client is different and needs bespoke advice. This is especially evident when I take on a new client. Invariably they come with a portfolio of existing investments and in most cases it would be wholly inappropriate to sell them all to be reinvested into a model portfolio of my creation on a platform of my choice. It is far too disruptive. Good funds may end up being ditched or a capital gains tax (CGT) charge may be generated inadvertently. Instead I will undertake a review and usually make changes to the asset allocation, platforms or fund selection slowly. It is invariably a gradual change by evolution not revolution.

Given this, it is not unreasonable to conclude a CIP works better if the new client comes to you with cash as you don't have the problem of untangling a pre-existing portfolio of investments held on an array of different platforms or with providers direct.

A bespoke approach means I can work with the "baggage" clients come with including old legacy products and platforms they hold their investments, even if I would not ordinarily recommend these to clients. In many cases the platforms are reasonably good and I may not be able to justify transferring a client's holdings to one of my preferred platforms given the cost of advice.

As a result of a bespoke investment advice process the portfolios my clients have look very different to each other in terms of the product mix, the asset allocation, the platforms used and funds held. Many portfolios will include legacy products such as with profits bonds, old style pensions or ISAs held direct with a fund manager. Transfers and re-registrations may be recommended if appropriate and cost effective. The benefits are consolidated administration and access to clean share classes with lower OCFs. However clients may be best served by retaining with profits investments whilst ditching pensions with guaranteed annuity rates is very likely to be bad advice.

My second issue with CIPs are the fixed or inflexible asset allocations that undergird them. They may be entirely unsuited to current stock market conditions and asset valuations.

I gave an example above for a cautious risk investor where the default "ideal" asset allocation might look something like this - 55% fixed interest, 30% equities, 10% property and alternatives and 5% cash. This is clearly a high level division as the fixed interest tranche could be split between gilts, investment grade corporate bonds, index linked and high yield whilst equities could be divided between the UK and global, or developed and emerging markets.

Irrespective of the how the investment cake is cut up this asset allocation is unsuitable for the prevailing market conditions in 2019 in my opinion. Since the global financial crisis bond yields have fallen sharply through very accommodative central bank monetary policy i.e. quantitative easing and ultra-low interest rates. Bond prices rose sharply as a consequence, driving down yields. Currently in general much of the bond market especially in developed markets and investment grade now offers very little value. In fact I see a skewed risk reward profile with little upside potential but a risk of a fall in bond prices from interest rate rises. Consequently I have rarely recommended bond funds in recent years, although they still have a role in providing portfolio diversity and income. Government bonds are also important as a safe haven asset.

In summary although in general fixed interest carries less risk than equities as measured by volatility of prices there is too much risk in the bond market for me - interest rate or duration risk for government bonds and investment grade corporates and default risk for high yield bonds. With fears of recession default rates could rise.

I take the view that the risk of different asset classes relative to each other is not fixed and advisers must take account of current market conditions, valuations and asset specific risks before deciding their recommended asset allocation.

As I therefore see more overall risk in fixed interest than equities I can't envisage I would recommend a portfolio composed of 55% fixed interest at this time, except perhaps for selected income investors and where inclusion of high yield bonds will be suitable for the clients' risk profile.

I stated the FCA expressed concern about inconsistent asset allocations. They found that portfolios labelled as moderate or balanced had bond allocations of less than 5% and up to 60%! This apparent disparity may actually highlight a different point than inconsistency. The portfolio consisting of 60% in bonds may be a classic example of an asset allocation that is rigid and that takes no account of market conditions, valuations or the specific risks of fixed interest assets. On the other hand the adviser proposing 5% in bonds might have tactically and radically adjusted the portfolio asset allocation taking all these factors into account. In my view this allocation is more tactically astute. If I was a long term investor with a balanced risk profile I know what portfolio I would prefer. Currently my SIPP is predominantly equity based although that should be caveated by the fact that that I am an aggressive risk investor.

In conclusion I think only bespoke investment advice can take account of individual needs. In my experience no two clients are alike, although to be fair I have never advised twins! Every client will come to you with some financial planning in place - whether it is an existing collection of investments and pensions or a unique set of financial needs and objectives, attitudes, timescales and values. You have to work with what you have in front of you rather than shoehorn their existing arrangements into your CIP. We need to adapt to our clients not expect them to adapt to us and our processes.

Giving bespoke advice is a problem for advisers who have decided to work on a percentage fee basis. The fee is fixed and is determined in advance by the amount of money to be invested or managed. This does not sit well with bespoke investment advice as the adviser knows it will take longer to carry out the work compared to an off the shelf CIP, which he or she may have used many times previously.

In contrast for me charging by the hour I am fully remunerated for the extra work and complexity that bespoke investment advice entails. It is also much more varied and interesting as a result compared to churning out the same stuff for multiple clients, year in year out.

Finally I should say that although I don't use CIPs I frequently use the same funds for different portfolios if appropriate. For example if I identify a high quality Japanese equity fund I may recommend it to more than one client if the fund is suitable and market conditions are favourable. There is no point in reinventing the wheel. Although you will find favoured funds in lots of my client portfolios each portfolio will look very different. In no way is this a CIP.

Active v Passive

Whether active fund management is better than passive index tracking or the other way around is another controversial issue in the advice industry. Increasingly, advocates of passive investment have been more vocal and evangelical in arguing their case. As a result passive investment has grown in popularity and index tracking assets under management are rocketing, unwittingly aided by the regulators who are obsessed in driving down investment costs.

It is true that whilst investment returns are not known in advance, fund charges are. That said they are not fixed and can go up. However in an environment of low investment returns paying an OCF as low as 0.06% p.a. for an equity tracker or ETF is a tangible benefit compared to paying 0.75% p.a. or more for an actively managed fund. That is a fair point but as I will explain later differences in fund charges are much smaller than differences in fund performance and therefore in my view charges are not the prime determinant in achieving good investment returns.

What we can categorically say however that paying 0.75% p.a. or more for a closet tracker is indefensible. A closet tracker is one that is ostensibly actively managed but in reality it hugs the index closely. The fund manager does that to follow the crowd, avoid going out on a limb and getting his or her stock selection all wrong. His or her goal is to avoid falling to the bottom of fund rankings. If average performance is an outcome that is deemed acceptable, it is hardly an inspiring investment vision. The conclusion is if you are going to pay a higher OCF than a tracker then you need to ensure the fund is truly actively managed. A closet tracker simply won't do.

Aside from low fund management charges advocates of passive investment argue few active fund managers beat the market. However the evidence I have seen for this comes from highly efficient markets only, such as the S&P 500 in the USA, where analyst coverage of listed companies is so comprehensive there is little scope for pricing anomalies that stock picking fund managers can exploit. All the information about companies or pretty well all of it is out there in the public domain. However in many other markets analyst coverage is minimal or absent, notably with smaller companies. Pricing anomalies are common and active stock picking fund management rewards investors.

Another point to note is that evidence for index tracking outperforming actively managed funds comes from periods when stock markets are rising steadily, notably in the 1980s and 1990s which were generally golden years for equities and after the global financial crisis in 2008. With the latter when central banks slashed interest rates and used QE to inject liquidity into the market, share prices rose uniformly and indiscriminately across the board. It was an example of the principle that "a rising tide floats all boats." During this period good and bad stocks rose together.

The converse is expected as liquidity is withdrawn, investors will buy and sell based on company fundamentals. Correlations will break down and dispersion of stock returns will increase.

It is my observation that when markets move sideways index tracking underperforms. That makes sense to me. In such an environment the index will go nowhere fast. If you look at a graph of the FTSE 100 index you will see that the index rose steadily through the 1980s and 1990s.[31]

The index peaked at 6,930 at the end of 1999. The technology bubble then burst and share prices fell sharply. This was followed by a recovery triggered by what was referred to as the Baghdad Bounce in March 2003, named after the invasion of Iraq. Then we had the global financial crisis in 2008 which sent markets plunging again.

Although an economic recovery started in March 2009 it has generally been weak outside the US. Following the sell-off at the end of 2018 the FTSE closed at 6,728 on 31/12/18. In other words the FTSE 100 moved sideways for 19 years. True an investor would have received dividends during this time over this period but that is the yield only and nothing else - no capital growth. These are the sort of returns you expect from bonds held from issue to maturity. A FTSE 100 Index tracker would have been a rotten thing to have invested in in that 19 year period.

The FTSE 100 had a better year in 2019 and closed at 7,542, a rise of just 8.8% in 20 years excluding dividends.

The question is did active fund managers do better? Research undertaken by Trustnet showed the answer is yes.[32]

Trustnet analysed data for UK equity funds over a 20 year period between 30/6/1998 and 30/6/18. The FTSE All Share Total Return (TR) i.e. with reinvested dividends rose 196.66%. Please note the FTSE All Share index is a composite of the FTSE 100, the FTSE 250 and the FTSE Small Cap indices. As medium and smaller companies historically outperform larger companies the FTSE All Share will have outperformed the FTSE 100 index in the last 20 years.

To illustrate this outperformance I calculated using data from Swanlow Park[33] that £1,000 invested for 15 years from 2003 to 2018 would have returned £3,091 from the FTSE 100 TR compared to £3,417 from the FTSE

---

[31] https://www.ukvalueinvestor.com/2016/06/ftse-100-valuation.html/
[32] https://www.trustnet.com/news/835254/uk-growth-funds-that-have-stood-the-test-of-time-part-1
[33] http://www.swanlowpark.co.uk/ftseannual

All Share TR.

Now I appreciate the 20 year period Trustnet looked at differs from this 15 year period but all the data I have seen shows the same outcome over the long term. It is true over the short term smaller and mid-caps usually underperform when markets sell-off but it is the long term picture we are interested here, through multiple market expansions and contractions. All the evidence shows smaller companies outperform.

Anyway back to the Trustnet research whilst the FTSE All Share TR index returned 196.66% over 20 years the average IA UK All Companies fund delivered 193.83%. So the index just beat the average UK equity fund, a result that is not unsurprising. The IA All Companies sector is large and competitive and consists mainly of actively managed funds but some passive trackers too. I would have expected the returns of the index to be roughly equal to the average performance of all funds in the sector. The slight outperformance of the index is not surprising given the index has no costs and fees but funds do, even trackers.

It is not stated in the article how many funds have 20 year records but at 7/4/19 Trustnet data showed there were 200 with a 10 year track record. Even if there were just 100 funds with 20 year track records many would be expected to have delivered returns greater than the FTSE All Share TR, if again the index only just beat the IA UK All Companies average. Trustnet itself identified consistently good performers in the long term. The following funds were highlighted with their total returns:

- Axa Framlington UK Select Opportunities - 409.08%
- Marlborough UK Multi-Cap Growth - 502.85%
- Schroder UK Recovery - 569.07%.

These and other funds trounced index returns over the same 20 year period.

It is important to note that these are 20 year cumulative returns, the change from the start date to the end date. They don't tell you what happened in between i.e. the profile of those returns, how smooth or lumpy they were and if there were periods of underperformance.

However the Trustnet methodology shortlisted funds based on 61 rolling five periods over the 20 years and only shortlisted funds with very low decile rankings, in other words those which delivered returns consistently over the 61 five year periods. So it was not just that these funds beat the index they delivered returns in a relatively smooth and consistent way.

So what can we conclude? Firstly active fund managers have outperformed the FTSE All Share TR index in the long term. That is a fact. It seems entirely logical to me that if a good stock picker can avoid the deadwood and value traps and pick companies with strong fundamentals, active fund management will outperform the market.

The converse is also reasonable to me. I can't see the logic of investing in a company, if it is a basket case just because it is in the index. Surely there has to be a sound investment case to hold each stock.

I also find it odd and even churlish for advocates of passive investment to effectively discount all stock picking fund management skills and assume any outperformance is down to luck. This is to suggest all analysis of geo-politics, global economics, stock markets, currencies or company fundamentals including balance sheets and the quality of the management is a worthless exercise and you would be better off sticking a pin in the share pages of a newspaper to choose which stocks to invest in. To dismiss all technical analysis and research and stock selection as worthless feels like something coming from advocates of a flat earth.

I do however accept there are active funds and fund managers where the hype does not match the reality and who do not outperform the market. However there are plenty of great ones out there that do.

For advisers who mainly use actively managed funds as I do, your role is to identify fund managers who understand their market, have a clear investment strategy and have the guts to back their convictions and make decisions even if it means going against the crowd. It does not necessarily mean following a star fund manager when he leaves his role especially if the investment processes which have delivered the outperformance are embedded in the fund management and will be continued by a new incumbent. As Trustnet explained, the manager of the Axa Framlington UK Select Opportunities, Nigel Thomas, in charge since 2002 was set to retire in March 2019 after 40 years in asset management.

> "After this, the fund will be taken over by Chris St John, who has worked alongside Thomas for several years and will continue to do so over a transition period; in a recent FE Trustnet article, St John explained why investors will see little change in how the fund is managed once he takes the helm."[34]

Sticking with star fund managers unstintingly has its risks. Many great fund managers lose their star qualities and have periods of underperformance, sometimes serious and prolonged. Sometimes fund managers go off the boil due to poor asset allocation and stock selection decisions but it may also be because the fund's investment style is temporarily out of favour.

If a star manager loses his or her touch and it is time to ditch their funds that's OK. An adviser can identify other funds to invest in. There are always high quality alternatives and other good managers available. Funds which would have been first on the team sheet when creating new portfolios in the past may subsequently get put on the bench or ditched completely.

The principle here has similarities to being a professional football manager. Your star striker may give you good seven years, banging in the goals consistently. Then he starts to lose his edge as he becomes older and slower, and the goals dry up, so you bring in a new striker from another club who has already proved his worth or who is a prospect from the youth academy and showing real promise. He might go by the name Harry Kane.

The point is you stick with a fund manager as long as he or she is delivering the goods. When things go wrong you need to decide whether this is just a short term blip or whether it time to find a substitute. An adviser who is picking funds for their clients and favours

---

[34] https://www.trustnet.com/News/835254/uk-growth-funds-that-have-stood-the-test-of-time-part-1 - 4/9/18

active management needs to be flexible and decisive. They should review performance and be willing to rotate fund managers if necessary. In that way you should still be able to stay ahead of the game and consistently outperform the market and beat the IA sector averages.

As an aside with a growing trend towards team management there is perhaps less emphasis on individual managers - the contrarian maverick with a magic wand coated with star dust. You often find good funds managed by two or more people with complementary skills. However in these circumstances you don't want the underlying successful investment strategy and individual convictions and skills being blunted by the team or strict top down house constraints. You have probably heard the one about a camel being a horse designed by a committee.

I suggested earlier that my observation was that index tracking works in efficient markets. The contrast is most notable amongst smaller company funds. In e-mail correspondence in March 2019 with someone in the industry who strongly advocates passive investment I wrote:

> *"Moving onto market efficiency the lack of passive investments in smaller companies is notable. As you know research and broker coverage is much less than for large caps and in some cases for example with Japanese smaller companies there is no analyst cover at all. The lack of research contributes to pricing inefficiencies which makes active fund management and stock picking much more rewarding. Trustnet shows amongst OEICs and unit trusts there are seven Japanese smaller company funds. Not one is an index tracker. The same is true of the 16 North American Smaller Companies funds and the 24 European Smaller Companies funds. Finally I can't see a single index tracker amongst the 51 UK Smaller Companies funds.*
>
> *My point is that if passive investment is so good why are there no index trackers in the smaller companies space? Some ETFs are available. My conclusion is that no fund manager has the conviction to launch a fund that is likely to be trounced by every active fund in the sector. There are bound to be other inefficient markets where index tracking is likely to do poorly."*

We have seen that one of the principle benefits of index trackers are the very low fund management charges, and there is strong pressure from the regulators, the financial press and the consumer lobby to drive down costs. We see it in other industries too such as the energy market. The stealth tax industry spawned by successive governments is the notable exception of course. The trend of ever lower costs is driven by the view that consumers need to be protected from rapacious fund managers. The campaign is undergirded by a *fact* that charges eat into returns. This is indisputable but equally there is also a *fallacy*, a weakness in the argument which says that you are more likely to get the best investment performance by curbing costs.

I think this is misguided as differences in charges are always smaller than differences in fund returns. Take for example the IA UK All Companies sector. The Fidelity Index UK, a FTSE All Share tracker has an ultra-low OCF of 0.06% p.a. for the P share class. Data from Trustnet (8/4/19) show the fund returned 38.4% over five years. The average fund in the sector returned 33.7% over the same period. There were 233 funds with a five year track record.

Although the return of the Fidelity Index UK fund was better than average as an adviser you should not be satisfied that your clients achieve average or just better than average, you should want to see superior performance. In fact 75 UK equity funds returned more than the Fidelity Index UK over five years, a couple yielded more than 90% and 26 delivered returns in excess of 50%.

All of these returns are net of all fund charges - annual management charges, other fund costs such as auditor and custodian fees and transaction expenses. Ignoring the very worst 10 and the very best 10 performing funds to remove the impact of the extremes, the 11th best fund returned 61.1% and the 223rd delivered just 15.3% a difference of 45.8%. The 11th best fund also beat the Fidelity Index UK by 22.7% over five years. Even over one year the best fund returned 15.5%, the worst -18.7%, the average 4.4% and the Fidelity Index UK gained 7.1%.

Now I can't say which is the highest charging fund in the sector, but many actively managed UK funds have OCFs of less than 1% p.a. The Liontrust Sustainable Future (SF) UK Growth was the 11th best fund over five years with a return of 61.1%. It has an OCF of 0.91% p.a. and estimated transaction costs of 0.74% p.a. taking the total cost of fund ownership to 1.65% p.a. These transaction costs are much higher than average incidentally. In contrast the Fidelity Index UK has an OCF of 0.06% and estimated transaction costs of -0.01% p.a. Don't ask me to explain that. Taking it at face value we have over five years:

	Cost of Fund Ownership[35]	Five Year Return[36]
Liontrust SF UK Growth	1.65% p.a.	61.1%
Fidelity Index UK	0.05% p.a.	38.4%
Difference	1.60% p.a.	22.7%

Over a five year period cumulatively a charge of 1.60% p.a. would reduce a £100 investment to £92.25 i.e. by 7.75%, much less than the excess return of 22.7% over the same period of time. Bear in mind too that the returns are net of all fund charges.

You will see this consistently that differences in performance are much greater than differences in charges. In the same way that the tax tail should not wag the investment dog so the charges tail should not wag the investment dog. Our investment dog has two tails, which can wag independently. This is not to say that I don't think fund charges are important. If I can identify a great active fund with low costs then that is an ideal combination.

Although I favour active fund management I occasionally use index tracking funds. For example after a sharp stock market sell-off I will occasionally recommend a tracker to buy the index at a low level and leverage a recovery in the index when it comes. If you are lucky it will be V shaped and rapid. I may then sell out once the recovery has delivered decent profits.

I may also use passives to provide diversity. This may include multi-asset fund of funds which blend active and passive investments. Finally I may use passives to access strong asset allocation skills of a fund manager. I am thinking of Vanguard's LifeStrategy fund series here. These are fettered fund of funds, investing solely in Vanguard index trackers. What they have done very well for my clients to date, is to get

---

[35] Fidelity FundsNetwork
[36] Trustnet (8/4/19)

the asset allocation right whilst keeping charges low. It demonstrates a principal that every investment adviser will be schooled in, that asset allocation is the prime determinant of good returns, not stock selection. So what you typically find is the worst performing fund in the best performing sector will outperform the best performing fund in the worst performing sector. However it will never always be true given the existence of extreme outliers in most sectors.

To address an apparent anomaly here, if asset allocation is more important than stock selection surely it seems as if I am suggesting passive investment is best. No. Most passives are single sector funds tracking a single index e.g. the FTSE 100, the S&P 500 or the Nikkei 225. There is no asset allocation, the trackers merely replicates the index. In contrast the Vanguard LifeStrategy funds are a blended portfolio of passive funds. To create the right mix the fund manager must decide which trackers to include and in what proportions. That is an asset allocation skill.

In conclusion the active v passive debate is complex and nuanced and you will need to develop your own convictions on what is right. For me active fund management is generally best.

Strategic Asset Allocation

Strategic investment is about long term asset allocation. As an example consider a client age 30 likely to work for the next 35 years and starting to save for retirement. I would normally take the view that even if he or she is a cautious risk investor they should invest 100% into pure equity funds for the first 25 years at least. There are two key drivers that reduce risk for such a client - the long term nature of the investment and multiple monthly contributions with its risk reduction and the potential benefits of volatility as explained in Chapter 5.

To remind you, at the troughs and other low valuation points monthly investors pick up units cheaply and hence buy more of them for their fixed contribution compared to higher valuation points. My strategy is undergirded by the view that although share prices go up and down, in the very long term equity markets rise and they outperform other asset classes notably cash and fixed interest. You can trace this trend back for more than 100 years, for example from the excellent annual *"Barclays*

Equity Gilt Study."

Strong advocates of a buy and hold investment strategy argue that it is futile and potentially costly to try and time the market. Selling equities at the top of the market and buying back in at the troughs is very difficult. You have got to get two calls spot on. Selling out too early means you miss the gains if the markets continue to rise in the following months, before the downturn hits.

When the crash comes, a quick and sharp V shaped recovery may mean you buy back in after the rise has commenced and you miss out on the early gains.

I have made this point previously. There is plenty of evidence that missing the best days in the market slashes your returns. Data I saw from Vanguard Asset Management Ltd, quoting FactSet shows that investing in the FTSE All Share Index between 1986 and 2016 would have turned £100,000 into £1,828,115. However if an investor missed the best 10 days the return would have been slashed to £969,239.[37]

Timing the market carries a lot of risk and success requires exceptional skill or luck. In the end it is generally best to stay in the market and ride the volatility.

Picking funds & fund managers

In my view this is part science part art. The science bit is the research. It is about objectivity and facts. I look at fund performance and volatility data from Trustnet, an excellent free to use online fund information service. In addition I check the fund fact sheets or make enquiries direct to investment companies if the information I am looking for is not shown. I am interested in a variety of things for example asset and sector allocations, small cap exposure, duration for bond funds and cash positions.

I also use Morningstar Analyst (formerly Old Broad Street Research, OBSR) ratings. What I like about these is they are independent

---

[37] https://www.vanguardinvestor.co.uk/articles/latest-thoughts/investing-success/time-in-the-markets

assessments of the quality of the fund management process and do not just focus on past performance, as with other ratings.

The ratings are based on five pillars:

1. *Process:* What is the fund's strategy and does management have a competitive advantage enabling it to execute the process well and consistently over time?

2. *Performance:* Is the fund's performance pattern logical given its process? Has the fund earned its keep with strong risk-adjusted returns over relevant time periods?

3. *People:* What is Morningstar's assessment of the manager's talent, tenure, and resources?

4. *Parent:* What priorities prevail at the firm? Stewardship or salesmanship?

5. *Price:* Is the fund a good value proposition compared with similar funds sold through similar channels?[38]

The best funds are awarded a Gold, Silver or Bronze rating. However few achieve ratings and they are therefore highly prestigious. Although most funds are unrated Morningstar allocate a Neutral and Negative rating to some funds. The definitions can be found on their website.

I don't only pick funds with good Morningstar Analyst ratings i.e. Gold, Silver or Bronze even though they are prestigious and rarely awarded. Often I discover funds that are cracking investments which have delivered consistently good performance over many years but which have not been recognised by Morningstar Analyst for whatever reason. The Axa Global Distribution is one such fund. It is an IA Mixed Investment (20-60% shares) with a unique asset allocation investing in global equities and index linked bonds.

At the date of writing on 11/4/19 data from Trustnet show it has

---

[38] http://www.morningstar.com/InvGlossary/morningstar-analyst-rating-for-funds.aspx

trounced the sector average over one, three, five and 10 years. For example over the last five years it returned 47.2% compared to the sector average of 25.2%. Some of my clients have held the fund for many years and have been richly rewarded.

The unique asset mix of the Axa Distribution fund range, including an ethical fund, has been in place since the 1980s and it has generally delivered strong absolute and relative returns through many market cycles. It is an example of a fund that clearly has a set, repeatable and successful investment strategy.

Then there is the art bit. When choosing investments I frequently buy fund managers rather than funds, which is why I like to listen to them at webinars and seminars and read their missives as much as possible. If they clearly understand their markets, have compelling investment philosophies and strategies, can articulate their thinking well and they can enthuse me I am likely to recommend their funds for suitable clients.

I can't always put my finger on what it is that attracts me to certain fund managers but it adds up at times to what seems like a gut instinct. They are often contrarians managing funds with high active share. They don't follow the crowd although the crowd might follow them once they have been successful for long enough.

The best fund managers stand out from the crowd. Usually there will be times when I really like what I hear. Something clicks. It's a kind of love at first sight, a Eureka moment. It is hard to pin down but the investment strategy chimes with my own convictions. I remember sometime around 2010 listening to Jeremy Gleeson manager of the Axa Framlington Global Technology fund and feeling this is a guy who really understands his market. I also liked the fact there was greater exposure to smaller companies than most technology funds. I concluded this was a fund I would be happy to recommend to my clients, assuming technology was a suitable investment for them.

I am glad I did. My clients have done incredibly well with the Axa Framlington Global Technology fund. Over five years the fund was up 195% (Data from Trustnet, 11/4/19) compared to the sector average of 129.4%. For me Jeremy Gleeson has been a star fund manager for the last

5-10 years. Moreover I can identify other such funds.

I normally stick with those I consider excellent fund managers for the long term. Some are value investors that have not always outperformed their peers but I am prepared to give them time with an expectation of good long term performance. Others have been remarkably consistent performers and have served my clients very well.

Of course star fund managers lose their touch or I occasionally recommend duff funds to clients. No-one is perfect and no adviser will get their fund selection right all the time. The key point though is to spot these early enough and be willing to ditch funds that have significantly underperformed and don't have reasonable prospects for improvement.

As an example during reviews in 2018 I identified a variety of poor multi-asset, absolute targeted return and other cautious risk funds. I recommended they were replaced as they failed to deliver returns in excess of inflation over three years. The benchmark for inflation I used was the retail prices index. This was the minimum return I could deem acceptable, on the basis that a failure to match RPI would mean clients lost money in real terms.

In some cases I will stick with struggling funds or fund managers on the principle that form is temporary but class is permanent and that pretty well all good managers go through difficult periods. This may be because their investment style is out of favour or even the best make occasional wrong calls on asset allocation and stock selection.

On occasions I will recommend funds that may have only delivered average returns or have underperformed their peers but where the asset allocation is unique and therefore the fund provides diversification benefits. A fund that fits this category is the Investec Cautious Managed fund, run by Alastair Mundy. Like the Axa Global Distribution fund it is located in the IA Mixed Investments (20-60% shares) sector but the two funds have completely different asset allocations and investment strategies.

Mundy is a contrarian value investor who certainly backs his convictions. For a long time he has held investments in Norwegian government bonds and gold. At the time of writing in April 2019 the fund has underperformed its IA sector average over one, three and five years. Despite this the very long term returns have been excellent. Investec stated annualised returns of 6.9% have been achieved since launch in 1993 to 31/3/19 with about half the volatility of UK equities.

Looking at the asset allocation at the end of February 2019 the fund held 24.9% in UK equities and 20.5% in cash and short dated government bonds. The latter is a very defensive position but permits tactical investment from cash or when bonds mature. UK equities were lowly valued, in large part due to Brexit uncertainty. Returns from gold have been dull in recent years but rallied in the second half of 2018 and into 2019. Given this and the fund's value investment style the underperformance in recent years is not unexpected. However I am not too worried about this as the fund has beaten RPI over three years with a return of 15.4% [39].

The Investec Cautious Managed[40] is a fund I am happy to include in client portfolios for the long term. It is defensively managed and it is offers significant diversity from most other multi-asset funds. Not every fund I recommend has to deliver shoot the lights out performance. Steady Eddies with good long term figures are welcome additions to my portfolios.

Finally I want to address the issue of consistency of performance. John Husselbee is head of multi-asset at Liontrust and a very experienced investor. He argues that consistency of performance is nigh on impossible over the longish term. In other words funds that outperform over a set time frame rarely continue to do so over subsequent periods. Moreover he cites one study by Morningstar which found few top quartile funds over 10 years actually posted three consecutive years of top quartile outperformance during this period. The lack of consistency would appear to add weight to investing in passives. However Husselbee explains this is not necessarily so as the study showed that trackers were less likely to post three consecutive top quartile returns

---

[39] Trustnet (12/4/19).

[40] In April 2020 Mundy stood down from his fund manager role due to illness. I wish him well. Investec is now branded Ninety One

than actively managed funds!

Husselbee rightly concludes whilst consistency of performance is virtually impossible, consistency of the fund management process is an absolute necessity and this is what he looks for in the funds he selects for his multi-manager portfolios. The majority of funds he picks are managed by contrarians who back their convictions. This approach chimes with me.

Once you have backed your chosen fund managers he suggests the need for patience, accepting periods of underperformance will occur. Husselbee eschews trying to time the market with tactical investment strategies, instead he advocates the old adage, *it is time in the market that counts*.

Once I have made my fund selection I supply my clients with fund fact sheets, Key Investor Information Documents (KIIDs) and an investment proposals document. I have attached an example as an appendix at the end of the chapter. It summarises the key details of my recommended funds including investment costs and a brief description. In some cases more information about selected funds is included in the accompanying letter.

Use of discretionary fund managers (DFMs)

There is an increasing trend for advisers to outsource investment management of client portfolios to DFMs. In large part this is due to the complexity and costs of doing it in house. It is a variation of the use of centralised investment propositions (CIPs) which minimises work for the adviser. In these circumstances it is the DFM that runs the CIP not the adviser.

There is an argument that outsourcing investment permits advisers to concentrate on financial planning, their prime skill set. I can see there is a distinction between investment management and financial planning but for advisers to withdraw from provision of investment advice is a concern for me.

Clearly outsourcing investment management has its benefits especially for small firms with limited research capabilities or ability to monitor portfolios regularly. This is especially true as most advisers do not have discretionary powers and cannot transact investment purchases and sales without giving advice and obtaining the consent of the client.

There is no doubt client portfolios get much more attention from a DFM than they would from many IFAs operating on an advisory basis. I include myself here. On the other hand I am not sure it really matters bearing in mind that our clients are long term investors. Buying and holding equities for the long term is a powerful and successful investment strategy especially if combined with regular reviews, a subject covered below. In my view advisers should not be micro-managing portfolios with day to day tactical investment and short term trading.

The other issue I have with the use of DFMs is the double charging. The DFM may charge 1% p.a. or more plus VAT for the investment management. In addition the adviser may take an additional fee of 0.5% to 0.75% p.a. As noted in Chapter 4 percentage fees are expensive for large portfolios. Given the adviser's role is secondary, liaising with the DFM and monitoring what is going on. It is not much of a work load and I am not sure the whole package is good value for the client. It also raises the question why should the client involve the adviser at all? What value do they bring to the table? Couldn't they be removed from the arrangement with its attendant cost savings?

I very rarely use DFMs. Where I do it is to run specialist portfolios such as AIM (Alternative Investment Market) shares which I neither have the training, skills or authority to deal in. These investments are excellent for inheritance tax (IHT) planning as many AIM stocks qualify for Business Relief. This provides tax exemption after two years.

I don't use DFMs to manage portfolios of collective investments. That is what I do. My use of DFMs is complementary and it enables me to access specialist investment advice that I cannot provide.

Reviews

Reviews are of course essential for efficient portfolio management and to ensure investments are still suitable for clients. So what might have changed since the investments were first set up or since the last review? Firstly the asset allocation may no longer be suitable for current stock market conditions. Alternatively the client's circumstances, especially their risk profile may have changed.

Even if there are no such changes the portfolio will naturally drift up the risk scale if adventurous risk equity funds outperform. This is of course expected in the medium to long term. The relative size of such investments will increase and rebalancing may be required. If this sort of portfolio drift doesn't occur you have another problem with your investment strategy, one that is arguably more serious. Your clients have been exposed to unnecessary risk by investment in adventurous funds with no compensation from enhanced capital growth that was expected.

Secondly reviews are also important to crystallise profits, add investments in new sectors with compelling fundamentals and valuations or to identify dog funds and laggards. Retaining failing funds for too long will be a drag on portfolio returns especially if they are sizeable holdings.

Portfolios are dynamic and are constantly changing and need frequent if not constant monitoring. The latter is of course beyond the capabilities of small firms without discretionary permissions. Most advisers simply lack the resources to review investments monthly let alone weekly or daily. For most advisers reviews will need to be agreed with their clients at regular intervals – perhaps yearly or bi-annually. Mine are normally undertaken annually with occasional bi-annual or *ad hoc* reviews.

Investment reviews and portfolio management are activities that are akin to gardening. Left to itself a garden gets out of shape, slowly but surely. It becomes untidy and weeds grow. The grass becomes too long and the edges of the lawn ragged. On a day to day level you don't see much change but over a period of time the changes can be dramatic. A garden needs maintenance and work to restore its balance and beauty. It is similar with portfolio management.

At the start of an investment review I obtain an update on the client's circumstances, including any changes to their risk profile or requirement for income. However I take the view, one that may be unpopular with the regulator and the compliance industry, that reviews are not just about meeting clients' financial objectives and needs. Often clients tell me nothing has changed. Consequently investment reviews can be driven solely by a long term requirement for efficient portfolio management and fund changes can therefore be warranted for investment purposes only.

For example consider a client who has a UK equity fund that has performed poorly. After investigation I may recommend a switch to an alternative UK equity fund if I conclude it is appropriate to maintain the existing asset allocation. If the client's personal circumstances have not changed then the fund switch is undertaken solely for investment purposes i.e. to get shot of a bad fund. Investment change does not have to be driven by or justified because the client's financial needs or objectives have changed. That's too simplistic.

The next step in the review is to provide a client with an updated investment valuation statement. Over the years I have created and maintained spreadsheets with details of all of a client's investments. It shows their holdings on all platforms. Of course clients get individual statements direct from the providers but the values may be weeks out of date by the time they land on their mat. Mine are hot off the press, usually same day valuations or just a few days old.

Aside from the fact that my valuation statements include investments held with multiple platforms and providers they are different in other ways. Firstly I show the amounts originally invested into each fund and its profit or loss figure. Not all platforms I use do this, notably Fidelity and Alliance Trust Savings. AJ Bell Investcentre do, but they don't show the date of the original investment and they adjust the book cost for earlier disposals.

I think the start dates are important as it puts the profit and loss figures into context. A fund that is down 10% over one year is less of a concern that one that is 10% off over five or 10 years. Conversely a fund that is up 10% over one year will get a pat on the back but one that is up 10% over five years is likely to raise concerns that investment returns have been too dull and have failed to match inflation.

Secondly my investment valuation statements include a notes column and separate comments at the bottom. The notes column relates typically to an investment account or a specific fund. For example it might show if income is being paid out from the account or a specific fund, what one-off disposals have been made or the origin of a fund, e.g. it was switched from XYZ on such and such date or it was acquired as a result of a bed and ISA deal. The notes at the bottom are general clarifications for example to explain what abbreviations such as OEIC, Inc or Acc mean or to highlight that profit figures exclude regular income paid out but include one-off amounts switched out of or sold to cash.

In a covering letter to accompany the valuation statement I normally compare the portfolio value with the previous statement and explain why it has gone up or down. It is important to remind a client that they may have sold £10,000 of investments to fund a holiday or new car six months' ago and this has contributed to a drop in overall portfolio value. I will also remind them if natural income has been paid out or they have a regular withdrawal plan set up. This is important so that clients appreciate the value attributable to their portfolio is more than just capital returns.

Then I explain how stock markets have fared over the reporting period and how this has affected their portfolio, highlighting particular sectors or funds that might have done particularly well or bad.

The next stage is to identify if profit-taking and risk reduction is required, if the asset allocation needs adjusting or rebalancing or if specific funds need replacing.

In deciding whether a fund should be sold I take into account a number of factors.

1. Past performance

This is about the numbers. Past performance tells us what a fund delivered in cash or percentage terms. These are absolute returns. However it is also important to see how a fund has fared compared to its peers. These are relative returns.

Whilst of course, *"past performance is not necessarily a guide to future returns,"* it can't be ignored. Most marketing for funds in adverts and client facing documents normally highlight strong investment returns. Whilst there are regulations in place to ensure such marketing is fair and not misleading, the regulators are conflicted in my view on this issue. On one hand they think past performance is a poor indicator of the future and shouldn't be relied on. On the other they permit past performance to be marketed which is an implicit acceptance that it has value. You can't have it both ways in my view.

The problem here lies in the interpretation of the wording. *"Not necessarily,"* may mean it might or might not, leaving readers to make a judgement call on how likely is the might and how probable is the might not! By sitting on the fence and trying to be all things to all men the FCA leave investors confused as to what the reality is and precisely what side they are coming down on. Arguably it is lazy regulation. Moreover the wording of past performance risk warnings differs from provider to provider, adding to the complexity and confusion. Here are some examples from three funds:

> *"Past performance should not be taken as a guide to the future."* Investec Cautious Managed.
>
> *"Past performance is not necessarily a guide to future performance."* Fundsmith Equity.
>
> *"Past performance is not a reliable indicator of future results."* Schroder European Recovery.

There are subtle variations of wording and meaning in the caveats here. The Investec risk warning is the strongest. The message is don't use past performance as a guide. Discount it completely. It begs the question then, why do they quote any performance data at all! The other two risk warnings don't shut the door to past performance data having value but warn against it with differing strengths of feeling. The Fundsmith Equity is most benign. It is neutral - it may be a guide, it may not be. It is kind of 50:50. The Schroder one is more negative. Like lending money to an unreliable person where past experience tells you there is a good chance he or she won't repay you, so on the balance of outcomes you can't rely on past performance.

My view is that past performance can be a useful indicator of future returns but it is a not guaranteed indicator. Why do I say this? To say future returns are not guaranteed based on the past needs no explanation for obvious reasons. Very little in life is guaranteed except death and taxes. Unless you have a crystal ball you cannot predict the future with certainty. However if a fund has delivered outstanding returns consistently over five years, I don't think it is unreasonable to ask, why would you not expect this outperformance to continue in the future?

If the fund has been managed with clear, compelling and consistent investment management processes and these are still in place there is good reason to assume the outperformance will carry on. This assumes the lead fund manager and team is still in situ and there is no threat to the fund's investment style falling out of favour.

This is a different way of looking at past performance which has been too readily discounted.

In other cases you can look at a fund and find very good reasons why the outperformance is unlikely to continue, in which case past performance should be discounted. A star fund manager or key team members have left, the fund is no longer being managed according to its core principles or the fund has a strong style bias which is no longer in favour.

In assessing past performance I look at one, three and five year returns and judge performance of a fund to be good or excellent if:

a) In absolute or cash terms the net returns over three and five years have exceeded cash and inflation as measured by RPI and/or

b) In relative or comparative terms the fund has outperformed its peers in the Investment Association (IA) sector it is located in. The outperformance can be considered in a variety of ways, for example a top ranking in a sector, first quartile returns over one, three and five years or beating the sector average over all these periods. The latter is a less challenging benchmark.

It needs to be remembered that for some IA sectors relative performance is absolutely meaningless. For example the IA Specialist sector may include funds that invest in India, global financials, commodities, Latin America and bonds. Similarly funds in the IA Volatility Managed and Targeted Absolute Return sectors are so varied in their asset allocations, target returns and risk profiles to make comparisons of performance unhelpful or downright dangerous.

It should also be noted that one, three and five year performance data has its limitations because the returns are cumulative. In other words the one and three year figures are included in the five year totals. Cumulative figures don't tell you what happened over that five year period i.e. about the consistency of returns and how much volatility there was. A top fund may have had one or two cracking years but three or four mediocre or poor years. Cumulative returns can mask these. In contrast discrete year performance for example over separate calendar years tells you more about the consistency of returns.

So to conclude this sub-section where can you find fund performance data? There are many sources. Each adviser will have their favourites. Trustnet is a one good free to use website. I also subscribe to Investment Week, receiving a digital copy although the figures are a couple of weeks out of date by the time it hits my inbox.

2. Understanding past performance

I don't always recommend ditching poor performing funds. After all future returns may be different. The past performance caveat should be used with consistency and therefore applies equally to the bad funds as well as the good. We shouldn't assume a fund firing blanks currently won't load up with live bullets in the future.

It is important to understand why a fund has had delivered poor returns and whether there is a potential for a turnaround. To do this I find it helpful to talk to the fund management group to understand what is going on under the bonnet. In my experience most of the broker reps I deal with have very good knowledge of their funds, they will own up to mistakes in fund management and if they don't know the answer to a question they have access to the fund manager or their team. Normally the answers I get back are comprehensive and fair despite the temptation to put gloss on to make a poor fund look better than it is in reality.

What I am looking for is evidence that the fund managers are aware of the problems, they are not making excuses or refusing to accept responsibility, they are addressing the issues so I can reasonably expect a turnaround in the fund's performance. Signs of early improvement may be found in short term performance data over three or six months but it may take longer.

3. Fund ratings

If a fund has lost its Morningstar Analyst rating or it has been downgraded that would be a concern and it will be a factor in my decision whether to recommend a client retains a poor performing fund. It suggests the quality of the fund management processes has deteriorated.

4. Fund management changes

A fund that has previously performed well has done so for a reason. I think luck is too simplistic an assumption but it is essentially what the passive zealots would have you believe. If the fundamentals of the fund management philosophy, processes and structures haven't changed that gives me confidence to continue to back the fund.

5. Client needs

Clearly if a client's circumstances and financial needs have changed a fund may no longer be suitable even it is highly rated with a strong performance record. That said I very rarely ditch these although I might trim the size of the holding by partial switches to other funds.

A client may require more income from their investments or their risk profile may have changed or there is a need for portfolio risk reduction as the client approaches retirement. This is not necessarily a given as I explain in Chapter 13.

In conclusion when I review a client's portfolio I identify which funds to retain, usually the majority and which to switch out of. For the latter I then present my recommendations for replacement funds. I typically deliver my advice in the form of a spreadsheet which details the key data about each fund. An example is shown at the end of the chapter. You will see it includes full MIFID II fund charge disclosures including estimated fund transaction costs and a risk profile which is my own assessment. As stated the notes column gives some information about the nature of the fund, for example if it has a targeted return, performance information and why I have recommended it. The spreadsheet is accompanied by fund fact sheets and KIIDs.

Once the client has agreed to the investments fund switch instructions are placed and a final suitability letter is sent. However the latter is principally a summary of advice that has previously been provided in writing. At each stage there is an e-mail or letter with commentary on the portfolio, market conditions, individual fund reviews and recommended replacement investments.

Finally contract notes are checked and the changes to the portfolio are updated on the client's investment valuation statement.

Ethical investment

Many of my clients want ethical investment, not necessarily for all their holdings but for some. You could argue that a mixed approach is somewhat hypocritical. If your principles and conscience dictate avoiding investment in companies with business activities you disapprove of surely you should invest only in ethical or environmental funds. However there is a balance to be struck here between a pragmatic and purist approach. There are risks of reduced returns from investing solely in ethical investments and I can understand why people may wish to make a contribution here without going the whole hog. After all their investments are for their financial benefit not just for the environment and good causes.

Moreover adopting a purist approach may necessitate a change to bank accounts, insurance policies, pension plans and low risk with profits investments. It would be highly disruptive, expensive and could distort a portfolio and make it unsuitably high risk that no longer meets the investor's needs. This is because ethical funds are generally not suited to low risk investment. Firstly the fund manager has a restricted investment universe to select stocks and secondly ethical funds tend to hold more in smaller companies than other funds.

Originally ethical investment focussed on negative screening and exclusions, avoiding for example investment in arms producers, tobacco manufacturers, pornography and trade with oppressive regimes. This is traditional "dark green" ethical investment.

The other more modern approach is the inclusion of socially responsible investments (SRI) in a portfolio, for example environmental funds or where fund managers select companies based on positive criteria, those that are best in class or where the fund managers use engagement with companies to improve social responsibility. This is the concept of the modern "light green" ethical investment. More recently environmental, social and governance (ESG) fund management has become the buzz phrase.

I wonder if ESG is just a repackaging of SRI, but looser in its ethical definition to be more inclusive. I might be wrong but it is interesting a number of companies notably L&G Investment Management and Vanguard have come in for criticism recently for so-called "greenwashing." A study by wealth manager SCM Direct, of Gina Miller fame found for example the L&G Future World ESG UK Index fund contained tobacco, gaming and defence stocks. This is shocking. There is not much that I agree with Gina Miller but here we are on the same page.

I have clients in both camps - those who want ethical investment and those that don't. However those requiring a total dark green ethical screen for all of their portfolio holdings are generally in the minority.

It is essential for advisers in their fact finding processes not only to ask whether clients want ethical investment but to find out what issues they are especially concerned about. Most of my clients generally will cite avoiding investment in arms producers, tobacco, oppressive regimes or pornography, the so called sin stocks. They don't normally have single issue concerns. However one of my best clients has a particular focus on avoiding animal testing and over the years it has been a challenge to find suitable funds for her. Surprisingly few funds labelled as ethical avoid animal testing completely. Many invest in companies that test on animals for human medicine but avoid those that test for cosmetics. Only traditional dark green funds with strict negative screens are acceptable for my client as they operate a blanket ban on all companies testing on animals.

The problem I have faced from an investment perspective is that the universe of suitable funds is very small given few funds labelled as ethical or socially responsible have a strict negative screen on all animal testing. It has therefore been difficult to avoid concentration of investment into a few qualifying funds resulting in a lack of portfolio diversity and heightened risk. This is especially an issue as my client has a very large investment and pension portfolio.

To address this problem over the years I have used two strategies. The first is a concept that I call ethically neutral investment. Here I identify funds that invest in specialised sector specific funds which do not have an ethical label but by definition avoid animal testing. Examples are property funds, a Robotics fund, physical gold and silver Exchange Traded Commodities (ETCs), financials and a water fund.

This is not a perfect solution because there is always the potential for animal testing to creep in by the back door. Consider a property fund. Typically the underlying properties are commercial premises - offices, factories or warehouses. An office could be let to a company that is directly involved in animal testing or a company occupying a property may manufacture equipment or supply parts used in animal testing. Auditing the business activities of all parties down the supply chain becomes nigh on impossible and advisers and investors will have to draw the line somewhere. Absolutely purity of investment cannot be achieved.

Similarly a financial fund invests in banks, insurers or asset manager. Who knows if one of the banks lends money to an animal testing company or an insurer covers their business? The point is that compromise is invariably required and investors may have to accept some conflicts of interest. Another example is ethical funds that exclude tobacco manufacturers. These funds however may invest in supermarkets which sell cigarettes. The stated ethical criteria will normally say something to the effect that a company with sales of less than 10% from tobacco can be included in the fund.

The second strategy for my client was to outsource parts of her portfolio to discretionary fund managers (DFMs) to invest directly in stocks and shares with a screen for animal testing. My client has two such portfolios. One is an AIM share portfolio which also serves a purpose of reducing my client's inheritance tax liability using Business Relief (previously Business Property Relief). The second is a more traditional managed portfolio of stocks and shares investing mainly in UK larger companies.

One issue that may not be clear to ethical investors is that they do not invest money into the underlying companies that their funds hold. They merely buy units or shares in those funds. The manager then uses investors' money to purchase shares of companies from a third party market-maker, not usually from the companies direct. These shares are usually in existence already i.e. they are second-hand. Thus an investor does not invest money into the company itself. An exception is a rights issue, where a company issues new shares to raise cash.

However it is clear that an investor benefits from companies' business activities and profits, in the form of dividends received by the fund and the appreciation of the share price.

This distinction may not matter to clients but some may be happier to understand that none of their money goes direct to companies whose business activities they disapprove of.

Conclusion

Giving good investment advice should be highly rewarding for both advisers and their clients. When your clients see their capital grow it is a highly visible and tangible benefit. It is also very satisfying for advisers to see their investment choices work well. Happy clients may recommend you to their friends and family.

That said advisers who manage their clients' money which runs into hundreds of thousands of pounds or more if you are lucky, have a huge responsibility to undertake due diligence, make good investment decisions and manage client expectations especially if markets are tumbling.

To be a competent and successful investment adviser you face various important choices on how to do it. You will need to consider a number of key issues. Do you think active fund management is best or you going to stick to passives? Which is better, bespoke tailored portfolios or centralised investment propositions? Are you going to outsource to a DFM or keep investment advice in house? Will your investment advice be restricted or independent, advising on the full range of retail investment products? How are you going to charge for your advice - percentage fees or an hourly charge?

For aspiring financial advisers you will need to develop convictions on these key choices. So listen to the arguments, consider the pros and cons, weigh it all up in your head and then follow your heart.

Appendix – Investment proposals document 12/11/19

Fund	IA/AIC Sector	Risk Profile	Investment	OCF	TC	TCO	Notes
Artemis Corporate Bond	Sterling Corporate Bond	Cautious	£15,000	0.40%	-	-	New fund due to be launched soon. Managed by an excellent and experienced fund manager, Stephen Snowden. The fund will be able to invest nimbly and have high levels of liquidity
Architas Multi-Asset Blended Intermediate	Volatility Managed	Cautious	£10,000	1.06%	0.10%	1.16%	Fund of funds which blends passive and active investments. Steady returns. Over three years it returned 17.3%.
ASI MyFolio Market III Platform	Volatility Managed	Cautious	£15,000	0.36%	0.02%	0.38%	A multi-asset fund of funds investing mainly in index trackers. Adds diversity to portfolio as most funds are actively managed. Excellent record of returns over three and five years
Capital Gearing Investment Trust	Flexible	Cautious	£11,000	0.90%	0.10%	1.00%	Mixed asset investment trust with large weighting in index linked bonds and equities. 6.5% annual return in last five years to 31/10/19
Dodge & Cox Worldwide Global Bond	Global Bond	Cautious	£15,000	0.49%	0.09%	0.58%	Global bond fund with good track record of returns and low volatility. Fund has a creditable Silver rating from Morningstar Analyst. Includes some emerging market debt which adds diversity
Royal London Sustainable Managed Growth Trust	Mixed Investments (0-35%) Shares	Cautious	£15,000	0.68%	0.06%	0.74%	Mixed bond and equity fund investing mainly in the UK. Low volatility and strong one, three and five year returns which are well above inflation. Managed with socially responsible criteria, Bronze rated by Morningstar Analyst
Time Commercial Long Income (A Gross Acc) PAIF	UK Direct Property	Very Cautious	£15,000	1.34%	-	1.34%	Invests in long commercial leases and ground rents. Very low level of volatility and excellent returns. A good portfolio diversifier. See note at bottom and accompanying letter. Initial charge is 1% not 3% as per the KIID. The latter is a maximum
Unicorn UK Income	UK Equity Income	Balanced	£10,000	0.81%	-0.11%	0.70%	Replacement for ASI Equity Income Unconstrained fund. UK equity income fund, maintains exposure to undervalued sector with strong recovery potential. Excellent record of returns
Vanguard LifeStrategy 20% Equity	Mixed Investments (0-35%) Shares	Cautious	£15,000	0.22%	0.05%	0.27%	Global equity and bond fund investing in in house Vanguard index tracker funds. Good asset allocation and strong returns low fund charges. Gold rated by Morningstar Analyst
			£121,000.00				

Notes

- A PAIF is a Property Authorised Investment fund, a tax efficient structure.

- The IA is the Investment Association which group funds with similar investment strategies or markets, permitting meaningful comparisons of performance.

- The AIC is the Association of Investment Companies for investment trust, and is equivalent to the IA.

- The OCF is the ongoing fund charge, which includes the annual management charge and additional fund expenses. These include auditor fees and custodian charges. OCFs may change in the future.

- The TC is the transaction costs and is an estimate for the next 12 months. The -0.11% figure for the Unicorn UK Income is absurd but a reporting requirement.

- The TCO is the estimated total cost of ownership. It is the OCF+TC.

- Transaction cost reporting does not apply to direct property funds. Consequently the OCF does not include the costs of property purchases, legal fees and stamp duty.

- Overall charges are therefore high but returns are net of all costs (see letter).

- Ratings are from Morningstar Analyst which assess the quality of fund management.

- Risk ratings are my own assessments and these may vary from those ascribed by the fund managers or ratings shown in the KIIDs.

- Cautious risk funds do not guarantee to protect 100% of capital in all market conditions. They will limit downside volatility compared to pure equity funds although in some circumstances values may rise when markets are falling.

- Reference to past performance is typically over the last five years and data is either from fund fact sheets or Trustnet (11/11/19).

12. Principles of protection advice

Financial protection can be divided into two main categories:

1. Life assurance

2. Income protection

Critical illness insurance can fit into either of these categories. It can be combined with life assurance cover or sit alongside and complement income protection as I will explain below.

Life assurance

Life assurance is for the benefit of others. Last time I checked you can't take money with you when you die. Usually life assurance is to provide financial protection for your dependents principally to replace your lost income. It is also used to provide cover for non-working spouses or partners to cover child care and household costs that would arise from their death.

Life assurance is also commonly used to pay off a mortgage or other loans and can be used to cover an inheritance tax liability (IHT) for older clients.

One of the key tasks of a financial adviser is to calculate a suitable level of life assurance for your clients. This can be a complex exercise for income replacement purposes although it is easily determined to cover an IHT liability or mortgage.

1. Mortgage protection

A mortgage protection policy is a type of decreasing term assurance that fits hand in glove with a repayment mortgage. The amount of life cover tracks the declining capital balance of the mortgage i.e. what is still owing to the lender at any point in time. This declines slowly at first as most of the monthly mortgage payments goes to paying interest. As time progresses the balance shifts towards paying off capital and in the latter years the outstanding mortgage balance declines rapidly to zero.

Providing the interest rate on the mortgage does not exceed the policy interest rate the pay out from a mortgage protection policy is guaranteed to be at least equal to the mortgage balance. Policy interest rates are typically 5% to 7% p.a. well in excess of current mortgage rates so there is plenty of leg room if mortgage interest rates go up.

Naturally a financial adviser may need to review clients' mortgage life cover if additional borrowing is taken out, the term of the mortgage is extended or they move house and take on a different mortgage. Modern life assurance policies normally permit increases to the sum assured within certain limits and without a need to provide additional medical information, following certain events such as marriage, having a child or increasing a mortgage. This is called guaranteed insurability. The terms and conditions vary with insurer.

2. Family protection – factors to consider

Calculating the right amount of life cover for family protection purposes is more difficult. One important issue is deciding how long cover should last. The principle is to ensure the life assurance benefit will provide for a breadwinner's family until they are no longer financially dependent. This might be until the youngest child reaches age 18, or 21 if they go to university and if a stay at home partner or spouse will be able to find work after the kids have flown the nest. This of course may not be possible if the surviving partner no longer has the skills for the job market or the health for work and this risk may need to be taken into account in deciding when cover should end.

The interaction with work related life assurance, death in service pensions and state benefits will also need to be taken in account in determining the correct amount of life cover. For example an employer may provide up to four times an employee's salary in life assurance. This is where good fact finding and holistic financial planning comes in play.

Context is vitally important here because financial planning is rarely undertaken in isolation, whether it is investment management or protection advice. There are invariably existing financial elements in place or benefits that can be claimed that have to be assessed alongside the new arrangements you as an adviser recommend are put in place.

Moreover it is not just enough to understand the facts. An assessment of the significance of the facts and risks needs to be made. For example the fact that your client's employer provides £100,000 of life cover to him or her as an employee on a £25,000 p.a. salary does not automatically mean it should be taken into account when assessing a suitable level of additional family protection. The life cover will be lost if your client loses their job. A new employer may not be so generous and what if your client decides to become self-employed?

In contrast a personal life assurance policy is portable and permanent, at least until the end of the term of the contract - assuming premiums are maintained.

In assessing a client's attitude to risk, I explained in Chapter 5 that I consider both investment and insurance risk. A client with a low risk attitude to insurance may conclude they do not wish to chance the loss of their employer's life assurance and therefore may decide to discount it. Someone who has a high risk attitude to insurance, looking for low cost cover might prefer to take employer's cover into account.

3. Lump sum cover v family income benefit

When considering life assurance products for family protection I suspect family income benefit policies are underused by advisers. I reckon they have largely been eschewed in favour of lump sum life cover such as level term assurance or whole of life. Clearly a six figure life assurance benefits looks highly attractive to clients especially for very small premiums and for advisers it is an easy sale.

In some ways there is a parallel here with defined benefit pension transfer values, which have reached eye watering amounts in recent years with falling gilt yields. In both case clients can be seduced by a pound sign with lots of numbers after them.

In the case of pension transfers unwary investors can be seduced by the value of their pension and the accessibility that flexi-access drawdown (FAD) offers. They don't necessarily stop and work out how much income that lump sum transfer value can secure when invested. Neither may they query whether the transfer value will be sufficient to ensure their income is inflation proofed and sustainable in the long term. If they did they might discover the reality that they can't secure from FAD the same level of inflation proofed and secure income their defined benefit pension provides.

The problem with level term or whole of life assurance is working out how to convert this big fat lump sum into income. Firstly you have to assume a rate of investment return taking into account any tax on the investment. Then you have to build in index linking to account for inflation. Finally you have to decide whether the capital will be drawn on to fund the required post death income or if the survivor wants just to live off the interest or dividends the capital can generate.

If capital is gradually withdrawn, at the end of the dependency term the lump sum may be fully depleted. This is fine; the life cover has done its job, providing a replacement income over the period of dependency. If however your clients want the capital itself to be left untouched it increases the amount of life cover that is needed and hence the premiums.

On the first point the rate of investment returns you assume will depend on whether the lump sum is kept in cash or is invested. Cash is highly unattractive given current interest rates are so low but at least there is no investment risk or a need for ongoing investment advice. However given the pay-out will be used over a long period of time the case for investing the lump sum is strong. This means there is a need for advice and ongoing reviews which will incur adviser fees.

To determine the correct lump sum life assurance that is required I use a bespoke spreadsheet life assurance calculator. An example is at the end of the chapter. The document shows that in order to provide £2,500 p.m. gross interest before tax over fifteen years, a lump sum of £400,000 earning 1.5% p.a. would be required. It is assumed here that the money is kept in cash. You will see the capital is fully used up at the end.

I can tinker with the figures by starting with the income required and then calculating the level of life cover needed or taking the lump sum that is available and then working out what income it can generate. Naturally the term can be varied. For clients with young families these are typically 15-20 years depending on the ages of their kids.

A variation is to add indexation of income, let us say by 2% p.a. The spreadsheet calculator indexes it monthly. If we do this the capital is depleted after month 156. To ensure it lasts for the full 15 years the life cover needed increases from £400,000 to £462,000. You can have a lot of fun playing around with the figures and amending the assumptions although there is a certain amount of trial and error involved in determining the right level of life assurance.

When discussing the correct level of life cover for a breadwinner, if the dependent partner and potential beneficiary of a large lump sum pay out from a term assurance or whole of life policy is an adventurous risk investor, if and when the time comes he or she may prefer to consider investment rather than a cash savings account to generate a higher level of income. If so the assumed investment return in my life assurance calculator can be set at a higher rate, for example 4% p.a. rather than the 1.5% p.a. that I assumed for cash in the two examples above. This will result in a lower level of life assurance that will be needed.

It should be clear there are complexities and assumptions when using lump sum life assurance to provide an income which is why the use of family income benefit (FIB) plans is so much easier. When a claim is admitted the policy pays out a set level of income on a monthly basis to the end of the policy term. This is tax free and no investment advice is required.

In the scenario above having decided that your clients need £2,500 p.m. on death of the breadwinner a FIB plan is set up for that sum. The level of cover can be set to be indexed prior to and during a claim to offset the effects of inflation. It is as simple as it gets. You don't have to estimate interest rates on cash or investment returns on funds to determine the level of life cover that is needed. Moreover the regular monthly income removes a temptation for the recipient to splash the cash from a huge lump sum pay out and exhaust the fund thereby putting at risk the long term income the policy was intended for. However it should be noted that the payments from a family income benefit policy can normally be commuted to a reduced lump sum so that the temptation is not entirely removed.

A FIB is a type of decreasing term assurance and like all decreasing cover plans the value of the life assurance benefit declines with time. It means for a client who dies 13 years into a 15 year term, a FIB policy for £2,500 p.m. pays out just £60,000 (£2,500 p.m. x 12 months x 2 years) whereas if death occurs one year after the start the pay-out is £420,000. I have assumed here that cover is level. In contrast a level term assurance pays out the same sum assured whether the life assured dies one day after the policy starts or one day before it ends. However a level term assurance policy is more expensive as the sum at risk for the insurer is greater compared to a decreasing term assurance except at the very start. In addition with the latter the sum assured decreases as the life assured gets older and the risk to the insurer decreases, further contributing to lower premiums.

FIB and other decreasing term plans are the lowest cost form of life cover and are excellent for people on a tight budget. You could argue that these policies represent poor value in the latter years given the sum assured has declined sharply but this misses an important point. The FIB policy has done its job. It was there to protect your client's dependents in the event of his or her death. The fact that a policy only paid out say for two years doesn't matter - it met the actual need for financial protection in years 14 and 15 when your client's family were still financially vulnerable and it would have done so earlier had the breadwinner died at a younger age.

Whilst the equivalent level term assurance would pay out £450,000 on death after 13 years, only £60,000 of this would be required to cover the last two years of financial dependency. The rest is "surplus to requirements." If this is desirable all well and good but it takes the concept of life assurance to a different arena. Matching life cover to actual financial need, to replace the loss of income is the goal of protection. With a FIB the deceased's family will be no worse off financially but they will not be better off from the breadwinner's death. In contrast a level term assurance which pays out in the latter stages of the policy provides not only for the residual short period of financial dependency but a big fat bonus on top. My view is that wealth creation should not be a goal of life assurance which is one reason I like FIB plans. If your clients however prefer level term assurance that is their choice. They will of course pay more in premiums.

Naturally family income benefit plans are not suitable for paying off a mortgage. True the monthly income would permit mortgage payments to be maintained but that is not the point. Your clients will almost certainly want to get shot of the debt itself and therefore a policy that pays a lump sum on death, for example a decreasing term assurance is essential.

4. Life assurance & critical illness insurance

Life assurance can be combined with critical illness insurance and there is a strong case to include the latter given the risk of people aged under age 65 dying is much less than them having a serious illness. The problem with having life cover only is that your clients insure themselves against the least likely risk. That said critical illness insurance is much more expensive than life cover and a financial adviser will need to come up with a suitable protection plan that is within your client's budget and that is affordable in the longer term.

Combined life cover and critical illness insurance makes sense when covering a mortgage. Cover is best arranged on an accelerated basis. This means the sum assured is paid out on a first event basis. There is no point in having separate pay outs for critical illness and death, given the additional premiums, if the purpose of the protection is to pay off a mortgage.

Critical illness insurance is also useful for family protection purposes and for single people with no financial dependents. For the latter stand-alone critical illness insurance is available either on a lump sum or a family income benefit basis.

Income protection v critical illness insurance

At this point I want to consider the differences between income protection and critical illness insurance and the roles they play in personal protection.

In the event of long term illness or disability an employer may only pay your client for three to six months depending on their contract. Amongst the best benefits I have seen is six months' full pay, followed by six months' half pay. Employer payments will include Statutory Sick Pay (SSP) for up to 28 weeks. SSP is taxable. Thereafter Employment and Support Allowance (ESA) or Personal Independence Payments (PIP) may be your client's only sources of long term income. ESA is complex with various elements and it may be taxable. PIP is not taxable and is not means tested.

Some other state benefits may also be payable for example means tested Income Support and Housing Benefit. These benefits are beyond the scope of this book but state payments are invariably minimal, at subsistence levels, meaning long term illness results in a significant reduction in income and standard of living for many people.

Income protection is the most common type of health insurance used to provide a replacement income in the event of long term illness or disability that prevents people from working.

A fully index-linked *income protection policy*, in contrast to SSP and ESA will pay a substantial proportion of your client's earnings tax free after a short waiting period, called a deferred period. This typically may be 8, 13, 26 or 52 weeks. The policy is designed to kick in when earnings cease. Some providers permit a split plan to be set up with two deferred periods to fit in with staged employer sick pay.

The self-employed often choose shorter deferred periods for obvious reasons although depending on the nature of their work there may be a lag period between completion of a job and receipt of their fees, allowing for a longer deferred period.

Please note only the benefits from a personal income protection policy are tax free. If cover is provided by a group scheme set up by an employer the benefits are taxable under PAYE, including a liability for National Insurance contributions.

Cover can be set to rise with inflation and the pay-out continues until retirement or recovery. Payment may therefore be made for many years which contrasts with an *accident or sickness policy*, associated with mortgages and other loans where benefits are paid for a maximum of one or two years. However the latter normally include redundancy cover unlike an income protection policy. I guess with the scandal of much maligned PPI (Payment Protection Insurance), no-one sells this type of insurance any more.

The definition of disability that applies with the best income protection policies is an inability to perform your *own* stated occupation. However some people do not qualify for an own occupation definition of disability. Instead benefits are payable if you are unable to follow a *suited* or *any* occupation. For example a surgeon would normally receive a suited occupation definition as minor damage to their hands or eyes may prevent them working as a surgeon but not necessarily as a GP or a hospital doctor at an equivalent grade.

For people not in employment a house person's policy may be purchased. This recognises the fact that a stay at home partner has an indirect financial contribution to a family's finances and the loss of their ability to perform household tasks through illness or disability has a significant cost. The definition of disability that has to be satisfied before a claim is admitted is normally based on tests against certain *activities of daily living* or *life* tasks for example washing, dressing or feeding.

A final feature of income protection policies is that cover remains in place after a claim and the policyholder has recovered and returned to work. The insurer cannot cancel the contract which is why it is also called permanent health insurance (PHI), although this term is less frequently used than in the past. Perhaps if you read the permanent bit as referring to health as opposed to insurance you could be tempted to think PHI is a preventative cure for all life's afflictions!

The alternative or complementary health insurance policy is of course a critical illness contract which normally pays a single tax free cash lump sum in the event of *diagnosis* of certain critical illnesses (e.g. heart attack, cancer, stroke), disabilities (e.g. loss of sight, coma) or surgery (e.g. angioplasty, major organ transplant).

Payment of the benefit is usually irrespective of whether the condition prevents your client from working, unlike income protection. The main uses of the contract and the lump sum paid out are to enable people to pay off a mortgage, pay for home modifications, partially cover loss of earnings especially for the self-employed, utilise the cash for private medical treatment, rehabilitation costs or a long holiday. The cash can also be invested for income. As noted above critical illness insurance may also be combined with life assurance.

An important variant of critical illness insurance is a family income benefit policy where instead of a lump sum pay out, the claimant receives a fixed or escalating monthly payment up to a selected end date, normally retirement. As noted these plans have cheaper premiums than comparable lump sum plans because the insurer is not required to pay out the whole sum upfront.

In summary we can compare and contrast the two types of health insurance in broad terms, ignoring minor exemptions as follows.

INCOME PROTECTION	CRITICAL ILLNESS
Pays out if plan holder is unable to work	Pays on diagnosis of specified conditions irrespective of an ability to work or not
Benefit payable after a long deferred period typically	Benefit payable after short waiting or survival period
Benefit is capped and pay out may be restricted by any ongoing income	On admission of a claim the sum assured is paid out with no restrictions. There is no assessment against ongoing income or capital resources

Pays a monthly income which is tax free[41]	Pays a single tax free lump sum but an income option is available i.e. family income benefit
Provides a long term income replacement	Provides for shorter term capital needs or longer term income if the lump sum is invested for income or if a family income benefit option is chosen
Unsuitable for large capital expenditure	Suitable for large capital expenditure for example to pay off a mortgage, if it is a lump sum policy
Permanent. Insurance continues after a claim	Plan ceases after a claim and may mean the client is now uninsurable.

Consider now some specific medical conditions:

Heart attack, cancer - on diagnosis these are covered under a critical illness policy but not an income protection policy unless the illness keeps the insured off work longer than the *deferred* or *waiting* period, potentially up to 26 weeks.

Critical illness conditions typically have short survival periods after diagnosis of just 14 or 28 days although claims for some disabilities have longer waiting periods.

Back problem, depression - these are not usually covered under critical illness plans as back problems or depression are not deemed critical or life threatening conditions. In contrast they are the most common causes of claims under income protection plans. However one cross-over condition covered by critical illness plans is called *Total Permanent Disability* (TPD) which is the main or only condition to be related to an inability to work or to perform life or work tasks. All other conditions are payable on diagnosis of a medical condition or requirement for surgery.

A depression or back problem may be covered in some circumstances

---

[41] The pay-out is tax free from a personal plan but taxable if from an employer's group scheme.

under TPD but the condition must be *permanent* i.e. with no prospects of recovery. In contrast an income protection plan will pay out if the back problem or depression is *temporary*. That is a crucial difference. What this means is the criteria for a claim for TPD is stricter than for income protection.

Consider a serious road traffic accident in which your client is seriously injured. They may be in hospital for six months with a further six months recuperation and physiotherapy before a return to work. The disability is total but temporary. An income protection policy will pay out after the deferred period for example after 8, 13 or 26 weeks. In contrast a TPD claim will not be admitted on a critical illness policy if the doctors say the injuries are not permanent and recovery is expected.

Multiple Sclerosis - this could be covered by both policy types.

Early retirement pensions

If your client is a member of an occupational pension scheme the trustees may permit an early retirement pension to be paid. However this is only likely if the medical condition is deemed *permanent* with no prospect of recovery, similar to TPD, although each scheme will have its own qualifying rules. Similarly an early retirement pension may be available from a personal pension plan. These sources of income however may restrict the pay out from an income protection policy.

Early retirement pensions due to ill health can be paid before the normal retirement date and it may be possible to take the whole pension pot as a tax free lump sum before the age of 75. This is where you have less than a year to live and you do not exceed the pensions' lifetime allowance (£1,055,000 in 2019/20 for most people).

In summary both income protection and critical illness insurance policies have pros and cons and their complementary features mean that if fully comprehensive cover is needed both plan types can be purchased. In my view an income protection policy is most important as it only pays out in the event of a loss of income whilst a critical illness plan may pay out without a financial loss. For example consider someone who receives six months' full pay from their employer in the event of sickness or disability. If he or she suffers a heart attack but makes a full recovery and is back at work on a full time basis within six months, they have suffered no immediate direct financial loss but their critical illness plan has still paid out a capital sum.

Arguably in this example however the critical illness benefit may be useful in paying for private medical treatment, rehabilitation expenses, a long holiday before return to work or it may permit reduced working hours subsequently. In addition the illness may reduce the chances of future promotion or alternative employment so a financial loss may occur indirectly at a later stage.

In contrast in these circumstances an income protection plan would not have paid out if the policy had a deferred period of six months. This demonstrates the principle behind this plan; if there is no loss of income there is no pay out from the policy. We are returning here to the principle that the role of protection is to ensure a financial loss is mitigated, not to make your clients or their dependents better off.

Finally there is a similarity here as noted in the comparison between family income benefit on one hand and level term or whole of life assurance on the other. The latter two pay out lump sums. In the same way that family income benefit is not ideally suited to cover mortgages nor is income protection. A lump sum critical illness assurance only is able to clear the whole debt.

In selecting suitable critical illness insurance for your clients you need to take into account a variety of factors, a key one naturally are the premiums. Whilst reviewable rate policies are cheaper than those with guaranteed lifetime premiums I generally recommend the latter for certainty. If however you recommend a reviewable rate plan because your client has a limited budget you need to warn them that the premium will be reviewed from time to time and it could go up, potentially by a lot. As a result they may end up paying more in the long run.

To compare premiums on protection policies I use the Exchange system from Iress. It is cheap, functional and comprehensive.

Critical illness insurance & medical conditions

Apart from premiums another key consideration in recommending a suitable critical illness insurance policy are the medical conditions covered and their definitions. Defaqto a leading provider of financial product reviews make an important point that in recent years, critical illness insurers have been in a conditions race, adding more and more rare illnesses and disabilities to their policies despite the fact the vast majority of claims are for four conditions - heart attack, cancer, stroke and multiple sclerosis. In their assessment of the quality of critical illness insurance contracts Defaqto no longer take into account the number of conditions a policy covers but they focus on the likelihood of a pay out and the quality of the definitions.

On the point of quality Defaqto argue that ABI+ definitions add very little value. The ABI is the Association of British Insurers and they have minimum standard definitions. An ABI+ definition is better than standard but as Defaqto argue it is a crude label as it does not tell you in what way is it better. In contrast they claim that their comparison tool called *CIC Compare* uses a more sophisticated points system.

One of the problems advisers have is how to understand and assess the medical conditions covered by policies including definitions and claims criteria. Take for example Aviva's critical illness plan. At the date of writing in late May 2019 they cover 54 medical conditions. Normally you will find two sorts of documents issued by insurance companies. One is a sales aid or policy summary. This merely lists the names of the conditions covered. The second is a technical document with full medical definitions. Taking the first, it lists illnesses that I have never heard of i.e. Devic's disease and systemic lupus erythematosus. The latter has a brief note that says *"of specified severity!"* Well I am glad that point was made clear. It is a hypochondriac's nightmare. I never knew my body could go wrong in so many ways.

When it comes to cancer, the cause of around 60% of all critical illness claims, Aviva's brief list has a note that says that less advanced cases are excluded. Some of these are covered separately in what are referred to as their additional critical illness benefit, for example low grade prostate cancer with specified treatment or cancer *in situ* of the breast requiring surgery to remove the tumour. Upon a successful claim for these conditions a partial pay-out will be made. This is the lower of £25,000 or 25% of the sum assured. This two tier claim structure to separate out low grade critical illness conditions, resulting in partial pay outs is now common amongst insurers.

Aviva also have a more comprehensive policy conditions document with full medical definitions. It is full of legalese. The one for cancer is complex. It explains that tumours of the prostate are not covered unless they have a Gleason score of at least seven or above or having progressed to at least a TNM classification of T2bN0M0. Well I don't know about you but this is all above my pay grade and I certainly don't remember TNM scores coming up in my O Level Human Biology exam in 1972!

Royal London, another major provider is clearer on their coverage of cancer. I found this on their website relating to their Serious Illness Benefit product, a basic policy that covers just six conditions:

> *"Cancer is one of the illnesses covered by our Serious Illness Benefit. We define it as cancer that has progressed to at least pathological TNM classification equivalent of stage 2 as diagnosed by an oncologist or pathologist. The term cancer includes leukaemia, lymphoma and sarcoma.*
>
> *The following will not be paid under this definition:*
>
> - *Small cancers that are only present in the organ in which they started*
>
> - *Benign tumours, and*
>
> - *All cancer of the skin except cancerous moles (melanoma) that have spread beyond the skin.*

When the policy would and wouldn't pay out

Not all cancers are the same. The TNM classification of cancer staging describes the severity of an individual's cancer. This is based on the size of the original tumour as well as the extent to which the cancer has spread through the body. Some cancers are classed as early stage or less advanced.

They are more easily treatable and less likely to invade tissue and spread to other areas of the body. These are not covered by this policy.

Cancers that have progressed to stage 2 and beyond are typically larger in size and may have started to spread to other parts of the body. They are likely to have a larger impact on an individual life and are usually treated with a combination of surgery, radiotherapy, chemotherapy and other drug therapies. These are covered by this policy." [42]

Royal London then describes in detail various stages of cancer from 0-4, typical treatments that may be required and what stages their plan covers, i.e. 2-4.

Royal London also has a comprehensive critical illness policy, a different product to their Serious Illness Benefit. It defines cancer as follows:

"Cancer – excluding less advanced cases

Any malignant tumour positively diagnosed with histological confirmation and characterised by the uncontrolled growth of malignant cells and invasion of tissue. The term malignant tumour includes:

- *Leukaemia;*
- *Sarcoma; and*
- *Lymphoma (except cutaneous lymphoma –lymphoma confined to the skin).*

For the above definition, the following are not covered:

- *All cancers which are histologically classified as any of the following:*
    - *pre-malignant;*
    - *non-invasive;*

---

[42] https://www.royallondon.com/life-insurance/serious-illness-benefit/cancer/

- cancer in situ;
- having borderline malignancy; or
- having low malignant potential.

- Malignant melanoma that is confined to the epidermis (outer layer of skin).

- Any non-melanoma skin cancer (including cutaneous lymphoma) that has not spread to lymph nodes or metastasised to distant organs.

- All tumours of the prostate unless histologically classified as having a Gleason score of 7 or above, or having progressed to at least TNM classification T2bN0M0."[43]

Whether Royal London's cancer definition is identical to Aviva's is anybody's guess. I suspect not, although at least there is consistency about Gleason scores and TNM classifications. That said Royal London appear to have a different definition of cancer (or at least they use different terminology) with their Serious Illness Benefit than their Critical Illness Cover plan which seems a bit odd given the less advanced cancers are excluded from both.

Subtle differences will also invariably lie with ABI+ definitions. All the major financial adviser insurers have ABI+ definitions for cancer but they are likely to vary. Royal London's describes their enhancement as follows:

"We cover non-melanoma skin cancer which has spread to lymph nodes or distant organs. In addition, we have extended the cover to chronic lymphocytic leukaemia where a clear diagnosis is made but not progressed to Binet Stage A."

All this highlights the complexity of comparing the quality of the definitions and critical illness products. IFAs not only have to be financial advisers but arguably doctors and lawyers as well,

---

[43] https://www.royallondon.com/life-insurance/serious-illness-benefit/cancer/

understanding, interpreting and assigning significance to complex medical descriptions and terminology.

Aside from differences in medical definitions or claims criteria there are multiple additional factors to take into account when considering critical illness insurance, notably plan terms and conditions, additional benefits automatically included as standard and add on options, children's cover, cover increase options, waiver of premium, indexation and health support services.

The claims records of the insurers are also very important. Most providers say they are excellent although occasionally the press or consumer lobby pick up on cases where claims are refused, at first sight unfairly. These may stick in the throat of potential but sceptical clients which is why showing a client the totality of claims statistics for your recommended provider may be useful.

I take the view that the industry is not riddled with insurers doing their level best to avoid paying out claims but there will always be contentious cases where the strict conditions are not met or there was evidence of non-disclosure.

It would be fair to say that it is a slog working through all the different products available but fortunately there are tools to help advisers. These include the Exchange from Iress for comparative quotes and comparison tools offered by Alan Lakey's CI Expert and Defaqto's CIC Compare.

I have had Exchange for many years but I have no experience of the other two tools. If you frequently consider critical illness insurance you may need to consider one of these research tools to effectively filter down to the most suitable product for your client.

As an aside here the Exchange is a remarkable tool. I use it mainly for protection quotes but it can be used for other things such as annuity quotes. The basic package for a single user is just £16.80 p.m. which represents excellent value. I pay a reduced rate of £15.12 p.m. through my membership of a service provider, in my case SimplyBiz.

There are also a few free resources out there to assist you. Here are a selected few I have found:

1. Royal London has a website sales aid for advisers in their protection literature called, *"How our definitions compare in the market."*[44] It is a comprehensive table of leading providers, the conditions their policies cover and whether they meet ABI conditions or have ABI+ ratings.

2. Defaqto assesses policies using star ratings.[45]

Most IFA insurers have the highest five star ratings including Aviva, Aegon, L&G and Royal London. It is interesting to see the list of one and two star products. These are dominated by the banks and no doubt are sold direct to the public. I don't think any adviser will touch the one star rated Post Office Money or the two star Halifax Scottish Widows Plan & Protect Life & Body Cover plan with a ten foot barge pole. Lloyds Bank offers the same product.

Incidentally the Scottish Widows Protect Personal plan is five star rated which means the bank products they underwrite are lower quality budget plans.

These Defaqto ratings are good independent evidence that consumers will get the best products and (hopefully advice too) by using an independent adviser.

3. Canada Life's critical illness definition guide.[46]

I like this document. For each illness or disability it describes the condition and the plan definition, if relevant what is excluded and any ABI enhancements. Here is an example for coma:

> *"About the condition*

---

[44] https://adviser.royallondon.com/globalassets/docs/protection/P1L0187.how-we-compare-in-the-market.pdf
[45] https://www.defaqto.com/star-ratings/life-and-protection/critical-illness-level-term/
[46] http://documents.canadalife.co.uk/individual-protection-critical-illness-definitions-guide.pdf

A coma is a state of deep unconsciousness where the person affected can't be woken. A coma can be caused by damage to the brain following an accident or illness. The person affected may experience permanent nerve damage.

Plan definition

A state of unconsciousness with no reaction to external stimuli or internal needs which:

- *requires the use of life support systems; and*

- *results in permanent neurological deficit with persisting clinical symptoms.*

Excluded

- *a medically induced coma; or*

- *a coma resulting from excessive use of alcohol or drug abuse.*

- *loss of consciousness or concussion that does not require intubation and mechanical ventilation.*

ABI+

The ABI definition covers comas that last at least 96 hours. We have removed the time limit."

Conclusion on critical illness insurance

In considering the subject of critical illness insurance I am left wondering whether excessive research can be justified especially if you charge on a time cost basis. Is it worth the client paying for significant additional advice costs and higher premium costs for a marginally better definition of cancer or overall superior (on paper) policy when the chances are it is highly unlikely to benefit them?

Moreover since it is the case that 10 leading adviser insurers all offer ABI+ definitions for cancer, heart attack, stroke and multiple sclerosis which account for the vast majority of claims (Source: Royal London, see above) I wonder if the differences between the policies are so small that is impossible or even beneficial for advisers to be able to trawl through the definitions, understand them, place value on them and then assess whether any additional price the client will pay will justify the extra value. Given that a search for the perfect can be the enemy of the good it seems not unreasonable that a competitive guaranteed premium from a five star Defaqto rated plan would be a major determining factor when researching and selecting a policy for clients. It should also satisfy the compliance requirements of due diligence and research.

Finally returning to the theme of being client focussed which is at the heart of all good financial planning there is a case for asking clients considering critical illness insurance if there are any conditions they especially want to be covered or covered well. There may be a family history of a certain illness, perhaps a lesser known one or one where claims are rare. Prevalence may have been due to genetic factors or purely by chance two or more family members had the same condition. It may be subjective but your client may want to ensure their policy will cover that condition even if it is something uncommon or generally unknown such as Devic's disease.

Miscellaneous comments on protection

To finish this chapter I want to cover a few important miscellaneous issues and potential hazards that advisers face when giving advice on protection policies.

Indexation of benefits

If you recommend a policy where benefits are automatically indexed each year prior to and during a claim, it is important to understand how this works. First of all here is the good news. There is no medical underwriting involved, similar to the guaranteed insurability options, described above. However Guardian state:

> *"You can ask us to remove the Increasing Cover at any time too. Just ask and we'll remove it at the next policy anniversary. If you've removed your Increasing Cover option, you can ask us to add it back on again but this may be subject to underwriting. New increases will only take place from the*

next policy anniversary date."

Aviva increase cover by RPI (retail prices index) up to a maximum of 10% p.a. The premium rises however by RPI x 1.5% (the same as Guardian's plan). So if cover goes up by 2% p.a. premiums will rise by 3.5% p.a. Year on year the cumulative effect of the premiums rising faster than the cover will be significant.

L&G also cap RPI increases at 10% but state:

> "We will contact you at least three months before the policy anniversary to tell you what the increase in the amount of cover and premium will be."

I couldn't find any more information here but I bet premiums rise more than the cover.

Canada Life's key facts document also doesn't state how much premiums will increase by although they do say:

> "Your premiums will increase at a higher percentage than the cover as the cost of providing cover gets more expensive with age.
>
> If you decide not to increase the cover amount we won't offer to increase it again."

L&G also have a similar policy if the offer to increase the cover is not taken up.

Scottish Widows raise the premiums for lump sum protection products by a factor of 1.4x the increase in cover but there is no loading on the premiums for indexation of monthly income plans. I suspect this latter treatment is uncommon. In any event it is to be applauded. They also remove the option to increase cover annually if on two consecutive anniversaries the automatic increases are cancelled. This is more generous than Canada Life's and L&G's terms.

Zurich's Personal Protection plan enables customers to choose cover that increases each year by 3%, 5%, or in line with the RPI again up to a maximum of 10% in any year. Premiums go up each year by 1.5% for each 1% increase in cover.

They state:

> "If you ask to keep your cover and premiums the same three times during your policy term we'll remove increasing cover from your policy and you won't be able to add it back on. Your policy will then become a level cover policy."

In my brief survey and research Zurich's terms on indexation were the most attractive that I found. I like the fact you can fix increases at 3% p.a. or 5% p.a. as well as by RPI as well as the greater flexibility on taking up benefit increases.

When I first started out as an adviser in the 1990s some insurers indexed premiums at an identical rate to the benefit whilst others raised premiums based on the current age of the insured. This meant that premiums went up faster than the benefit. The example of Scottish Widows' FIB was the only example I found in my recent research of selected providers where cover and premium escalate at the same rate. That said I do not claim my review was comprehensive enough to conclude no other providers have the same terms.

What this all means is that when making an assessment of the cost of a policy an adviser must take into account how indexation increases affect the premiums. You will also need to do this for income protection policies. What might start out as a competitive premium at outset may become expensive in time with indexation costs.

Rebroking

On occasions advisers will need to rebroke existing cover. There may be several reasons to do so. A new client may come to you having bought a poor protection policy direct. It may be a low quality bank product or the premiums may be very expensive and is no longer affordable.

Care is needed. First you should tell your client not to cancel an existing protection plan until the new policy is in force. That should be obvious.

Secondly you need to check whether the client has experienced any new health and lifestyle issues or medical conditions arising after the original policy was set up as this could affect the client's eligibility for cover or result in hiked premiums. These are called ratings. In addition exclusions may apply. In the past I saw these especially with income protection policies.

Thirdly medical definitions may have changed over the years and have become less favourable. For example low grade cancers might be covered under an old critical illness policy but not with new ones. The following article from the Money Mail is worth reading.[47]

It gives an example where an old pre-2002 policy from Pegasus Assurance (now part of Royal London) would pay the full sum assured on diagnosis of prostate cancer, even for Gleeson scores of 2-6. In contrast modern plans only pay the whole sum assured with a Gleeson score of 7 or above. Lower grade prostate cancers are either not covered or only trigger a partial pay-out as described above. The old policy had a valuable benefit and the loss of this will need to be taken into consideration in the cost benefit analysis.

Finally be aware there may be an exclusion cause for suicide in the first year of a new policy. If you recommend a replacement life assurance policy and the client takes their own life, their dependents may have a valid claim of negligence or mis-selling against you. Clearly you need to protect yourself against this risk but at the same time you have to be very sensitive as to how you broach the subject. I don't think you should be asking clients whether they have ever attempted or are contemplating suicide. However I suggest you set out in writing before the replacement policy goes live what the disadvantages are of the new plan, notably that suicide is excluded in the first 12 months.

Selling the need

In Chapter 2 I said a good financial adviser should be a bad salesman. The exception here is with life assurance and other forms of protection. The need for cover has to be "sold." It is why the ban on commission with the RDR did not extend and rightly so to pure protection. The FCA

---

[47] https://www.thisismoney.co.uk/money/bills/article-5139179/Health-policies-changed-check-critical-cover.html

understands that the UK population is very under-insured and protection is rarely bought.

People need a nudge, gentle or a bit firmer to buy it. I do however make a distinction between selling the need and selling the product. In the old days advisers were primarily salesmen not financial planners. They were largely interested in flogging products for the commission the business brought. Today if you sell the need correctly the product will follow.

Bad selling in my view is trying to persuade someone to buy something they don't need, don't want or can't afford, or all three.

Good selling starts with a full fact find to identify what protection needs the client has, what financial arrangements they have in place that address those needs and what are the gaps and risks. An adviser then must make their clients fully aware of their findings, explaining the protection need the client has in a clear and compelling manner. In most cases they will concur and agree action needs to be taken.

Done properly, unless your client is stubborn or worse or genuinely cannot afford the premiums it will be a frictionless exercise with a good outcome for all concerned. You client will buy one or more protection policies and they and their families will be financially better off.

You will have done a good job and be paid for your advice. However there will be something to consider. You will be paid a commission, often a handsome one. Even if you don't do what I do, that is fully credit all initial commission to the client as I explained in Chapter 4, in my view you still owe it to your clients to treat them fairly. To remind you, I use the initial commission to cover my time charge. If there is an excess it stays on the client's timesheet as a credit to be used against the cost of future work or I pay it to the client in cash.

In any event I think you need to be able to justify full retention of a big commission payment which could be in excess of £2,000 and explain what you are paid is reasonable for the work you have done or the value you have added. After all the client is paying the commission through their premiums and you have to disclose it. There is no magic commission tree growing in the back garden of the life assurance company offices that is an independent source of your remuneration. If you can't or won't justify what commission you retain arguably there is a still a bit of the bad old salesman in you.

Can't pay, won't pay

Some of your clients may see the need for protection and genuinely cannot afford the premiums. In these circumstances you may need to explore your clients' budgets and see if cost savings can be made elsewhere. Otherwise you will need to explore limited budget policies for example Royal London's Serious Illness plan or an income protection policy with a limited pay out. As an example LV= offer a Budget Income Protection policy with a maximum two year pay-out. Whilst budget solutions offer limited cover and may not be ideal they are better than doing nothing and leaving your client totally uninsured.

Finding creative solutions to budget restraints is part of a financial adviser's job. Other options to reduce premiums are to select a longer deferred period, advise an income protection policy that terminates at age 60 rather than say at 66 or 67, your client's expected retirement age, or opt for a family income benefit plan rather than a level term assurance.

Making applications

In my time as an IFA, life assurance and other protection policy applications have become increasingly longer, more complex and more intrusive. The amount of information requested by medical underwriters is enormous and it feels excessive at times. Clearly insurers only want to take on clients if the risk of a pay-out is minimal. Someone once said that insurance is only available for those that don't need it! You can see their point. Cynically you could conclude life assurers are looking to find reasons to reject applicants or to apply ratings. On the other hand there is less chance of unintentional non-disclosure, so the amount of information that is required should help protect applicants from this risk.

As an example of the length of protection applications I recently sent one to a client to complete for a small critical illness mortgage protection policy. The PDF ran to 42 pages, although a few pages were general notes and guidance and there were blank pages at the end. Of course some of the information requested was standard stuff, name, address, the details of the insurance being applied for, declarations and bank details but the medical and lifestyle pages ran from pages 11 to 32.

Completing a form is relatively easy if your client is in rude health, has never had serious medical conditions and lots of "no" boxes can be ticked. Even so the questions are intrusive and detailed and applicants may need to make some guesses about their own health. Here are some examples:

"Do you now have or have you ever had the following:

- *Diabetes or sugar in urine*

- *Chest pain, palpitations, heart murmur...or disease or abnormality of your ... pulse, veins or arteries*

- *Any disorder of the eyes (including blurred or double vision) or the ears (including impaired hearing)*

You can ignore sight problems corrected by glasses or contact lenses."

The form asks for obvious maladies such as heart attack, cancer and epilepsy but how are people expected to know if they have ever had sugar in their urine or if they have never had diabetes? Do varicose veins need reporting as an abnormality? And who hasn't had mild and temporary blurred or double vision at times? Does frequent ear wax count as a disorder?

The next page asks for information on conditions (not previously stated) that have occurred in the last five years whether a medical practitioner has been consulted or not:

- *"A lump, growth or cyst of any kind, or any mole or freckle that has bled, become painful, changed colour or increased in size.*

- Anxiety, depression, stress, fatigue... or work-related stress.

- Any arthritis, gout, joint or muscle problems, including the knee(s), shoulder(s), neck, back or spine."

These are comprehensive medical complaints some of which may have been temporary and deemed insignificant at the time. Pretty well everyone will have experienced symptoms of some of these for example work related stress or a backache. Strictly they should be reported even if no medical advice was sought. This creates a dilemma for advisers and their clients to decide if symptoms which were trivial and one-off and should be ignored or should be reported on the application form.

The level of detail required is much less than when I started out as an IFA in 1992. On this point I want to briefly take a side track to make a more general point about change in the financial services industry. It is a kind of life lesson. Some years ago I bought an original health and lifestyle report hand written by a "private friend" of an applicant to the Scottish Widows' Life Assurance Society. It would have been for life assurance. Income protection and critical illness insurance didn't exist in those days. The application was dated August 9th 1860! It consisted of a single long page and it had 11 printed questions. Here are some of them:

"Have you ever known or heard of (him) being seriously indisposed?"

"Is (he) at this time, to the best of your knowledge in a good state of health?"

"Are (his) habits and mode of living regular and temperate?"

And for the medics amongst you:

"Have any of (his) near Relations died of Consumption or other Pulmonary complaints?"

By the way there was no gender bias, the application form had blanks for the friend to insert the correct pronoun of the applicant. If the answer to a question was yes there was a space to supply details.

It is quite possible that the applicant, an ironmonger from Ealing in west

London was asked to complete his own form. If so it almost certainly was written in the same quaint style with very limited information asked for. How things have changed. Complexity, detail and legalese have gone off the Richter scale.

Coming back to the side-track. The life lesson can be summarised in the saying:

> *"If you want to know what water is, why is the fish the last person you would ask?"*

The answer is because a fish has been immersed in water all its life and has known nothing else. It is incapable of understanding and critically assessing its environment. Old timers like myself who have been advisers for many years and been around the block a few times have experienced much change. We are well placed to make an objective assessment of the current situation, to understand what has changed and judge what has got better or worse for both advisers and their clients.

For new advisers all you will know is the present market and compliance regime. You have nothing to compare it to and you have less experience in which to make a fair assessment on how good or bad the industry is. In time you will.

In my view clients have never had it so good in terms of transparency, quality of products and low investment and policy charges, as explained in my review of compliance in Chapter 7. For advisers you could argue the opposite, never has it been so difficult and onerous.

To understand how good customers have it today you need a historical context, to understand how far we have come. If all you hear are the negative comments from the financial press, the regulator and the consumer lobby about what a rotten deal customers are getting and how the industry is ripping them off you'll end up with a skewed view. So my advice for aspiring or new advisers is talk to your more experienced colleagues and find out how things have changed for the better and the worse. Take time to understand the history of the financial advice industry. You'll then gain a better understanding so you can see how good the advice and regulatory regime currently is.

Back to the main issue of making protection applications, because of their complexity I much prefer to complete paper forms. I go as far as to say I detest online applications. A paper application is easier to record health details and allows the client to answer the medical and lifestyle questions themselves. This has two benefits. Firstly accurate information is more likely to be recorded on the application form compared to the client relaying information to you verbally, for you to complete. There is less chance of a Chinese whisper occurring or important details being missed off. Secondly your client takes full responsibility for the information disclosed or withheld. In the event of a claim being declined due to non-disclosure no blame can be laid at your feet.

An additional benefit for my clients paying me on a time charge basis is that completing forms themselves saves on my fees compared to me completing the form online, for example in a long telephone conversation call or sitting down with a client at my office.

My main problem with online applications is that often the drop-down lists don't include the answer I want and there is little no scope to add freeform text. I find this frustrating and concerning that something important will be missed.

Protection for business

My target market is personal clients, not businesses or limited companies. If you advise corporate clients you may need to consider issues such as share holder protection and key man insurance. This subject is out of scope for this book.

One thing to bear in mind when you give advice to limited companies is that your client and their company are separate legal entities, even if your client is the sole director and shareholder. If you take on someone like this you will need a personal and corporate fact find and your advice will need to be suitable to the needs of each entity and in the context of differing legal, tax and regulatory rules that apply. Your anti-money laundering checks will also be different.

Conclusion

On reflection there is more complexity in advising on protection business than at first sight. For young advisers it is likely that protection will be a major element of your business as it was for me when I first started out in the early 1990s so you'll need to get it right. Today my client bank is much older and most of my work is investment advice. I rarely advise on protection these days. Most of my clients have no need for such.

In writing this chapter it seems as if there are plenty of trip hazards for advisers who arrange protection policies. There is potential for claims for mis-selling or negligence if you make a major error for example when rebroking an existing policy or if a claim fails from non-disclosure. Selecting the right policy options and explaining how premiums could rise in the future is also important to avoid potential complaints.

Appendix

Capital	£400,000
Interest Rate p.a.	1.50%
Interest Rate p.m.	0.00125
Initial Withdrawal p.m.	£2,500.00
Income Increase p.a.	0%
Income Increase p.m.	0
Income Increase Factor	1
Term (years)	15
Term (months)	180

MONTH	CAPITAL	INTEREST EARNED	WITHDRAWAL
1	£400,000	£500	£2,500
2	£398,000	£498	£2,500
3	£395,998	£495	£2,500
4	£393,992	£492	£2,500
5	£391,985	£490	£2,500
6	£389,975	£487	£2,500
7	£387,962	£485	£2,500
8	£385,947	£482	£2,500
9	£383,930	£480	£2,500
10	£381,910	£477	£2,500
11	£379,887	£475	£2,500
12	£377,862	£472	£2,500
13	£375,834	£470	£2,500
14	£373,804	£467	£2,500
15	£371,771	£465	£2,500
16	£369,736	£462	£2,500
17	£367,698	£460	£2,500
18	£365,658	£457	£2,500
19	£363,615	£455	£2,500
20	£361,569	£452	£2,500
21	£359,521	£449	£2,500
22	£357,471	£447	£2,500
23	£355,418	£444	£2,500
24	£353,362	£442	£2,500
25	£351,304	£439	£2,500
26	£349,243	£437	£2,500

27	£347,179	£434	£2,500
28	£345,113	£431	£2,500
29	£343,045	£429	£2,500
30	£340,973	£426	£2,500
31	£338,900	£424	£2,500
32	£336,823	£421	£2,500
33	£334,744	£418	£2,500
34	£332,663	£416	£2,500
35	£330,579	£413	£2,500
36	£328,492	£411	£2,500
37	£326,402	£408	£2,500
38	£324,310	£405	£2,500
39	£322,216	£403	£2,500
40	£320,119	£400	£2,500
41	£318,019	£398	£2,500
42	£315,916	£395	£2,500
43	£313,811	£392	£2,500
44	£311,703	£390	£2,500
45	£309,593	£387	£2,500
46	£307,480	£384	£2,500
47	£305,364	£382	£2,500
48	£303,246	£379	£2,500
49	£301,125	£376	£2,500
50	£299,002	£374	£2,500
51	£296,875	£371	£2,500
52	£294,746	£368	£2,500
53	£292,615	£366	£2,500
54	£290,481	£363	£2,500
55	£288,344	£360	£2,500
56	£286,204	£358	£2,500
57	£284,062	£355	£2,500
58	£281,917	£352	£2,500
59	£279,769	£350	£2,500
60	£277,619	£347	£2,500
61	£275,466	£344	£2,500
62	£273,310	£342	£2,500
63	£271,152	£339	£2,500
64	£268,991	£336	£2,500
65	£266,827	£334	£2,500

66	£264,661	£331	£2,500
67	£262,492	£328	£2,500
68	£260,320	£325	£2,500
69	£258,145	£323	£2,500
70	£255,968	£320	£2,500
71	£253,788	£317	£2,500
72	£251,605	£315	£2,500
73	£249,420	£312	£2,500
74	£247,231	£309	£2,500
75	£245,040	£306	£2,500
76	£242,847	£304	£2,500
77	£240,650	£301	£2,500
78	£238,451	£298	£2,500
79	£236,249	£295	£2,500
80	£234,044	£293	£2,500
81	£231,837	£290	£2,500
82	£229,627	£287	£2,500
83	£227,414	£284	£2,500
84	£225,198	£281	£2,500
85	£222,980	£279	£2,500
86	£220,758	£276	£2,500
87	£218,534	£273	£2,500
88	£216,307	£270	£2,500
89	£214,078	£268	£2,500
90	£211,845	£265	£2,500
91	£209,610	£262	£2,500
92	£207,372	£259	£2,500
93	£205,131	£256	£2,500
94	£202,888	£254	£2,500
95	£200,641	£251	£2,500
96	£198,392	£248	£2,500
97	£196,140	£245	£2,500
98	£193,885	£242	£2,500
99	£191,628	£240	£2,500
100	£189,367	£237	£2,500
101	£187,104	£234	£2,500
102	£184,838	£231	£2,500
103	£182,569	£228	£2,500
104	£180,297	£225	£2,500

105	£178,023	£223	£2,500
106	£175,745	£220	£2,500
107	£173,465	£217	£2,500
108	£171,182	£214	£2,500
109	£168,896	£211	£2,500
110	£166,607	£208	£2,500
111	£164,315	£205	£2,500
112	£162,020	£203	£2,500
113	£159,723	£200	£2,500
114	£157,422	£197	£2,500
115	£155,119	£194	£2,500
116	£152,813	£191	£2,500
117	£150,504	£188	£2,500
118	£148,192	£185	£2,500
119	£145,878	£182	£2,500
120	£143,560	£179	£2,500
121	£141,239	£177	£2,500
122	£138,916	£174	£2,500
123	£136,590	£171	£2,500
124	£134,260	£168	£2,500
125	£131,928	£165	£2,500
126	£129,593	£162	£2,500
127	£127,255	£159	£2,500
128	£124,914	£156	£2,500
129	£122,570	£153	£2,500
130	£120,223	£150	£2,500
131	£117,874	£147	£2,500
132	£115,521	£144	£2,500
133	£113,165	£141	£2,500
134	£110,807	£139	£2,500
135	£108,445	£136	£2,500
136	£106,081	£133	£2,500
137	£103,714	£130	£2,500
138	£101,343	£127	£2,500
139	£98,970	£124	£2,500
140	£96,594	£121	£2,500
141	£94,214	£118	£2,500
142	£91,832	£115	£2,500
143	£89,447	£112	£2,500

144	£87,059	£109	£2,500
145	£84,668	£106	£2,500
146	£82,273	£103	£2,500
147	£79,876	£100	£2,500
148	£77,476	£97	£2,500
149	£75,073	£94	£2,500
150	£72,667	£91	£2,500
151	£70,258	£88	£2,500
152	£67,845	£85	£2,500
153	£65,430	£82	£2,500
154	£63,012	£79	£2,500
155	£60,591	£76	£2,500
156	£58,166	£73	£2,500
157	£55,739	£70	£2,500
158	£53,309	£67	£2,500
159	£50,876	£64	£2,500
160	£48,439	£61	£2,500
161	£46,000	£57	£2,500
162	£43,557	£54	£2,500
163	£41,112	£51	£2,500
164	£38,663	£48	£2,500
165	£36,211	£45	£2,500
166	£33,757	£42	£2,500
167	£31,299	£39	£2,500
168	£28,838	£36	£2,500
169	£26,374	£33	£2,500
170	£23,907	£30	£2,500
171	£21,437	£27	£2,500
172	£18,964	£24	£2,500
173	£16,487	£21	£2,500
174	£14,008	£18	£2,500
175	£11,525	£14	£2,500
176	£9,040	£11	£2,500
177	£6,551	£8	£2,500
178	£4,059	£5	£2,500
179	£1,564	£2	£2,500

13. Principles of pensions advice

The subject of giving pension advice is a massive topic and like investments it could be a book in its own right. I will only comment on a few issues here.

Pensions simplification

I have always found pensions to be the most technically challenging subject even after the so called "pensions simplification" regime that was introduced in April 2006, which at best failed to do what it said on the tin and at worst was a downright lie and has since become a dystopian nightmare.

Of course it may have been well intentioned but it did not account for unintended consequences and the tendency of the Treasury to fiddle with the rules, make things more complex and back track on tax breaks and allowances. Remember in 2006/07 the year of the launch of "pensions complication," the annual allowance was a whopping £215,000. It rose to £255,000 in 2010/11 but now stands at £40,000 p.a. for most people. It is tapered to £10,000 for high earners and reduced to £4,000 p.a. for those subject to the money purchase annual allowance (MPAA). This applies to people who have accessed pension benefits flexibly in excess of tax free cash. So someone taking a pound of taxable flexi-access drawdown (FAD) income will be subject to the MPAA as will those using uncrystallised funds pension lump sum (UFPLS) – see later in the chapter.

Over the years advisers and their clients have had to get to grips with the lifetime allowance, enhanced protection, fixed protection, pension input periods, carry forward, adjusted income and tapered annual allowances to name just a few. For me though the greatest injustice about the whole pension system is the lifetime allowance and its sting, the lifetime allowance charge, levied on excess pension values. This is as high as 55%. I can understand why the Treasury would want to restrict pension contributions that attract tax relief i.e. why an annual allowance is needed, but penalising people purely for enjoying good investment returns makes no sense to me. It is unfair to regulate and tax both the input i.e. the tax relieved pension contributions as well as the output, what is achieved from investment.

In my view the lifetime allowance should be scrapped but there is a fat chance of that as long as Treasury coffers are being swollen by pension taxes.

Pension transfers & drawdown

I never took the high level G60 or AF3 specialist pensions' exams from the CII so I am not qualified to give pension transfer advice from defined benefit or final salary pension schemes. However I take the view the default position for most people is it is best not to transfer their pension to a SIPP or personal pension in order to go into income drawdown, aka flexi-access drawdown.

The facts are clear. It is almost certain over the long term the income from guaranteed index linked defined benefit pensions, especially public sector schemes, can't be matched by a personal pension arrangement in drawdown and therefore people who transfer out are taking a huge amount of investment risk and a gamble on the sustainability of their long term income.

Transfers from defined benefit pensions to personal pensions or SIPPs might have great allure if there is a large six figure transfer value but it is a false security. Personal pensions or SIPPs are subject to the vagaries of the stock market and pension values are subject to significant capital erosion from sharp or sustained markets sell-offs. A pension pot can be damaged irrevocably by poor returns threatening your client's income and their long term livelihood. Unlike life assurance where the principal risk is dying too soon, in retirement people have the opposite problem, living too long and their money running out.

If fund prices remain depressed for a lengthy period an investor may experience what is called "pound cost ravaging." This is the evil twin of "pound cost averaging," which benefits monthly investors during the accumulation stage when they are building up pension assets.

Pound cost ravaging occurs when fund prices fall. Unless the personal pension or SIPP has sufficient cash to fund drawdown payments a larger number of units or shares have to be sold each month to provide a fixed income and this can have a devastating effect on capital values if it goes on for too long. After the global financial crisis in 2008 I had to advise two clients to suspend income drawdown from their pensions to avoid capital losses. From memory this lasted about 12-15 months. Of course a V shaped recovery in markets is much less damaging than a prolonged depression. To be clear neither of these clients had transferred from defined benefit schemes but from other personal pension plans.

Whilst pound cost ravaging can be avoided by drawing on SIPP cash for income when markets have fallen sharply, keeping too much cash is a drag on portfolio returns when stock markets are rising and interest rates are low. So there is a downside however it is done.

With the recent pension mis-selling scandal of British Steel workers in Port Talbot the regulatory spotlight has quite rightly fallen on pension transfer business and the market has tightened in part due to the FSCS limits being raised to £350,000 in April 2019. Fewer advisers are prepared to give advice on defined benefit transfers given the high risk involved whilst professional indemnity insurers are ratcheting up premiums or refusing to cover this type of business.

I would not say that pension transfers from defined benefit schemes are never in clients' best interests. A single person in poor health with short life expectancy and no financial dependents, suspecting their defined benefit pension will pay out only for a minimal length of time before they die may wish to access their pension pot. Please note however that if death occurs within two years of transfer it could result in an inheritance tax charge. This would arise if HMRC considered a transfer of value has arisen if there is evidence of an intention to confer a gratuitous benefit. This is a subject for you to study if necessary.

Similarly a widow or widower, with no financial dependents and with other secure income may be keen to leave an inheritance for their children. Individual factors will determine whether transfers are in clients' best interests.

I do have some sympathy with people concerned about the financial security of their private sector pension scheme given so many are in deficit. This means a scheme's liabilities to provide pension benefits, exceeds their assets, or their ability to meet their obligations when they are due. In my view the deficits are the result of a major failure of regulation which has required defined benefit pension providers to be invested far too cautiously over many years. The requirement to hold large amounts of government gilts, both conventional and index linked has been a disaster in an era of ultra-low interest rates. Since the global financial crisis Quantitative Easing (QE) has driven down bond yields to historically low levels.

Had pension schemes been able to be more heavily invested in equities the problem of deficits would not have arisen or at least they would not have been as bad as they are at present. Writing in 2019 it has been a cracking 11 years for equities since the global financial crisis and arguably pension schemes that were properly funded should have surpluses.

This is a classic example where being too cautious and pessimistic has been highly damaging for investment in the long term, something advisers should take note of when dealing with overly cautious risk clients. There is no such thing as a risk free investment strategy. Those who have kept their money in cash for many years will have learnt that lesson the hard way as interest rates collapsed. Investors always have to choose which risk they take. It is something the regulators don't seem to understand.

Accumulation - saving for retirement

For younger people building up pension funds is the priority. This is called accumulation, gathering assets for retirement. The earlier people start to save the better the long term results. Consider four people who save £200 p.m. gross but start at ages 20, 25, 30 and 35 years. Retirement is at age 68 for each of them. Assuming a 6% p.a. return net of charges the results are as follows:

	Fund (F)	Contributions (C)	F/C Ratio
1st person (20-68)	£667,493	£115,200	5.794:1
2nd person (25-68)	£484,015	£103,200	4.690:1
3rd person (30-68)	£348,861	£91,200	3.825:1
4th person (35-68)	£248,291	£79,200	3.135:1

The first person contributed to his or her pension for 48 years. Despite paying in just £12,000 more than the second person, an extra £183,478 pension pot results. Compared to the third person £318,632 more pension is accumulated, for an additional outlay of £24,000 only.

The F/C ratio shows us the efficiency of returns on a £1 investment. A higher F/C ratio means the greater the efficiency of returns. This is the power of compounding. Early gains themselves are invested and grow.

Now consider contributions that rise by 3% p.a. compound the funds that are calculated are:

	Fund (F)	Contributions (C)	F/C Ratio
1st person (20-68)	£1,005,672	£250,580	4.013:1
2nd person (25-68)	£743,628	£205,161	3.625:1
3rd person (30-68)	£517,649	£165,982	3.119:1
4th person (35-68)	£354,738	£132,186	2.684:1

Indexing contributions massively boosts the final fund values with the same observations as for level contributions, the earlier you start to save the greater the benefit of compounding. However it is interesting to see that the F/C Ratios are lower. This is due to the impact of higher contributions being made at the later stages meaning there is less time for them to compound returns.

The lesson is of course is the earlier your clients start to save the better the long term outcome. Moreover if they can complement their monthly savings with a lump sum contribution as well they'll get a big boost. Consider a pension contribution of £10,000 made at the same time as monthly savings start, the results are as follows assuming a 6% p.a. return:

	Fund (F)	Contributions (C)	F/C Ratio
1st person (20-68)	£163,938	£10,000	16.394:1
2nd person (25-68)	£122,504	£10,000	12.250:1
3rd person (30-68)	£91,542	£10,000	9.154:1
4th person (35-68)	£68,405	£10,000	6.840:1

For a five year extra period of time that the money is invested i.e. from 43 to 48 years an extra pension fund of £41,434 results. Moreover the bang for your buck i.e. the F/C ratio sky rockets for single contributions compared to monthly savings. It should be easy to figure out why.

In these examples the figures for monthly savings were obtained from a spreadsheet calculator I have used for many years, I think written for me by an actuary friend in the distant past. It just shows how old I am that I can't remember these things, although I should have had a clue when some people tried to blow the candles out on my birthday cake. They were driven back by the heat!

The lump sum figures were calculated using the google calculator.

It should be said this is a simplistic analysis in that the calculation assumes steadily rising stock markets and for monthly investment it ignores any potential uplift from pound cost averaging where volatility can boost returns especially if market prices are depressed for a long period of time. In these circumstances the investor buys units cheaper compared to a steadily rising market and therefore acquires more units for their fixed monthly contribution. Crucially though prices need to rally at the end for the investor to benefit. Of course it can work the other way, where investors buy fewer units because prices remain high for long periods of time but then collapse at the end of the savings period.

Moreover the average 20 year old is unlikely to have a spare £160 p.m. (for a £200 p.m. gross contribution) given the financial pressure on young people today. They may be students and once they graduate, find employment and start earning money, saving for a deposit for a house or paying off debt will invariably take a higher priority. It takes a lot of vision and discipline to save for an event 40-45 years in the future, or put it another way, to start financial planning for the end of your working life when you are just starting out in your first job and awaiting your first or second pay cheque. That said it helps that auto-enrolment has raised the profile of saving for retirement. In the 2019/20 tax year minimum auto-enrolment contributions are 8% p.a. with 3% of this coming from the employer. It is important to note here the 8% contribution typically is applied to earnings above the lower earnings limit of £6,136 not an employee's gross salary, so the real rate is less.

These figures are still small compared to defined benefit pension scheme. For example in the NHS employer contributions are 14.38% with employees paying 5% to 14.5%. Great work if you can get it. Of course over the years many defined benefit schemes especially in private sector have closed to new members or have moved to a pension that is based on career earnings rather than final salary. We have been witnessing the slow death of defined benefit pension schemes.

Savings for pensions in context

When I advise clients on how to split their savings budget I generally recommend using three buckets - short, medium and long term. The short term bucket is cash savings, for emergencies and short term needs. The latter could be for known one-off expenses in the next 6-12 months for example a holiday or work on the house.

The long term is for retirement, saving into pensions. Employer pension schemes or auto-enrolment contributions can be taken into account but unless your client is a member of a gold plated defined benefit scheme additional pension contributions will be required to ensure a decent level of retirement income.

The medium term bucket is harder to pin down but it could include a variety of things, saving for a deposit for house purchase in three to five years' time, children's education in 5-10 years, a replacement car or a special holiday.

The point is if your client say has a savings budget of £500 p.m. from surplus income you don't want to recommend it is all saved for retirement in 30-40 years even though there is tax relief on the contributions, potentially at the higher rates. People will normally want to see some of the benefits of their hard work and savings at an earlier stage.

Once pension contributions have been decided your client will need to allocate some of their surplus income to cash savings especially if they have none. The balance can be invested into a stocks and shares ISA for medium term capital growth for specified or unspecified purposes. How a client's budget is allocated will be determined by a host of factors including their budget, their age, personal preferences and existing arrangements, but in my view they should allocate money to short, medium and long term needs.

How much to save for retirement

Your clients may ask how much they should be savings towards retirement to get a decent income or you may want to raise this as a subject for discussion. Is £100 p.m. enough or is £500 p.m. required? There are a number of rules of thumb out there but I generally don't use these (an exception is below) nor do I have the space to discuss them here. I suggest you google the subject, if you want to learn more about retirement rules of thumb.

What I do is to undertake calculations and projections. First you need to discuss with your client what percentage or fraction of their current earnings do they want to achieve from their pension pot at retirement. Two thirds or three quarters is a reasonable target, given mortgages are likely to have been repaid, their children should be financially independent and a couple in retirement may not need to run two cars.

Consider someone who is self-employed, for simplicity, to avoid the complications of working out the benefits arising from potentially multiple employer pension schemes. So let's us say your client is aged 30 and is earning £60,000 p.a. gross and intends to retire at age 68. We need to take into account inflation and make some assumptions. Let's say this person's earnings will rise by 3% p.a. This may be somewhat optimistic but I chose this figure for illustration purposes as you will see.

A google or scientific calculator will show that in 38 years' time at retirement the £60,000 p.a. salary will now be £184,487 p.a. Now we compare this with pension fund projections we considered earlier on the subject of accumulation. The second table showed a 30 year old saving £200 p.m. indexed by 3% p.a. will accumulate a pension fund of £517,649 assuming 6% p.a. net returns.

The question then is how much income can that pension pot generate? To answer that question you could use current annuity rates to calculate a reasonable figure or we can use a rule of thumb. A common one is the 4% rule. It says an investor can draw a 4% income each year from a pension pot and that should be reasonably sustainable. Therefore a fund of £517,649 could produce an income of £20,706 p.a. This is just 11.22% of the client's final salary of £184,487. Saving £200 p.m. simply won't do.

To produce a retirement income that is 2/3rds of £184,487 i.e. £122,991 p.a. the investor will require a pension fund of £3,074,800, assuming the 4% rule. My calculations show savings of £1,188 p.m. will be required to hit this target. For most people it will be way beyond their budget. In many cases therefore you will need to say to your client the ideal is not practical and you will simply need to save as much as you can afford.

There of course so many assumptions this sort of analysis involves, inflation, investment returns, the shape of those investment returns and taxation. On the latter point a salary of £60,000 in 2019/20 would be subject to 40% income tax whereas 2/3rds of this salary i.e. £40,000 would not. A pension fund north of £3 million also is subject to a lifetime allowance charge. Given the complexities and that life throws up all sorts of spanners and opportunities there are plenty of things that can throw the calculations out. However this sort of crude analysis can provide a useful ball park assessment.

Decumulation

This is the opposite of accumulation, converting pension funds into an income in retirement. Good financial advice needs to ensure a retirement income is sustainable, inflation protected and tax efficient.

A holistic approach is required to assess all potential income sources. It is not just about pensions. For example ISAs provide tax free income unlike pensions which are taxed as earnings. Regular monthly withdrawals from general investment accounts (non-ISAs) that invest in funds geared for capital growth are also tax efficient if the realised gains are within the annual capital gains tax allowances. The 5% p.a. allowances from investment bonds are also tax efficient. Finally transferring assets to a spouse who is a non-taxpayer with unused personal allowance will enable them to generate a tax free income.

Partial crystallisation of pension benefits may also be appropriate especially if your client phases their retirement. Hitting the go button on all sources of income may push your client into a higher tax rate bracket and it does not leave anything in reserve, for example uncrystallised pensions which can provide additional income in the future or an inheritance for the children. These are important considerations.

Defined benefit pension schemes

For members of defined benefit pension schemes their choices will be limited with their income calculated by a set formula based on final salary or career average earnings, years of service and an accrual rate, for example 1/80th for each year of service. Pre-A Day scheme rules may impact on maximum tax free cash and there may be an option to commute pension for tax free cash if it does not get paid automatically or provide additional cash if it is available.

As an aside technically tax free cash should be referred to as Pension Commencement Lump Sum (PCLS). The phraseology changed some years back. The cynic in me thinks that it a precursor to removing the tax free status of a PCLS. It will be much easier for a Chancellor to sneak this tax charge in with the name change. Until then I will still use the phrase tax free cash as that is what it still is.

Whenever I have looked at commutation I have found that the amount of pension sacrificed is too high to justify taking tax free cash or additional tax free cash. For example consider the NHS scheme with a commutation factor of 12. This means for every £12 of tax free cash, £1 p.a. of pension is foregone. So let's say the maximum tax free cash is £40,000, your client would lose £3,333 p.a. of pension income at retirement (£40,000/12). If the £40,000 cash is invested for income they would need a yield of 8.33% p.a. just to match the lost pension and that doesn't take into account indexation of pension benefits in the scheme that will be paid in the second and subsequent years.

In contrast the Universities Superannuation Scheme has a more generous commutation factor of 17, for some members at least. Using the figure of £40,000 for tax free cash the pension foregone will be £2,353 p.a. in year one. The hurdle rate to match this from investment of the lump sum is still a hefty 5.88% p.a.

As state and defined benefit pensions are indexed with inflation each year there is a case for vesting pensions from defined contribution schemes or annuities differently to provide complementary benefits. So I sometimes advise clients with secure core pension arrangements to opt for a level income for example from annuities. Although there is no inflation protection, the client has that built into their defined benefit and state pensions. Opting for a level annuity means clients enjoy a higher income at outset, reducing the cliff edge drop when they retire from their job. A level annuity also reduces the risk from dying too soon. The issue here is about breakeven points, the expected date when the amount paid out by an annuity equals the purchase price. Since an indexed annuity will pay a significantly reduced starting income compared to a level annuity the breakeven date is longer. I write more on this point later in the chapter.

Third way products and fixed term annuities

Although a number of third way products for crystallising personal pensions have come to market over the years such as investment annuities, fixed term annuities, (which interestingly fall under income drawdown rules) and flexible retirement plans which combine annuities and drawdown in a single account they have not gained much traction amongst advisers. As a result some providers have withdrawn their products from the market. Third way products are complex and in my view they require too much compromise. Investment based products often have unacceptably limited fund choices and the annuities offered are not necessarily the best in the market.

I have only ever arranged one fixed term annuity (FTA) and it was advised somewhat reluctantly. It seemed the least bad option at the time in 2013. The client was in good health and she didn't qualify for an enhanced lifetime annuity given her health was good and she did not want to take investment risk with her pension pot, ruling out income drawdown. An FTA meant she was not locked into a poor standard annuity for the rest of her life. It was designed as a temporary five year arrangement after which there was the possibility that at age 68 she might qualify for a higher annuity rate based on her being five years older, her health not being as good or there being higher annuity rates in the open market.

The way these products work is that a temporary fixed annuity is paid to the client and a pre-determined guaranteed maturity value (GMV) is due at end of the term. The GMV is calculated at outset to be sufficient to provide a guaranteed lifetime income equal to the temporary annuity. That's the theory. This expectation was not however met in my client's case. The client's fixed term annuity was £7,609 p.a. but at maturity on 1/8/18 the GMV was only able to provide an equivalent lifetime income of £6,834 p.a. a drop of more than 10%.

GMVs are calculated on an assumption that annuity rates will remain the same at maturity of the fixed term annuity as they were at outset. In fact they fell between 2013 and 2018 explaining why my client's GMV was unable to support an ongoing income of £7,609 p.a.

It is evident that FTA providers adopt a very cautious investment strategy in order to provide the GMVs at maturity. This results in low investment returns, undercooked GMVs and poor value in my view. Consider the figures in my client's situation:

Fund Value:	£189,176
Tax Free Cash:	£47,294
Adviser Charge:	£1,250
Fixed Term Annuity Purchase Price:	£140,632
Annual Payments:	£7,609
Total Annual Payments (TAP 5 Years)	£38,045
GMV:	£116,563
Total Paid Out (GMV +TAP)	£154,608
Gross Gain	£13,976

The gross gain is £154,608 - £140,632, some of which i.e. the annuity payments were subject to income tax at 20%. I calculated the gross return was 2.1% p.a. only marginally better than cash.

It would be interesting to learn how fixed term annuity providers invest capital to provide the policy benefits notably the GMV. I have no knowledge here but according to annuity specialist Billy Burrows they invest in cash deposits. Whatever, you can bet your bottom dollar the investments are highly conservative.

The problem here lies in the guaranteed bit of a GMV. Providers as in other scenarios have to protect themselves from the risk of having to make up shortfalls if they offer guarantees. It is why annuity and pension providers undergird their liabilities by securing guaranteed cash flows by holding government gilts. With an FTA a guarantee may make an investor feel secure but they should understand they are also guaranteeing dull investment returns and that a paltry GMV may fail to provide an equivalent lifetime annuity at maturity. Investors in FTAs are excluding themselves at outset from participation in strong stock market gains during the term of their temporary annuity.

I wonder if the fixed term annuity product could be improved if there was an option to forego the guaranteed capital bit and replace a guaranteed maturity Value (GMV) with a targeted maturity value (TMV) especially for longer term plans. These could aim for say a 3.5% or 4% p.a. net investment return. The pension provider would then invest the monies cautiously, though not as conservatively as a GMV requires because they are not bound to provide any capital guarantee at maturity. Given many cautious risk investors are familiar with investment in defensive multi-asset, targeted absolute return and volatility managed funds I don't think accepting the concept of a TMV is a big ask.

With a TMV the investor of course has to accept investment risk but not too much given a cautious investment strategy is still adopted. Over most five to six year periods investors should achieve returns of 3.5% or 4% p.a. from a TMV and hence higher maturity values than from a GMV. They may even be able to secure a higher lifetime annuity than what their FTA provided. That would be a pleasant surprise.

I am not sure if my idea is workable but I would envisage two options under a FTA, one with a GMV for ultra-cautious investors, the other providing a TMV for those willing to take some investment risk but where full blown income drawdown is unsuitable. Of course those with a TMV would still retain a guaranteed element, the annuity payments till the end of the term.

Now back to my client. Fortunately she was willing to invest £10,742 of her tax free cash into a stocks and shares ISA and she has benefitted from more substantial capital growth. The investments are worth £16,165 as I write in mid-July 2019, representing a return of just over 50%.

With the benefit of hindsight my experience has led me to conclude fixed term annuities are too cautiously invested and they carry a substantial risk that the GMV will not be sufficient to provide an equivalent lifetime annuity at maturity. This is an asymmetric risk, limited upside and substantial downside potential.

As fixed term annuities represent poor value I have no intention of recommending them to any other client, at least not in their current form.

For cautious risk investors in very good health, where standard annuity rates are poor I am likely to recommend flexi-access drawdown especially if the client has other forms of guaranteed pension income i.e. from a defined benefit scheme or state pension. I say this on the principle that the *objective* risk a client needs to take, to get a decent and sustainable income trumps the *subjective* risk they are inclined to take based on their attitude to risk. This was a subject I discussed in Chapter 5.

With the wisdom of hindsight from dealing with my client in 2013, in future I will be more assertive with cautious risk investors and not take it as read that income drawdown should automatically be discounted. This naturally takes into account that income drawdown may be a short term arrangement until annuity rates improve or the client gets older or their health deteriorates. In these circumstances they can buy a lifetime annuity.

New advisers need to bear in mind your clients can switch from income drawdown to a lifetime annuity but not the other way around. If your clients buy a lifetime annuity that is the end of the matter. There is no flexibility to switch to an alternative arrangement. In contrast income drawdown may be a temporary arrangement until a suitable time arises to buy an annuity. The attendant investment risk is not forever.

In conclusion, in my view the three main choices clients have at retirement is to buy a traditional lifetime annuity, go into income drawdown i.e. flexi-access drawdown (FAD) or opt for a mixture of the two. This enables you to find and recommend the best provider for each element. In the next section I cover these two options in more detail.

Finally we can throw into the mix another income option, uncrystallised funds pension lump sum (UFPLS). This was a further creation of the pension freedoms legislation in 2015. It is where a client crystallises a small portion of their pension only. Let us say a client has a pension fund of £100,000 and needs an income of £10,000 in the next year. They could use UFPLS to crystallise £10,000. A quarter or £2,500 is tax free cash whilst £7,500 is taxable income. If the client has sufficient unused personal allowance the £7,500 may not be subject to income tax. Please note without a tax code income tax will be deducted at source using a quirky week one/month one basis and will need to be reclaimed from HMRC.

It is grossly unfair taxation compared to the past where an emergency tax code to collect income tax at the basic rate applied. Here is an example for one of my clients, a non-taxpayer in 2019/20 with no income, who effected a one-off UFPLS payment of £16,000. Of this £4,000 was tax free cash. The residual £12,000 fell entirely in the personal allowance of £12,500 and would be tax free. However the tax calculation was as follows:

Annual Tax Band	Month 1	Tax Rate	Tax Deducted
Personal Allowance	£1,041.67	0%	£0
Basic rate band	£3,125.00	20%	£625
Higher rate band	£7,833.33	40%	£3,133.32
Total	**£12,000**		**£3,758.32**

Month 1 figures are 1/12th of the annual tax band. For example £1,041.67 is 1/12th of the personal allowance of £12,500 whilst £3,125 is 1/12th of the basic rate tax band of £37,500. For the higher rate band the maximum month one band is £9,375.

So my client with no tax liability had to fork out more than £3,750 in tax and go through the rigmarole of claiming it back from HMRC. Had an emergency BR code applied the tax deducted at source would have been £2,400.

Back to my theoretical client the residual £90,000 left in the pension remains uncrystallised and the same exercise can be repeated next year. The problem with UFPLS is that unlike with an annuity or FAD it does not set up a lifetime or potentially lifetime income. It just deals with income provision a year at a time.

Lifetime annuities

Whilst lifetime annuities offer guaranteed pension benefits and you cannot outlive them they have become increasingly unpopular in recent years due to ultra-low interest rates and hence annuity rates, their inflexibility and the attractions of flexi-access drawdown, introduced with pension freedoms. Someone who buys a lifetime annuity today is locking themselves into a poor annuity rate, unless they happen to qualify for a medically enhanced benefit. That said lifetime annuities may be suitable for ultra-cautious risk clients looking for certainty and who want to avoid investment based solutions, ongoing investment reviews and higher advice costs.

The suitability of a lifetime annuity will in part depend on your client's other pension arrangements and it should not be solely determined by their risk profile. If the bulk of their retirement income comes from their state pension and a defined benefit pension scheme then the purchase of a lifetime annuity from a personal pension arrangement merely adds another tranche of guaranteed income. It is more of the same. The client should consider the merits of FAD to add diversity to their retirement income strategy and the potential benefits of an investment based product i.e. medium to long term capital growth and a higher long term income.

Moreover as noted if a client has a state pension and a defined benefit pension any annuity may be best arranged on a level income basis. I want to explore this in more detail. Consider someone age 65 with a pension fund of £100,000 who buys an annuity. Assuming a five year guarantee and no spouse or dependent's pension the best standard annuities are[48]:

Level:	£4,654 p.a.
Escalating by RPI:	£2,685 p.a.

The inflation linked annuity has a starting income of 42% less than the level income. That is a substantial reduction. However the key question is what is the breakeven point? In fact there are two breakeven points - the first is how long does it take for income from the inflation linked annuity to match the level annuity. The second is how long will it take for the total gross payments to equal each other. In order to calculate these we need to assume a rate of inflation. We could assume 2% p.a. the Bank of England inflation target. However let's take RPI at 2.5%. Using a homemade spreadsheet annuity calculator the figures are as follows:

Year	Level	RPI @ 2.5%
1	£4,654.00	£2,685.00
2	£4,654.00	£2,752.13
3	£4,654.00	£2,820.93
4	£4,654.00	£2,891.45
5	£4,654.00	£2,963.74
6	£4,654.00	£3,037.83
7	£4,654.00	£3,113.78

---

[48] Hargreaves Lansdown (24/8/19).
https://www.hl.co.uk/retirement/annuities/best-buy-rates

8	£4,654.00	£3,191.62
9	£4,654.00	£3,271.41
10	£4,654.00	£3,353.20
11	£4,654.00	£3,437.03
12	£4,654.00	£3,522.95
13	£4,654.00	£3,611.03
14	£4,654.00	£3,701.30
15	£4,654.00	£3,793.83
16	£4,654.00	£3,888.68
17	£4,654.00	£3,985.90
18	£4,654.00	£4,085.55
19	£4,654.00	£4,187.68
20	£4,654.00	£4,292.38
21	£4,654.00	£4,399.69
22	£4,654.00	£4,509.68
23	**£4,654.00**	**£4,622.42**
24	£4,654.00	£4,737.98
25	£4,654.00	£4,856.43
26	£4,654.00	£4,977.84
27	£4,654.00	£5,102.29
28	£4,654.00	£5,229.84
29	£4,654.00	£5,360.59
30	£4,654.00	£5,494.60
31	£4,654.00	£5,631.97
32	£4,654.00	£5,772.77
33	£4,654.00	£5,917.09
34	£4,654.00	£6,065.01
35	£4,654.00	£6,216.64
36	£4,654.00	£6,372.06
37	£4,654.00	£6,531.36
38	£4,654.00	£6,694.64
39	£4,654.00	£6,862.01
40	£4,654.00	£7,033.56
41	£4,654.00	£7,209.40
42	£4,654.00	£7,389.63
Total	**£195,468.00**	**£195,574.88**

So, we find the income from the indexed annuity matches the level one in the 23rd year but the total pay-out from the two annuities takes a further 19 years to reach parity in year 42. From year 42 the annuitant with index linking is better off, but that it is a very long time.

If we assume higher inflation at 4.5% p.a. the figures are as follows:

Year	Level	RPI @ 4.5%
1	£4,654.00	£2,685.00
2	£4,654.00	£2,805.83
3	£4,654.00	£2,932.09
4	£4,654.00	£3,064.03
5	£4,654.00	£3,201.91
6	£4,654.00	£3,346.00
7	£4,654.00	£3,496.57
8	£4,654.00	£3,653.91
9	£4,654.00	£3,818.34
10	£4,654.00	£3,990.17
11	£4,654.00	£4,169.72
12	£4,654.00	£4,357.36
13	£4,654.00	£4,553.44
14	**£4,654.00**	**£4,758.35**
15	£4,654.00	£4,972.47
16	£4,654.00	£5,196.23
17	£4,654.00	£5,430.06
18	£4,654.00	£5,674.42
19	£4,654.00	£5,929.77
20	£4,654.00	£6,196.60
21	£4,654.00	£6,475.45
22	£4,654.00	£6,766.85
23	£4,654.00	£7,071.36
24	£4,654.00	£7,389.57
Total	£111,696.00	£111,935.49

The matching income breakeven point is in year 14 and the second breakeven point, the total income is in the 24th year.

It is clear if you think inflation will be low for the long term then an RPI linked annuity is a poor choice. The breakeven points are simply too distant. There is a high risk of your client dying too early resulting in a lower total pay-out compared to a level annuity.

There is also a certain irony here in that people who opt for an annuity because they don't want to take any investment risk still have to take a view on long term interest rates if they consider an index linked annuity, the very same thing investors in general and those who go into income drawdown may also need to take into account. So arguably investment considerations are relevant to annuities albeit indirectly!

Aside from the question of whether your clients opt for a level or indexed annuity there are other choices to make - whether to select a joint annuity, a guarantee period or value protection and the frequency of the payments. Generally I recommend payments monthly in advance to avoid the issue of "proportion." As you may have picked up in your studies an annuity that pays in arrears can be paid with or without proportion, which determines if there is a pay-out in the month of the annuitant's death. Proportion is another complexity, if possible to avoid.

If a joint annuity and a guarantee period is selected you will also have to explain to your client the issue of "overlap." Consider an annuity with a five year guarantee period and a 50% spouse's pension. If death occurs within the guarantee period let us say after three years an annuity with overlap will start to pay the second life's annuity immediately in addition to the income for the remaining two years of the guarantee period. An annuity without overlap will only commence payment of the spouse's annuity at the end of the guarantee period i.e. two years later. Naturally the starting annuity if overlap is selected will be less than if there is no overlap.

The point is that there are some tricky technical bits to annuities. There is no investment advice, other than having to take a view on inflation, unless you consider investment annuities, another third way product. Nonetheless there are choices you and your clients will need to consider. You will have to get these choices right bearing in mind once the annuity is set up the terms cannot be amended.

Enhanced annuities

Many people will qualify for an enhanced annuity based on their medical history and lifestyle issues. A combination of relatively less serious conditions such as high blood pressure, cholesterol and diabetes even if controlled may mean your client qualifies for an enhanced annuity. Moreover past illnesses and conditions that are healed or no longer present symptoms may also be relevant.

To assess whether a client may qualify for an enhanced rate you will need to find out something about your client's health and their spouse or partner, if a joint plan is required. This can be somewhat intrusive and sensitive. Ideally you should first try and get a broad picture by asking your clients for example:

> *"Do you have or have you had in the past any serious medical conditions?*
>
> *Do you have high blood pressure, cholesterol or diabetes?"*

If the answer is yes you should then ask the client to complete the personal and medical sections of what used to be called a "Common Quotation Form." It is now called the "Retirement Health Form (RHF),"[49]

It is a single form that in theory can be sent to five providers - Just (formed by the merger of specialist annuity and retirement providers Partnership and Just Retirement), Canada Life, Legal & General, Aviva and Scottish Widows. The adviser completes details of the pension fund available and the annuity options they want the quotes to be based on. It saves a lot of time compared to contacting the participants individually each with their different information requirements and forms.

I much prefer filling in a paper form and as noted in the previous chapter it is also much easier and practical for clients to disclose the medical information, fully and accurately.

Once completed you can e-mail the form directly to Just, Canada Life and Aviva. Unfortunately L&G[50] and Scottish Widows require you to submit the information via online portals such as Iress (The Exchange), Webline or Synaptic, which is quite frankly a pain. I won't do this for two reasons. Firstly it would double or treble the time taken compared to simply e-mailing the same completed form to them all. If like me you

---

[49] https://www.retirementhealthform.co.uk/Home/DownloadForm
[50] L&G have fortunately been willing to accept the RHF by e-mail when I explained my issue with online data entry.

charge for your time it greatly increases the cost to the client. Secondly as noted I have a real problem with online applications involving disclosure of highly detailed and complex medical information where binary responses or drop down lists may fail to capture the full picture. A client of mine expressed the problem well:

> "...some questions are binary when a true answer is not and any response I give to the question as asked would be inaccurate, obviating my ability to complete what is in effect an insurance proposal form with answers given in 'absolute good faith'."

Unfortunately the number of providers offering enhanced annuities has reduced. A few years ago around seven to eight companies were able to quote via the Common Quotation Form. It is a pity that competition has reduced at a time when there is more awareness of enhanced annuities.

I have to warn you the medical information requested on the Retirement Health Form is extensive and complex. In some cases it will require the client's GP to provide the relevant information. Readings for cholesterol and high blood pressure are required and some of the terminology is technical and largely meaningless to non-medical professionals. For example for cancer, the form asks what stage the tumour is, if known. Options include TNM, Modified Astler-Coller, Figo classification and Breslow thickness. It is a similar issue discussed in the previous chapter for the underwriting of insurance with you or your client having to get to grips with complex medical terms.

Naturally the poorer the client's health is the greater the chance of them securing an enhanced annuity, so it is important for as much detail to go down as possible. It is worth the effort to complete the form as qualifying for an enhanced annuity might be the deciding factor in a client's decision whether to opt for an annuity or income drawdown. Without an enhancement an annuity may be dead in the water but with a significantly enhanced annuity it may be an attractive option.

Flexi-access drawdown (FAD)

For many clients with defined contribution pensions FAD is the default option for drawing retirement benefits. An important consideration here is that the concept of investment will not be new to them. After all they may have spent 30 years or more saving into a personal pension with all the ups and downs of stock market volatility. This is radically different for members of defined benefit pension schemes who have little or no experience of the vagaries of the stock markets. The difference between a guaranteed pension arrangement with no investment risk on one hand and FAD with high levels of investment risk on the other are polar opposites.

For defined contribution investors prior to crystallisation the focus was on accumulation of assets and there was no income provision from the pension. It was a situation where money goes in and no money goes out. Decumulation is a 180 degrees about turn, no money goes in but money goes out. Despite the radical changes that retirement and drawing pension benefits involves it can still be a relatively seamless exercise especially if the personal pension or SIPP allows clients to move from accumulation to decumulation within the same contract and there is not a radical change of investment strategy.

The point is clients who go into FAD are invested before retirement and they are invested after retirement, so there need not be a cliff edge. That said the investment strategy will be different between the accumulation and decumulation phases. The latter carries more risk as regular income or *ad hoc* withdrawals are being taken. In a bear market with a long period of low equity prices this exacerbates capital erosion. This requires careful management. I write more on managing drawdown risk later.

During the latter years leading up to retirement conventional wisdom and practice involves protecting gains, reducing risk and focusing on capital preservation. It means selling equities and buying defensive investments such as bonds, mixed asset funds, targeted absolute return strategies and cash. You see this asset allocation shift most markedly with defined contribution company pension schemes that operate lifestyle programmes. Here members' investments are gradually shifted to cautious risk assets in the 5-10 years prior to their selected retirement dates. Lifestyling as it is called is normally the default investment option and is especially aimed at people who do not receive investment advice. It is low cost robo-advice.

Of course members can make their own investment choices from the available funds and opt out of a lifestyle programme but I suspect with auto-enrolment most people don't because of inertia or a lack of confidence and knowledge to manage their own investments.

Lifestyling might be suitable for more cautious risk investors who want to buy an annuity in retirement. Gradual risk reduction and a shift to defensive assets makes sense to protect pension pots from the ravages of stock market sell-offs in the years preceding retirement. This is because clients who buy an annuity need to encash 100% of their pension, 25% typically will be taken as tax free cash with 75% used to buy a lifetime annuity. Retirement and vesting of their pension is therefore a potential cliff edge with enormous investment risk. Lifestyling is a good though not the only investment strategy against the risk of a last minute stock market crash but it makes less sense for investors going into drawdown. With 75% of a pension fund remaining invested for potentially 25-30 years post retirement why undertake the radical investment changes that lifestyling requires in the years leading up to retirement? An equity investment strategy post retirement is as suitable as it is pre-retirement so lifestyling may be unnecessary. It is also potentially risky.

Consider a scenario where a pension pot predominantly for capital growth is mainly invested in equities. There is no lifestyling and the pension is seamlessly switched to FAD at retirement within the same contract. The portfolio can remain in mainly in equities in drawdown. This means capital growth potential does not need to be sacrificed in the last 5-10 years prior to crystallisation as with a lifestyle programme.

In contrast a client who has sold down equities under a lifestyle programme misses out on potential capital growth over this period and if stock markets are high when they start drawdown they will buy back into equities at high prices. They'll need to be invested in equities to a significant degree to avoid capital erosion in the longer term once they start taking income, rather than investing in a portfolio mainly consisting of bonds, cash and other defensive assets.

Naturally the opposite is true. If the investor with a lifestyle pension happens to be lucky with their timing and the switch to equities from bonds and cash when they enter drawdown corresponds with a bear market or a significant trough in equity valuations they will benefit by acquiring assets at low prices.

It is not strictly true that defined contribution investors going into FAD face no cliff edge. It is just not as great a potential fall compared to annuity purchase. What is at risk is the tax free cash. By definition it cannot remain invested in the pension. So if global stock markets fall sharply when tax free cash is withdrawn retirees will take a hit. If however the tax free cash will not be spent or gifted it can be immediately re-invested in equities in ISAs or general investment accounts and benefit when the market recovers. Alternatively, pre-retirement lifestyling could be applied to 25% of the fund only to protect tax free cash values being slashed from a last minute crash.

In conclusion I would advocate lifestyling for clients who anticipate buying an annuity but not for those who plan to go into drawdown, or just modest lifestyling for them. This is a reason to briefly discuss retirement options with your client 5-10 years before the big day. It will determine a suitable investment strategy in the intervening period.

Uncrystallised funds pension lump sum (UFPLS)

This was explained above. As noted it is a facility where a small portion of a pension pot, is crystallised and withdrawn fully. A quarter is taken as tax free cash and the balance is paid as a lump sum that is liable to income tax. The amount is set to provide a fixed income say for the next 12 months and the process can be repeated in subsequent years.

Here is an example from a planning scenario for a client of mine, relevant in the summer of 2019. My client, the one discussed above, retired a few years ago but he had not needed to draw on his pensions until now. He tasked me with setting up a regular income of £30,000 p.a. after tax from pensions and investments. For tax efficiency, bearing in mind he is a non-taxpayer, I presented two options in respect of pensions:

1. Flexi-access drawdown (FAD)

Crystallise £400,000 (a portion of his pension fund), take £100,000 tax free cash and use the residual £300,000 to go into FAD. Using a 4% p.a.

withdrawal rate an income of £12,000 p.a. would be payable. This taxable income would be covered in full by his personal allowance.

His income need was clearly more than £12,000 p.a. but this could be provided from existing ISAs and other investments plus tax free cash.

2. Uncrystallised funds pension lump sum (UFPLS)

Opt for UFPLS, crystallising £16,000 with £4,000 being tax free cash and £12,000 taxable income.

I wrote in reference to UFPLS:

> "What it means is you would only crystallise £16,000 in year one and £48,000 in total after year three as opposed to £400,000 (under FAD) ... However the problem is that there is no surplus tax free cash to top up your income to the required £30,000. To overcome this problem you could crystallise a separate sum into FAD. For example in addition to the UFPLS if you crystallised £60,000 in year one, took 25% tax free cash of £15,000 and went into 0% FAD with the balance this would make up the shortfall (in the first year) *without needing to draw on existing investments and set up new ISAs. It would also be very tax efficient and obviate the need to find a temporary home for cash (the £100,000 from FAD). Advice costs would also be lower using a combination of UFPLS and FAD, at least initially."

Hopefully you get the picture. It is thinking creatively about client situations and if necessary using a mix and match approach using the various pension income and investment options available to you.

Cash flow planning

This has become an increasingly popular financial planning exercise amongst advisers and various tools are available to create a grand plan for providing a long term income in retirement. I remain unconvinced however about the merits of cash flow planning, especially for periods longer than three or four years. I wonder if the drivers of its use are partly to justify high adviser charges i.e. to claim that cash flow planning is a highly technical added value service or an attempt to demonstrate how professional an adviser is. Some like to make a distinction between a financial adviser and a financial planner. The former is seen as traditional, old school with a focus on recommending products whilst a financial planner is more professional, offering a more sophisticated holistic service.

I suspect that subtly this reinforces the idea in the client's mind that they are getting great financial planning benefit, ergo the fees they pay must be justified. It is no different to a 25-40 page investment report where a much shorter one will do. A report the size of a house brick is likely to be full of general bumf, waffle and padding that the client does not need, read or understand even if they try to do so. Call me an old cynic.

My problem with cash flow planning from a technical and practical perspective is that there are too many variables, too many assumptions and too many things that can go wrong. Clients' plans and circumstances change whilst life has a habit of throwing up the unexpected and chucking spanners in the works. Someone once said:

"Life is what happens to you while you're busy making other plans."

I think a better approach is to discuss and agree a broad brush plan with your client that starts with meeting their immediate income need. If they semi-retire, reviews will need to be undertaken at key stages down the line, notably on full retirement or reaching state pension age.

That said I am not entirely dismissive of cash flow planning especially where it serves a valuable purpose, for example to bridge a gap of a few years before a state pension or a defined benefit pension kicks in or if this is something a client has requested. I prepared a three year cash flow plan for the client mentioned above, after he requested a target income of £30,000 p.a. income. It was fairly complex involving the use of tax free cash, drawdown and ISAs arranged in a tax efficient manner. The point however is I don't automatically provide this service, it has to be justified or requested.

Investment strategies for income drawdown

This is a big subject in its own right. A suitable investment strategy will depend on a variety of factors including the client's attitude to risk, their income requirements and stock market conditions. The investment goals are however clear:

1. To set a suitable level of income withdrawals that meets a client's immediate needs, taking into account other sources of income for example from defined benefit pension schemes, state pension or ISAs.

2. To ensure the level of withdrawals is sustainable in the long term. This means it cannot be set at too high a level. The 4% rule may be a useful guide here but depending on the asset allocation and risk profile of the client, slightly higher withdrawal rates can be considered for example 5% to 6% p.a.

3. To ensure your client's income will increase over time to offset the impact from inflation. Income growth requires capital growth in the medium term. This is why significant investment in equities is required. A simple way to understand this is to consider a UK equity income fund with a consistent dividend yield of 3.8% p.a. An investment of £10,000 will produce an income of £380 p.a. If capital grows to £13,000 after say three years but the yield is unchanged then the dividends will now be £494 p.a. If the fund manager is able to increase the yield as well there will be a further income boost. This is something that many investment trusts have achieved, increasing the dividend per share each year, in some cases for more than 40 or 50 consecutive years.

4. To ensure strategies are in place to protect the pension pot from capital erosion from high levels of income withdrawals or sharp stock market sell-offs. When these twin threats to capital are combined with regular unit sales it leads to the so called pound cost ravaging described earlier in the chapter.

In these circumstances it may be necessary to reduce or suspend income payments for a while unless it can be funded from SIPP cash. It is why cash savings, other capital or income sources are required as a backstop and to allow flexible financial planning.

5. To ensure a client's retirement income is as tax efficient as possible. Limits on withdrawals from pensions may be required to prevent the client being taxed at the higher rate. To make up any shortfall in income advisers need to plan holistically drawing income from ISAs or general investment accounts using capital gains tax allowances.

6. To ensure the arrangements put into place are still suitable. This is where regular reviews and flexibility come into play. A client's income needs may change but even if they don't advisers need to monitor the investments to ensure they are still performing well.

14. Closing comments

In Chapters 10-12 I covered principles of investment, protection and pension planning. Now I don't want you to think that an adviser's job is to just to deal with product oriented matters. A fee based adviser who provides holistic financial planning will give advice on other areas including inheritance tax planning, capital gains tax calculations and tax returns. I no longer complete tax returns for clients but I assist with queries or supply relevant tax information relating to investments to clients' accountants.

I also handle general queries from clients about all sorts of other things - savings accounts, National Savings & Investments and tax allowances, my assessment of apparently attractive investments they have discovered online for example risky unregulated high interest bonds, buy to let property as an investment or wills.

Ignoring the nonsense from over-regulation, being a financial adviser is a richly rewarding profession to pursue. It has given me a lot of self-esteem and purpose in life as well as great satisfaction especially when I have helped clients achieve good financial outcomes. I have enjoyed my dealings with people and have made some friendships. I am nearer the end of my career than the beginning and I am thinking about retirement.

For young aspiring financial advisers you don't need to be concerned about how you wind up your career and business in 35-40 years' time. You've got bigger fish to fry, but for any experienced advisers in their 60s reading this book it will be a major consideration. If you run your own business you should be able to sell it to an acquirer, potentially for a large sum of money. It should set you up for a comfortable retirement providing they don't come after you for your last penny following mis-selling claims, real or alleged.

On this point I probably need to say something to make this book idiot proof. I hope not but there could be someone who reads it who lacks the common sense to understand that hot drinks contain hot liquid. Much of what I have written is factual but facts change and I have provided many personal interpretations and opinions. Others will take a different view. Please come to your own conclusions and then take full personal responsibility for how you use the content.

It remains for me to say to aspiring advisers, I wish you well in your career. For more experienced IFAs I hope you can rekindle your love for your work. For regulators and the press please try to see the industry from the perspective of advisers and judge things by the outcomes and by understanding what really serves customers.

If you are an investor and have read this book to understand more about how to find a good IFA I hope it has helped.

Postscript note on Coronavirus

This book was written before the Coronavirus pandemic hit the global economy and stock markets for six. It was being prepared for publication during March 2020, a terrible month for investors, although the sell-off began at the end of February.

Of Dollars and Data, a personal finance data analysis website described March as the craziest month in stock market history[51]. This is an article worth reading. It brought the 11 year bull market to a thundering halt.

Despite the crash most of my clients were remarkably sanguine or at least if they were panicking they didn't tell me! I think they understood that investment is for the long term and that markets go through cycles. For my older clients it isn't the first. Fair enough this one is very extreme and it is not over yet. They also get they are sitting on paper losses and that real losses only occur when investments are sold. The vast majority of my clients did not dump equities, choosing to sit tight. To have such a positive outlook requires two things – time and cash. Time is a great healer and the history of stock markets crashes shows us that equities do recover eventually. Right now the debate is whether the recovery will be V, W, U or L shaped. It will depend on how long and deep the global recession will be.

Cash savings are crucial to investors primarily to protect investment portfolios. It is a buffer that shields investors from being forced sellers of

---

[51] https://ofdollarsanddata.com/the-craziest-month-in-stock-market-history/

equities at knock down prices. For adventurous risk contrarian investors cash also permits tactical investment if they are brave enough.

A few of my clients did decide to sell equities in a falling market fearing an even worse collapse in markets and a global depression on a scale which would rival that in the 1930s. Even though I did not agree with their strategy I couldn't tell them they were wrong. Who knows?

The role of an adviser in such crises is to engage with clients – my investment blog count hit a record in March. Facts, guidance and perspective are good antidotes to fear. For example pointing out that not all assets have collapsed. Initially gold and government bonds fell but they reasserted themselves as safe haven assets. Some defensive funds have held up well and not all equities have fallen to the same extent – cruise companies and airlines for example performed worse than supermarkets. Crucially clients need to be reminded that their portfolios are not the same as the index. Portfolios are in the main diverse, multi-asset and hold non-correlated investments. They have been cushioned to varying degrees from the worst of the downside and volatility.

At a practical level an adviser will need to manage investors' cash flow especially those in income drawdown. It helped one of my clients to learn he had enough cash in his SIPP to cover the next five months' payments whilst the requirement to raise cash thereafter can come from defensive funds, minimising the effects of pound cost ravaging.

In conclusion if you are an adviser you have a big opportunity during these times to help and reassure your clients and demonstrate the value of your investment advice. How portfolios hold up will say a lot about your investment skills and the value for money your fees have represented.

Finally had I written the book before the Coronavirus pandemic and the global stock market sell-off some of my comments on investment would have been different. For example the returns on funds I quoted are lower now and tactical investment would have been emphasised. Moreover the case for bonds, notably investment grade corporates is now more compelling. Hopefully you've cottoned on to those things by now.

Client Agreement

MONTGO CONSULTING LTD　　　　DA7

31 Beach Road, Eastbourne, East Sussex, BN22 7EY Tel: 01323 735303

Montgo Consulting Ltd is registered in England & Wales, Company No: 4918378
Registered Address as above

CLIENT AGREEMENT

1. This document sets out the basis on which we, Montgo Consulting Ltd, also referred to in this document as the Firm, will advise you, conduct business with you and charge for our services. Please read it carefully and if you are unsure of any of its terms please ask.

2. This agreement comes into force on acceptance of its terms by you. This may be prior to you signing the agreement, for example if it is necessary for us to commence work immediately. However a signed copy will be required subsequently.

3. Montgo Consulting Ltd is authorised and regulated by the Financial Conduct Authority (FCA) with a firm reference number 606440. You can check this on the FCA's Register by visiting the FCA's website at www.fca.org.uk/firms/systems-reporting/register or by contacting the FCA at 25 The North Colonnade, Canary Wharf, London E14 5HS or by telephone 0800 111 6768.

THE RANGE OF OUR ADVICE AND FINANCIAL PLANNING OBJECTIVES

4. Your adviser is an independent financial adviser (IFA) and acts on your behalf. We offer products and services as follows:

Investments - we offer an independent advice service. We will recommend retail investment products as defined by the FCA based on a comprehensive and fair analysis of the market. These include unit trusts, open ended investment companies, venture capital trusts, investment trusts, structured products, exchange traded funds and investment bonds.

We will place no restrictions on the investment markets we will consider before providing recommendations, unless you instruct us otherwise in writing. However we will not recommend unregulated collective investment schemes or other unregulated investments e.g. art, wine or stamps. We will only make a recommendation for an investment if we consider it is suitable for you.

Investment and non-investment based protection contracts - we offer advice from the whole market on protection products, specifically whole of life, term assurance, income protection and critical illness insurance.

Pensions - we offer advice from the whole market on personal pensions, self-invested personal pensions (SIPPs) and retirement planning products notably annuities and flexi-access drawdown. We give advice on certain occupational pension arrangements but not on transfers from defined benefit schemes.

General financial planning - including retirement, tax planning and investment reviews.

5. In order to provide you with personal financial advice and recommendations suitable for you we will need to ensure we understand your financial circumstances, objectives, needs and attitudes. We will normally ask you to complete a "personal financial questionnaire" (or fact find) to gather the relevant information to assess your requirements. Details of your stated objectives will be set out in a "suitability report" (or letter of recommendation) that we will issue to you to confirm our recommendations. Unless stated in writing, to the contrary, we will assume that you do not wish to place any restrictions on the advice we give you.

6. In the event of the Firm assisting you in the completion of any investment or insurance application or policy proposal forms you should ensure the information that is entered on such forms is correct and complete. Therefore you should understand that inclusion of incorrect information or omission of any material facts may result in the insurance, investment or policy to which the application or proposal relates to being adversely adjusted, made void and/or any claim(s) made against it being refused. The advice we give you will be based on the information you have given us and your stated investment objectives including the degree of risk you will accept and your capacity for loss. You should advise us of any changes to your financial circumstances and needs.

7. We will forward to you all documents showing ownership of your investments/contracts as soon as practicable after we receive them. Many product providers however will send them to you direct or post them online.

8. We will state at outset whether our advice will cover your entire financial planning needs or whether it will focus on a specific area, giving consideration to any restriction you place on what advice you want.

After the initial advice you will not be obliged to receive an ongoing advice service, for example an investment or financial review. However if you and the Firm agree to an ongoing review service this should normally be undertaken at least annually and should include confirmation of the ongoing suitability of the investments you hold.

If an ongoing review service is not agreed the Firm will remain your IFA. You may then at any time in the future request a review or other ongoing service or the Firm may recommend one. This will be on a one-off basis, as and when needed, for example if there is a change to your financial circumstances. This will be without any obligation to receive future annual or *ad hoc* reviews.

9. We normally require our clients to give us instructions in writing, for example to proceed with buying an investment that we have recommended, or we may confirm our understanding in writing, by post or by email, in order to avoid possible disputes.

CUSTOMER CLASSIFICATION OF YOU

10. The type of client category will determine the levels of protection afforded to you. The Firm proposes to classify you in accordance with FCA rules as a retail client for investment

business and a consumer for non-investment insurance. The regulatory protection available product provider, we will pass on the full value of that commission to you in one or more ways. For example, we could reduce our fee, reduce your insurance premium, or refund some or all of the commission to you in cash subject to certain conditions. Renewal commissions are treated differently (see 12.2c and 13).

In respect of any regular premium protection policy, which we may recommend, should you stop paying the premiums on the policy and as a result of your cancellation we are obliged to refund upfront commission that has been paid to us, we will charge you a fee representing the amount we have to repay. This claw back liability lasts for a period of up to four years after commencement of the policy and the fee will not exceed the amount of commission that was credited to you at outset. For example, assume a life assurance policy is arranged for you and the fee for the work was £700. Commission of £400 was paid by the provider to the Firm and the balance of the fee, £300 was paid by you by invoice. If after one year you cancel the policy and the Firm is obliged to repay 75% of the commission i.e. £300 then the difference between the cost of the work or the original fee, £700 and the amount retained by the Firm, £400 (£100 commission not clawed back plus the £300 fee) is £300 and this would be the amount the Firm would invoice you for.

We will write to you at the point of policy commencement in the suitability report, to confirm the maximum amount you may be liable for and the term over which this will apply.

12.4 Payment for Ongoing Services

You are not obliged to receive and pay for any ongoing services or reviews. However work that is agreed with you is charged on a time spent basis at £160 per hour. Where possible an estimate of the cost will be provided prior to commencement of chargeable work.

The cost of ongoing services and reviews can be paid for by invoiced fee, a product or adviser charge, certain ongoing commissions or a combination of the three.

If the work is terminated by you prior to completion the fee will be calculated based on the hourly rate and the time spent up to the point of cancellation.

TREATMENT OF ONGOING COMMISSIONS & EXCESS COMMISSION

13. Montgo Consulting Ltd may receive ongoing commissions of various types either from investments or plans the firm has arranged for you previously or that you have transferred to our agency. Ongoing commissions may be paid from several sources:

a) Renewal commissions from regular premium endowment, pension, critical illness, income protection and life assurance policies. Typically this is 2.5% of the monthly premiums and is paid after an initial period of up to four years.

b) Indexation commissions may be payable when a premium for certain policies listed above in 13a) is automatically increased at a policy anniversary.

c) Fund or trail commissions may be paid from investments such as ISAs or investment bonds or pensions. Typically this is at a rate of 0.5% p.a. of the value of the investment.

Fund or trail commission from investments and pensions (13.c) are credited to your timesheet (unless they are deemed trivial, see below) and are used to offset the cost of our work in whole or part.

Other commissions from policies with an investment element are also normally credited to timesheets whilst renewal commissions from pure protection policies are normally retained by the Firm due to differential treatment under the regulations.

Trivial commissions of typically £1 or less are not recorded as credits on timesheets given the disproportionate costs for the Firm to check, record and take account of these.

14. Trail commission from investments received by the Firm that exceeds the cost of work is not usually paid out to clients in cash. Instead it is retained as a timesheet credit to be offset against the cost of future work.

Cash rebates are deemed to be "annual payments," by HMRC and they will be taxable at your highest income tax rate. However if excess initial commission from a pure protection policy is paid to you in cash it is not deemed to be an annual payment and hence it is not taxable.

Cash payments to you from pension plans will not be made in any circumstances as they are unauthorized payments and will incur a penalty or a tax charge.

CLIENT MONEY

15. For your security we do not handle clients' money. We do not accept cheques made out to us unless it is in settlement of our fees or other charges or disbursements for which we have sent you an invoice. We do not handle cash. Payment by cheque for investments or insurance policies should always be drawn in favour of the investment or insurance provider.

ACCOUNTING TO YOU

16. We will make arrangements for all your investments policies and/or contracts to be registered in your name unless you first instruct us otherwise in writing. You have a right to inspect copies of contract notes and entries in our records in relation to transactions on your behalf. In that request we reserve the right to give you copies of such documents rather than access to the original records.

We will forward to you all documents showing ownership of your investments policies and/or contracts as soon as practicable after we receive them. Where a number of documents relating to a series of transactions is involved, we will normally hold each document until the series is complete and then forward them all to you.

FINANCIAL SERVICES COMPENSATION SCHEME

17. We are covered by the Financial Services Compensation Scheme (FSCS). You may be entitled to compensation from the scheme if we or a financial services provider we have recommended cannot meet our or their obligations respectively. This depends on the type of business and the circumstances of the claim. You will find up to date details of the FSCS's compensation limits, eligibility and details of how to make a claim on its website: www.fscs.org.uk.

The current limits are:

Investment

Most retail investments are covered up to a maximum limit of £85,000 per person. Investments into an Enterprise Investment Scheme (EIS), a Venture Capital Trust (VCT), an Exchange Traded Product (ETP) and Business Relief schemes are not covered by the FSCS. Advice on these schemes is however covered in the event of the Firm going out of business.

Insurance & Pensions

Insurance advising and arranging is covered for 100% of the claim with no upper limit.

Annuities

Cover is 100% with no upper limit.

Cash

Cover is £85,000 per person per banking institution.

COMPLAINTS

18. If you should have any complaint about the advice you receive or a product you have bought please write or call the Complaints Officer at Montgo Consulting Ltd, 31 Beach Road, Eastbourne, East Sussex BN22 7EY Tel: 01323 735303. Alternatively please e-mail Mike Grant at mike@montgo.co.uk .

If following our subsequent investigation and response you are still not satisfied you may contact the Financial Ombudsman Service (www.financial-ombudsman.org.uk; Exchange Tower, London E14 9SR. Tel: 0800 023 4567). Full details are contained within our internal complaints procedure, which is available to you on request at any time.

CANCELLATION RIGHTS

19. In most cases you can exercise a right to cancel by withdrawing from a newly entered into contract. In general terms you will normally have a 30 day cooling off period for a life, pure protection, payment protection or pension policy and a 14 day cancellation period for an investment.

For pure protection policies the start of the cancellation period will normally begin when you are informed that the contract has started, or later when you have received the contractual terms and conditions. Instructions for exercising the right to cancel, if applicable, will be contained in the relevant product disclosure information which will be issued to you by the product provider.

If you cancel a single contribution investment based contract you might not get back the full amount you invested due to stock market movements. This happens if the value of an investment falls between the investment and cancellation dates.

MATERIAL INTERESTS

20. We will act honestly, fairly and professionally known as conducting business in "Clients' best interest" regulations.

We are not connected to nor have any material interest in any product provider. If we become aware of any future potential conflict of interest for example if we or one of our other clients have some form of interest in business transacted for you we will write to you and obtain your consent before we carry out your instructions, and detail the steps we will take to ensure fair treatment.

RISK WARNINGS

21. Relevant risk warnings will be advised throughout the financial planning process and in your suitability report.

The value of investments may go down as well as up, and you may not get back the amount invested. The amount of income from investments may fluctuate. Non-readily realisable investments for example into an authorised commercial property fund will generally have a restricted market, and therefore it may be difficult to deal in that investment or to obtain reliable information about its value.

For insurance products, your insurance policy may lapse if you do not keep up with your regular premium payments and you will not be covered if a claim is made.

22. COMMUNICATIONS AND MARKETING

The Firm does not send out marketing communications other than occasional client newsletters and investment blogs. These communications are mainly for information purposes for example to explain changes in legislation or taxation. However issues relating to financial planning may be suggested for your consideration.

The Firm has no associated companies and will never pass on or sell your details to third parties for the purposes of marketing. You can opt in or out from receiving client newsletters and investment blogs by letting us know, preferably by e-mail or letter.

TERMINATION OF AUTHORITY

23. You or we may terminate our authority and/or this agreement to act on your behalf at any time without penalty. Notice of this termination must be given in writing and will take effect from the date of receipt. Termination is without prejudice to any transactions already initiated which will be completed according to this client agreement unless otherwise agreed in writing. You will be liable to pay for any transactions made prior to termination and our fees that are outstanding.

CLIENT CONSENT

31. This is our client agreement upon which we intend to rely. For your own benefit and protection you should read these terms carefully before signing them. If you do not understand any point please ask for further information.

I/We understand and consent to the terms of this client agreement and I/We hereby authorise the transfer of information, as described above, on a confidential basis when warranted between such third parties.

I/We authorise you to liaise with My/Our other professional advisers in exchanging relevant personal information pertinent to my/our financial planning requirements and to rely on any such information provided.

I/We agree that this Client Agreement will come into effect from the date you sign below or earlier if you require work to commence prior to this date.

Client Name(s) ....

Client signature(s) ....

Date ....

Signed for and on behalf of the firm:

Adviser : Mike Grant

M. Grant

Version 7- 25/5/18

Fact Find

MONTGO CONSULTING LTD
INDEPENDENT FINANCIAL ADVISER

31 BEACH ROAD, EASTBOURNE, EAST SUSSEX, BN22 7EY
TEL: 01323 735303
DIRECTOR: MIKE GRANT

PERSONAL FINANCIAL QUESTIONNAIRE

(FACT FIND)

Client(s)	
Date completed	

MONTGO CONSULTING LTD IS AUTHORISED AND REGULATED BY THE FINANCIAL CONDUCT AUTHORITY

MONTGO CONSULTING LIMITED IS REGISTERED IN ENGLAND & WALES 4918378

Personal Information

Name (You)	
Address	
Telephone	
E-mail	
Date of Birth	
Nationality	
NI Number	
Marital Status	
Preferred Title	
Employment Status (please tick)	☐ Employed ☐ Self employed ☐ Director of own company ☐ Unemployed ☐ Retired ☐ Other
Any other relevant personal information? (e.g. health or change of circumstances)	

Name (Spouse or Partner)	
Address	
Telephone	
E-mail	
Date of Birth	
Nationality	
NI Number	
Marital Status	
Preferred Title	
Employment Status (please tick)	☐ Employed ☐ Self employed ☐ Director of own company ☐ Unemployed ☐ Retired ☐ Other
Any other relevant personal information? (e.g. health or change of circumstances)	

Children & Financial Dependents

	1	2	3	4	5
Name					
Date of Birth					
Financially Dependent?	☐ Yes ☐ No	☐ Yes ☐ No	☐ Yes ☐ No	☐ Yes ☐ No	☐ Yes ☐ No
At Private School?	☐ Yes ☐ No	☐ Yes ☐ No	☐ Yes ☐ No	☐ Yes ☐ No	☐ Yes ☐ No
At University	☐ Yes ☐ No	☐ Yes ☐ No	☐ Yes ☐ No	☐ Yes ☐ No	☐ Yes ☐ No
Current cost of education p.a.					
Expected total future cost of education p.a.					

Miscellaneous comments

Earnings and Tax

You

Occupation	
Employee's Name	
	☐ Full time ☐ Part time
Gross earnings p.a.	
Net earnings after tax per month	
Income tax rate (if known)	
Employer benefits? (If so please list)	
Tax year end (If self-employed)	
Do you normally complete a tax return?	☐ Yes ☐ No

Spouse or Partner

Occupation	
Employee's Name	
	☐ Full time ☐ Part time
Gross earnings p.a.	
Net earnings after tax per month	
Income tax rate (if known)	
Employer benefits? (If so please list)	
Tax year end (If self-employed)	
Do you normally complete a tax return?	☐ Yes ☐ No

5

Other Income?
(E.g. pension)

You

	Source	Amount	Before or after Tax

Spouse or Partner

	Source	Amount	Before or after Tax

Budget
Please provide approximate figures for both of you for a typical month

Total net monthly income	£		
Total monthly expenditure	£		
Do you need additional regular income?	☐ Yes. If yes, how much? ☐ No		
Do you have any large one off expenses in the next six months?	☐ Yes. If yes, please list below. ☐ No		
Item		Amount	Date required

Assets

Please provide approximate amounts and supply a list of accounts and investments if you have one

	You	Spouse or Partner	Joint
Current account (typical balance)			
Cash ISA			
Premium bonds			
Other NS&I			
Other cash savings			
House value			
Investments			
Shares			
Other			

Liabilities

Please provide current outstanding balances

	You	Spouse or Partner	Joint
Mortgage	£	£	£
Credit cards	£	£	£
Personal loans	£	£	£
Do you pay off credit cards each month in full?	☐ Yes ☐ No		
Mortgage end date			
Mortgage repayment method			
Is the mortgage fully covered with life insurance?	☐ Yes ☐ No		

Retirement

	You	Spouse or Partner
Expected retirement date		
Hoped for retirement date (if different)		
State pension age (if known)		

Pension Arrangements

	You	Spouse or Partner
Member of company pension?	☐ Yes ☐ No	☐ Yes ☐ No
Date you joined		
Scheme type	☐ Defined benefit / final salary ☐ Defined contribution	☐ Defined benefit / final salary ☐ Defined contribution
Employer payments		
Employee payments		
Scheme retirement date		
Do you pay into any personal pensions?	☐ Yes ☐ No	☐ Yes ☐ No
If so how much?		
What is the plan value?		
Do you have any paid up pensions or past employers' pensions? If so please provided details including plan values or deferred benefits		

Miscellaneous

	You	Spouse or Partner	Comments
Have you contributed to any ISA this tax year – either to a stocks and shares or cash ISA? If so please provide details on page 10.	☐ Yes ☐ No	☐ Yes ☐ No	Please write on page 10
Risk profile for investment (See document supplied)			
Risk profile for insurance			
Is ethical investment required? (See document supplied)	☐ Yes – For all ☐ Yes – For some ☐ No	☐ Yes – For all ☐ Yes – For some ☐ No	Please state what issues concern you the most on page 10
Do you have a will?	☐ Yes ☐ No	☐ Yes ☐ No	
If so what are the main details?			
Do you have a Power of Attorney?	☐ Yes ☐ No	☐ Yes ☐ No	If yes please provide details on page 10
Inheritance due in the near future?	☐ Yes ☐ No	☐ Yes ☐ No	
Do you have any critical illness or income protection insurance? If so please provide details on page 10 stating who is covered.	☐ Yes ☐ No	☐ Yes ☐ No	Please write on page 10

Financial Objectives and Other Information

Please use the space below to record your financial objectives, what you require advice on, and your monthly budget for savings, pensions or insurance, details of any life assurance or protection policies. Alternatively provide copies of policy documents. If you are interested in ethical investment please state what issues concern you most.

Please continue on page 11 if necessary.

11

15. Glossary of abbreviations

ABI	Association of British Insurers, a trade body for you've guessed it, British insurance companies.
A-DAY	This was 6/4/06 when the rules on pensions were simplified into a single set of rules. In reality it has spawned a lot of complexity.
AIC	Association of Investment Companies, a trade body for UK investment trusts. Like the Investment Association (IA) the AIC place investment companies into sectors, permitting meaningful comparisons of performance and other data.
AIM	Alternative Investment Market, a junior London Stock Exchange for small companies not listed on the main market. Many of these qualify for Business Relief.
AMC	The annual management charge of a fund. It excludes additional fund expenses such as custodian and auditor fees. See OCF. The AMC also excludes fund transaction costs when the manager buys and sells stock.
CGT	Capital gains tax.
CIP	Centralised investment proposition, a set repeatable investment process for managing client portfolios.
CPD	Continuous professional development. Advisers must undertake at least 35 hours of CPD each year, 21 of which must be structured and 15 must be protection related.
CRP	Centralised retirement proposition, a consistent process for managing clients' income needs and pension investments.

DFM	Discretionary fund manager.
EIS	Enterprise Investment Scheme, a tax relieved investment which is a retail investment product, as defined by the FCA.
ETC	Exchange trade commodity, a debt security that enables an investor to track the spot price of commodities such as gold, silver, oil or cereals.
ETF	Exchange traded fund, a traded security that tracks a stock market index.
ESA	Employment and Support Allowance, a state benefit.
FAD	Flexi-access drawdown, the new term for income drawdown, introduced with George Osborne's pensions' freedoms.
FCA	Financial Conduct Authority, the main regulator of financial services since 1/4/13.
FIB	Family income benefit, a type of decreasing term assurance that upon a valid claim pays out a tax free monthly income to the end of the policy term.
FSA	Financial Services Authority, the predecessor of the FCA, prior to 1/4/13.
FOS	Financial Ombudsman Service which handles complaints rejected by investment and insurance companies and adviser firms.
FSCS	Financial Services Compensation Scheme which handles claims against firms in default. Not all investments are covered by the FSCS including EISs and VCTs, although regulated advice on these products is.
FTA	Fixed term annuity, a third way pension providing a guaranteed income for a set period of time and a

	guaranteed maturity value.
GABRIEL	This is "gathering better regulatory information electronically," and it is the FCA's online reporting tool all firms must use to provide regulatory data.
IA	Investment Association, a trade body that groups funds such as unit trusts into sectors that permits meaningful comparisons of performance.
IFA	Independent financial adviser.
IHT	Inheritance tax.
KID	Key information document, a standard disclosure document that must be issued to clients prior to investment in products that are governed by PRIIPS regulations, for example investment trusts and investment bonds.
KIID	Key investor information document, a standard disclosure document that must be issued to clients prior to investment into authorised open ended funds i.e. unit trusts and OEICs.
MIFID II	Markets in Financial Instruments Directive II, EU regulations that came into force on 3/1/18. This introduced strict charge disclosures for investments and other requirements.
MPAA	The money purchase annual allowance of £4,000. It restricts tax relieved pension contributions for people who have accessed pension income flexibly.
NURS	Non UCITS retail scheme, an open ended regulated fund with wider investment powers than OEICs, but which cannot be marketed throughout the EU.
NMPIs	Non-mainstream pooled investments. These unregulated investments cannot be marketed to retail investment

	clients. NMPIs include UCIS.
OCF	The annual management charge plus additional fund expenses, for example custodian and regulator fees. The OCF does not include fund transaction charges.
OEIC	Open ended investment company, an open ended authorised and regulated collective fund that can be marketed throughout the EU. This is likely to change with Brexit.
PCLS	Pension commencement lump sum, the replacement name for tax free cash.
PFS	Personal Finance Society, part of the Charted Insurance Institute with an aim of supporting the development of financial advisers.
PII	Professional indemnity insurance. All adviser firms must be covered by suitable PII.
PIP	Personal Independence Payment, a state benefit.
PPI	Payment protection insurance. Thank goodness there are no more of those annoying adverts for compensation but the claims industry has set its sights on investment advice. So watch out!
PRIIPS	Packaged retail and insurance-based investment products, EU regulations introduced on 1/1/18. See Chapter 3.
PROD	Product intervention and product governance sourcebook. Introduced by the FCA on 3/1/18 alongside MIFID II. A meaningless tick box exercise for IFAs whose advice is always bespoke and personalised and by definition is the most suitable it can be.
QE	Quantitative easing, central bank monetary policy of bond purchases. This has supported the global economy

	since the global banking crisis.
RDR	The Retail Distribution Review, a major change to the regulatory regime introduced by the FSA on 31/12/12. It banned commissions from sales of pensions and investments.
RIP	Retail investment product, a term borne out of the RDR. RIPs are the types of investment the FCA say IFAs should consider when advising clients.
SIPP	Self-invested personal pension.
SSP	Statutory Sick Pay, a state benefit.
UCIS	Unregulated collective investment scheme. See Chapter 3.
UCITS	Undertakings in collective investment in transferable securities. These are EU regulations that govern OEICs.
UFPLS	Uncrystallised funds pension lump sum, a facility born out of pension freedoms. Here an investor fully crystallises a small portion of their pension with 25% tax free cash and 75% taxable as income.
VCT	Venture capital trust, a tax relieved investment which is a retail investment product, as defined by the FCA.

16. Acknowledgements

This book has taken about a year to write, although in another sense I could say more than 29 years was closer to the mark. That is how long I have needed to acquire the necessary knowledge, experience and confidence before undertaking the project. During that time I have had many positive influences and thanks could go to a variety of people even though I am unlikely to meet them again, nor do I expect they will ever pick up and read a copy of the book. Firstly thanks to Berat Tekin (not his real name), manager at Liberty Life and others who provided me with a career opening into the industry and gave me a basic grounding as a financial adviser.

Then I want to mention David Flowers and others at the Investment Practice who introduced me to the world of independent financial advice and developed my love of investments. Next I should thank the many fund managers and economists who have educated me and shaped my thinking.

Aside from people in the industry the book would not have come into being without the co-operation of my clients over many years. Because of their incredible trust and willingness to permit me to manage their money I gained the necessary experience of investments and portfolio construction and therefore I have something to say.

Next I want to thank Louis Goacher, an aspiring financial adviser who I mentored informally for about 18 months. Louis is now authorised as an adviser and is settling into work with a firm of IFAs in Eastbourne. It was my experience in coaching Louis that inspired me to put my knowledge and thinking in writing for the benefit of others who may go down the same path.

Finally many thanks to Peter, my incredibly bright, insightful and articulate son. He read the draft and made many very useful comments and suggestions, lots of which were adopted. The credit for getting the book from a Word document to print, albeit self-published on Amazon is also down to him.

It remains for me to thank those who gave me permission to quote material from their publications. These include Money Marketing, a weekly newspaper which has kept me abreast of what is going on in the financial services industry. The FCA also permitted me to include small sections from their handbook. Thanks too to International Adviser; Cambridge Dictionary; Trustnet; New Model Adviser, Citywire Financial Publishers; Libertatem (now The Impartial Financial Advisers Association, IFAA); Andrew Goodwin, author of "The Happy Financial Adviser," Fidelity Investments and Vanguard Asset Management Ltd.

Requests to quote were made to other organisations but no responses were received. I have assumed either they had no objections or failing that, fair usage permitting me to quote small sections of their material applies. It was after all publically available on the internet and their organisations arguably get some free advertising.

Copyright: Mike Grant 2020

mwgrant54@gmail.com

Printed in Great Britain
by Amazon